Choosing Childcare For Dummies®

D0601077

What to Ask a Day-Care Center Director During a Phone Screen

- Do you have any spaces available? If not, how long is your waiting list?
- What are your hours of operation? Does the center have a limit on the number of hours a child can spend at the center each day?
- Are part-timers welcome, or do you accept children only on a full-time basis?
- What's the age range of children enrolled at the center? Do you group children according to age, or do you use mixed-age groupings?
- What is your caregiver-child ratio?
- Does the center shut down at certain times of the year?
- Do you have a trial period for new children?
- Has all center staff received appropriate training in first aid?
- What are your fees? Do you offer discounts or scholarships to families on limited incomes?
- May I bring my child with me when I conduct my onsite visit?
- What kind of information do you require in order to complete the registration paperwork?

Points to Consider When Visiting a Day-Care Center

- Is the day-care environment warm and welcoming?
- Is the day-care center designed to be secure?
- Does the day-care day have some sort of predictable rhythm?
- What kind of training has the day-care center staff received in working with young children?
- How long has the staff member who would be assigned to work with your child been working with young children? What are her child-care philosophies?
- What are the center's discipline policies?
- How does the center support parents who are toilet training their children?
- What are the center's basic operating policies and procedures?
- What are the center's policies regarding sick children?
- What kinds of meals and snacks does the center serve?
- Is the center director willing to provide you with the names and phone numbers of parents who are willing to speak with you about their families' experiences with the center?

For Dummies: Bestselling Book Series for Beginners

Choosing Childcare For Dummies®

Cheat Sheet

What to Ask a Family Day-Care Provider During a Phone Screen

- Do you have any spaces available?
- Where is your family day care located?
- What are your hours of operation?
- Are part-timers welcome?
- What are the ages of the other children?
- Does the family day care shut down during any time of the year?
- Do you have a backup provider lined up?
- Have you been trained in first aid?
- What fees do you charge?

What to Ask a Prospective Nanny

- What hours and days of the week are you available for work?
- What made you choose a career as a nanny?
- How long have you been working with young children?
- Are you legally permitted to work in the U.S.?
- What were your duties at your most recent position? What was your reason for leaving?
- What kind of training have you received?
- Would you be willing to do a bit of light housework?
- When could you start work?
- Would you be willing to undergo a background check and pre-employment medical exam at our expense?
- What ages of children do you have the most experience working with?
- Could you make at least a one-year commitment to our family?
- What are your salary expectations?
- Are you able to provide a list of references?

What to Ask When Visiting a Family Day Care

- What kind of training have you received?
- Are your immunizations up to date?
- Is your child-care license current?
- How long have you been working with young children?
- Are any other businesses being run out of your home?
- What are the ages of children you most enjoy working with?
- What's the maximum number of children you'd want to care for?
- What are your child-care philosophies?
- Do you have any written policies and procedures?
- Do you charge late fees if parents are late picking their children up?
- What approach do you take when toilet training children?
- What are your policies regarding sick children, naps?
- How much notice do you require if I decide to withdraw my child?
- Are parents welcome to drop by at any time unannounced?
- Are you willing to provide references?

For Dummies: Bestselling Book Series for Beginners

Choosing Childcare

FOR

DUMMIES®

Choosing Childcare
FOR
DUMMIES®

by Ann Douglas

WILEY

Wiley Publishing, Inc.

Choosing Childcare For Dummies®

Published by
Wiley Publishing, Inc.
111 River Street
Hoboken, NJ 07030-5774
www.wiley.com

About the Author

Ann Douglas is one of North America's most popular parenting writers. An award-winning journalist and the mother of four children, ages 6 through 15, Ann is the author of 24 books, including *The Mother of All Pregnancy Books, The Mother of All Baby Books,* and *The Unofficial Guide to Childcare.* (The next two books in Ann's best-selling "Mother of All Books" series — *The Mother of All Toddler Books* and *The Mother of All Parenting Books* — are scheduled for publication in 2004, along with the second edition of her highly successful book *The Unofficial Guide to Having a Baby.*)

Known for her lively anecdotes and real-world advice, Ann makes regular radio and television appearances and is regularly quoted in such publications as *Parenting, Parents, Fit Pregnancy, American Baby,* and *Working Mother.* She teaches online pregnancy and parenting courses for WebMD.com and Netscape's Online Learning Center as well as through her own Web sites, BellyUniversity.com and MomUniversity.com.

You can download copies of Ann's pregnancy and parenting tip sheets, access her online archive of parenting articles, join her parenting book club, sign up for her monthly parenting newsletter, or inquire about her speaking and consulting services by visiting Ann's Web site at www.childcare-guide.com.

If you prefer to write to her the old-fashioned way (via the post office), you can send her your letter care of:

John Wiley & Sons, Inc.
111 River Street, 4th Floor
Hoboken, NJ 07030-5774

Attention: Ann Douglas, Author,
Choosing Childcare For Dummies

Dedication

This book is dedicated to Lorrie Baird, our family's child-care provider for the past three years. Lorrie, I wouldn't have been able to find the time to write a single word about childcare, let alone more than 150,000 words, if it weren't for your willingness to take such great care of Ian so that I would have time to write books like this one. We certainly won at child-care roulette the day we found you. Thank you for going above and beyond the call of duty in so many ways and for being such a great person to boot.

Author's Acknowledgments

A book like this doesn't come together without a lot of behind-the-scenes efforts from a lot of very hard-working people. I'm almost hesitant to start naming names in case I accidentally leave someone out, but (gulp!) here goes.

First of all, I'd like to thank Tracy Boggier, my ever-supportive acquisitions editor, for coming up with the idea for this book in the first place and for thinking of me when the time came to start shopping for an author. All I can say is, you certainly went all out when it came to researching your subject matter, Tracy. Not every editor is willing to have a baby just so she has an excuse to check out child-care facilities! (Heaven help your poor husband if your next book ends up being on multiple pregnancy . . .)

I also owe a huge debt of gratitude to my project editor, Allyson Grove, who never let on how crazy I was making her when I had to break the number-one commandment in the Dummies Author Universe ("Thou shalt not miss a chapter batch submission deadline") time and time again. Granted, I had some rather extenuating circumstances to deal with (my mother passed away rather suddenly and unexpectedly during the writing of this book), but you were very kind to me, Allyson. I owe you big time.

I'd also like to thank Claire Lerner, the Director of the Learning and Growing Together Strategic Initiative for ZERO TO THREE: National Center for Infants, Toddlers, and Families, for serving as the technical editor for this book. Claire, I know how insanely busy you are and what a huge coup it was to convince you to play a role in this book. I will always be grateful to you for taking the time to comment on the manuscript and for sharing your tremendous knowledge of the world of childcare.

Finally, I'd like to thank Kristin A. Cocks, product development director, for her very helpful, up-front comments on my working table of contents; the book's two copy editors, Chrissy Guthrie and Michelle Dzurny, for having such a great eye for detail; and the countless unsung heroes in the production, graphics, editorial, publicity, and marketing teams at Wiley. Thank you for your unwavering enthusiasm for this project and your ongoing support of my writing career. Wiley rocks!

Publisher's Acknowledgments

We're proud of this book; please send us your comments through our Dummies online registration form located at www.dummies.com/register/.

Some of the people who helped bring this book to market include the following:

Acquisitions, Editorial, and Media Development

Project Editor: Allyson Grove

Acquisitions Editor: Tracy Boggier

Copy Editors: Michelle Dzurny, Christina Guthrie

Editorial Program Assistant: Holly Gastineau-Grimes

Technical Editor: Claire Lerner

Editorial Manager: Michelle Hacker

Editorial Assistant: Elizabeth Rea

Cover Photos: ©Laura Dwight/Stock Connection/PictureQuest

Cartoons: Rich Tennant, www.the5thwave.com

Production

Project Coordinator: Erin Smith, Ryan Steffen

Layout and Graphics: Kristin McMullan, Heather Ryan, Jacque Schneider, Shae Lynn Wilson

Proofreaders: Laura Albert, Andy Hollandbeck, Dwight Ramsey, TECHBOOKS Production Services

Indexer: TECHBOOKS Production Services

Publishing and Editorial for Consumer Dummies

    Diane Graves Steele, Vice President and Publisher, Consumer Dummies

    Joyce Pepple, Acquisitions Director, Consumer Dummies

    Kristin A. Cocks, Product Development Director, Consumer Dummies

    Michael Spring, Vice President and Publisher, Travel

    Brice Gosnell, Associate Publisher, Travel

    Kelly Regan, Editorial Director, Travel

Publishing for Technology Dummies

    Andy Cummings, Vice President and Publisher, Dummies Technology/General User

Composition Services

    Gerry Fahey, Vice President of Production Services

    Debbie Stailey, Director of Composition Services

Contents at a Glance

Table of Contents

Introduction

. . . .

*W*elcome to *Choosing Childcare For Dummies*, a guidebook for parents eager to scratch at least one of the items off their kid-related worry lists — namely the worry associated with finding a suitable child-care arrangement.

Shopping around for a suitable child-care arrangement can be anxiety-producing for sure, but it doesn't have to result in an express trip to the therapist's couch — at least not if you have a copy of *Choosing Childcare For Dummies* along for the ride! This book helps you weigh your various child-care options and make the decision that's right for your family. Trust me, this book is the closest thing to a ticket to child-care nirvana that you're likely to find!

One of the reasons I wrote this book was to eliminate some of the stress that goes along with choosing a child-care arrangement. I know what it's like being a parent who's completely panicked at the thought of leaving her child in someone else's care, and I want to help alleviate some of that worry for you. Around the time I was to return to work after the birth of my first child, I tuned into a really bad episode of a trashy daytime talk show. As luck would have it, the show was all about baby sitters who abuse or neglect the children in their care. This TV show scared me so much that I honestly considered rigging my daughter's diaper bag with a walkie-talkie so that I could spy on her child-care provider the first time I left her at day care. (Bear in mind that this was before nanny cams were invented — a time when parents were pretty much left to their own low-tech devices if they wanted to do any spying. Nowadays, you let teddy bears do your dirty work for you. Yep, some enterprising spy-gadget companies have actually stuffed nanny cams inside teddy bears!)

As it turned out, my daughter and I survived her first day at day care and the hundreds of days that followed, and her three younger brothers and I have made it through thousands of day-care days since. But I've never forgotten how scared I was leaving my baby in someone else's care for the very first time.

I don't want you to feel like that; I want you to feel confident about the child-care choices you're making — to feel that you've come to the best possible decision for your child and your family. This is the reason I wrote this book.

About This Book

Choosing Childcare For Dummies is designed to be fun to read — something that really helps set the book apart from the countless other child-care books on the market today. As you've probably noticed by now, most books about choosing childcare read more like someone's PhD thesis than a book you can actually sink your teeth into. I can't imagine reading such a book, let alone writing one, so I was more than a little relieved when my editor pointed out that having fun when writing a *For Dummies* book is okay. In fact, having fun is encouraged! It's a darned good thing that's how the folks at Wiley operate, because I don't think I have it in me to check my sense of humor at the door.

How to Use This Book

Of course, the tone of the book isn't the only thing that sets *Choosing Childcare For Dummies* apart from other child-care books. This book is also highly user-friendly. Not only is it equipped with a detailed table of contents and an index (features that help you zero in on the information you're looking for in a matter of seconds), but the entire book's also structured in a way that saves you tons of time. You can read any chapter on its own and get a handle on the key concepts being discussed, even if you never bother to read another page in the rest of the book. (Of course, I assume you want to read each and every word of my deathless prose, but that may just be wishful thinking on my part.)

Each chapter in a *For Dummies* book functions like a tiny building block — not unlike the building blocks that your child likes to play with, in fact. Although you can snap two or more building blocks together to create something bigger (in this case, a series of chapters or an entire book), each block (or chapter) is useful on its own.

Because this book can be read in bits and pieces, you can flip to the part that deals with the issues that are of greatest interest to you at any given time (for example, if you're interviewing a teenage baby sitter in half an hour, Chapter 14 is where you want to be right now). You don't have to waste hours of time wading through material that may be mildly interesting but isn't particularly relevant to your situation.

The book's modular, or "building block," structure also makes finding the information you need quick and easy — a big plus if, like many parents, the amount of time you have for reading is in chronically short supply. You don't have to flip from chapter to chapter to piece together the various chunks of material that relate to a particular topic. Most of what you need to know about a particular subject is pulled together in a single chapter. And if you do have to flip somewhere else in the book to find out more about a related subject, you can rely on me to provide you with clear directions on how to get there — much clearer directions than the hand-drawn map that Uncle Fred scrawled on that mustard-smeared napkin at last year's family reunion, I promise!

I've said a lot about what's in the book. Now let me tell you what's *not* in the book. As you can imagine, writing a well-organized book also means eliminating a lot of unnecessary fluff. (Fluff is, of course, the editorial world's equivalent to the filler that gets added to hamburger patties — stuff that helps bulk up the product but does absolutely nothing to improve the quality!) Because my editors and I recognize that time is a tremendously precious commodity for parents with young children, any material that was off-topic or irrelevant was eliminated. The result is a book that's jam-packed with need-to-know information, and nothing but.

Not-So-Foolish Assumptions

I've made a lot of foolish assumptions in my lifetime, but I don't think I've made too many during the writing of this book. Or, at least, I hope I haven't! (I've had egg on my face before, and it doesn't particularly suit my complexion.)

My key assumption in writing this book is that you're in the process of choosing childcare for the child in your life, be it a child, stepchild, grandchild, foster child, or the child of your significant other.

For reasons of sheer convenience (the need to avoid that horribly awkward "he/she" grammatical construct), I've made the assumption that the majority of child-care providers are female and proceeded accordingly in the pronoun department. (I realize that tons of truly wonderful men are working in the child-care profession, but in the interests of avoiding the need to say "he/she" seven billion times, I've chosen to stick with the female pronoun when referring to child-care providers. What the world really needs right about now is a nice, friendly unisex pronoun, I tell you!)

And in the interests of preventing *you* from making any foolish assumptions, let me remind you that no book can ever serve as a substitute for your own sixth sense as a parent. You're the best judge of what is — and isn't — in your child's best interests. If your gut instinct tells you that something's not quite right about a particular child-care situation, be prepared to go back to the drawing board.

How This Book Is Organized

I talked a bit about the book's modular structure earlier — how you can dive into any part of the book and still find the information you need. To save you even more time, here's a quick preview of what you can find in each of the book's five parts.

Part 1: Getting Started: Choosing Childcare 101

Choosing childcare can seem like an overwhelming task until you get a handle on what's involved. This part of the book walks you through the basic process of finding childcare, helps you weigh the pros and cons of your various child-care options, gives you an idea of what you can expect to pay for in-home versus out-of-home childcare, and answers your key questions about what constitutes quality on the child-care front.

Part 11: Out-of-Home Childcare: Evaluating the Big Three

The majority of children who require childcare are cared for in a location other than their own homes. In this part of the book, I zero in on the three basic out-of-home child-care choices — day-care centers, family day cares, and preschools — and talk about how you can go about evaluating each of these types of childcare.

Part 111: In-Home Childcare: Deciding Whether Nanny or Uncle Danny Can Do the Job

Some parents prefer to have their children cared for in their own homes. This part of the book discusses what's involved in hiring a nanny or other in-home caregiver, including a relative such as your child's grandmother. If you decide to go this route, you need to know how to cut through all the governmental red tape associated with being someone's employer, which is why I've devoted an entire chapter to the subject.

Part IV: Wanted: Part-Time and Occasional Childcare

In a perfect world, you never have to worry about your family day-care provider calling in sick or your nanny coming down with the chickenpox. But because you're not exactly raising your kids in a perfect world, you have to deal with these kinds of last-minute curveballs. Other real-world challenges that are discussed in this part of the book include finding childcare when you work nonstandard hours and finding a part-time baby sitter.

Part V: The Part of Tens

If you've read other books in this series, you know that the Part of Tens is a standard feature in any *For Dummies* book. These short chapters are always packed with practical tips and great information that invariably wrap up each book with a bang. In *Choosing Childcare For Dummies*, the Part of Tens focuses on getting your child started in a new child-care arrangement, feeling connected to your child's day-care "family," and spotting the signs that your child-care arrangement is in trouble. I also include a list of ten child-care resources and organizations you definitely want to know about.

Icons Used in This Book

To help you make the best use of your time as you're flipping through the book, I've spotlighted some of the information in the text by using a series of icons. Here's a rundown of the icons I use in the book and what each one means.

Tip icons draw your attention to some really nitty-gritty, practical information that can make the task of choosing childcare a whole lot easier. Just think of the tip icons as gold nuggets that I've buried in the text for you to find.

Remember icons highlight something in the text that you're likely to refer to at some point in the future. They're the next best thing to having me show up at your house with a highlighting marker, ready to draw your attention to the most important chunks of text.

Warning icons alert you to something of tremendous importance to your child's health or well-being. When you come across one of these icons, pretend that alarm bells are going off in your head, urging you to pay particular attention to what I have to say. I don't use these particular icons lightly.

Fridge Notes icons highlight chunks of material that you may want to make a note of and stick on your refrigerator — a child-care-related Web site you may want to visit, the 800 number for a child-care-related organization that may be helpful to you, and so on.

These icons highlight key definitions for bits of childcare lingo that you'll find sprinkled throughout the text. These are terms you'll want to master, not just because you'll impress the heck out of your friends, but also because understanding these terms can actually help to demystify the process of choosing childcare. (Hey, it helps to speak the language, right?)

Where to Go from Here

Because this book doesn't demand that you read it from cover to cover, you can pretty much open the book to any place you want. If you're in the market for something other than your standard, full-time 9 a.m.-to-5 p.m. day-care arrangement, then you can dive right into Part IV. If you know for certain that you want to go the out-of-home child-care route, then you may want to start by reading Part II. If you have a pretty good idea that in-home childcare is going to be the best bet for your family, then Part III is where you want to be. Of course, if you feel like you don't know enough about what's involved in choosing childcare and you want a quick crash course, then you may want to go the old-fashioned route and start with Part I. Just because a book is modular doesn't mean you *have* to read the chapters in random order. Remember, you're in the driver's seat.

Part I
Getting Started: Choosing Childcare 101

The 5th Wave — By Rich Tennant

"Hello, operator? Do you have a listing for Ringling Bros. and Barnum & Bailey Day-care Center?"

In this part . . .

Do you wish you had a compass to guide you through the child-care maze? Well, you're in luck! Part I of this book functions as a navigational aid of sorts, alerting you to the key challenges you can expect to encounter as you embark on your child-care quest.

If you quickly flip through the next few chapters, you'll notice that I cover a lot of important territory in this part of the book: what to expect from your child-care search; how to weigh the pros and cons of the various in-home and out-of-home child-care options; how to find a child-care arrangement that meets your family's needs; how to take advantage of tax credits and subsidies that can help take a bite out of your child-care expenditures; and how to size up a particular child-care arrangement.

Chapter 1

Getting a Bird's-Eye View of What's Involved

In This Chapter

▶ Finding out why the child-care search requires so much time and patience

▶ Discovering what you can do to make the process go more smoothly

▶ Seeing what's on the child-care menu

*1*f you're in the habit of comparing notes with other parents, you've no doubt heard your fair share of child-care horror stories by now — truly hair-raising tales of nannies caught hitting the bottle or hopping into the sack with their boyfriends while the tots in their care go completely unsupervised. Frankly, it's not unlike what happens when you announce that you're having a baby: People you barely know seem to take perverse delight in scaring you skinny with tales of their best friend's neighbor's 78-hour labor and foot-long episiotomy scar. Never mind the fact that these stories tend to be made up of 0.01 percent cold, hard truth and 99.99 percent urban legend. Why let something as boring as the truth get in the way of a rip-roaring story?

So if you're feeling totally shell-shocked by all the caregiver-from-hell stories that you keep being subjected to every time you dare to venture to the office water cooler, gas station, or grocery store, I'd like to offer you a bit of advice. Take these stories with a grain of salt. Finding a suitable child-care arrangement isn't going to be a cakewalk, but it's not going to be mission impossible, either. I promise.

As for the details of your child-care mission, well, that's what this chapter is all about. I talk about why the search for childcare can be frustrating and exhausting and what you can do to make the process a little less stressful. I walk you through the various options on the child-care menu, both out-of-home and in-home. And I discuss how your child-care needs may be affected by your family's unique circumstances. Just as there's no such thing as one-size-fits-all pantyhose (trust me, I know this from personal experience!), there's no such thing as a one-size-fits-all child-care solution. This chapter is about laying the groundwork for those child-care solutions. Sorry, you're on your own when it comes to the pantyhose . . . .

Understanding Why the Search for Childcare Can Be Frustrating

You don't have to be a rocket scientist to figure out why the search for child-care can be so frustrating. You've probably heard the child-care facts of life more than once by now, but just in case:

- Quality childcare is in chronically short supply.

- If you work offbeat hours, you can expect your child-care search to be more frustrating than average. Evening and weekend childcare is even harder to find.

- Even if you're lucky enough to find a spot, you may not necessarily be able to afford it.

- You need to line up backup care as well as regular care. No parent can afford to have all her eggs in a single child-care basket.

- If you and your partner don't see eye to eye when it comes to childcare, your child-care quest may become even more complicated.

What the quality child-care shortage means to you

You've probably seen the newspaper headlines talking about the shortage of quality childcare — in other words, childcare that meets or exceeds some basic standards for quality. (If you want a detailed breakdown of what constitutes quality childcare, by the way, flip to Chapter 5.) This shortage doesn't necessarily mean that you'll have trouble finding child-care spaces in your community (although, frankly, that can be an issue, too), but you can pretty much count on having trouble finding *quality* child-care spaces in your community, at least according to what the experts are saying.

If you're like most parents, you probably assume that child-care programs are carefully regulated and monitored for health and safety infractions. Although some programs are required to measure up to the kinds of standards that you and I have come to expect, other programs fall through the cracks — a lot of other programs, in fact. According to the Annie E. Casey Foundation (a non-profit foundation that researches child-care-related issues and other issues affecting the health and well-being of children), approximately 40 percent of child-care programs in America are legally exempt from state regulations that are designed to protect children. Forty percent! So if you're expecting some government bureaucrat to play the role of defender of good, you may want to give yourself a bit of a reality check. It may or may not happen in this lifetime — literally.

Because the United States has no countrywide child-care "system" in place, we've ended up with a patchwork quilt of regulations that don't quite mesh together the way they should. This is why so many child-care programs are exempt from the child-care legislation that's been put in place to protect children. And when centers aren't held accountable for the quality of care that they provide, serious problems can and often do result.

In recent years, national studies have identified some disturbing truths with the quality of childcare in this country — problems that should encourage every parent in America to scrutinize his or her child's child-care arrangement a little more closely. Here's a quick summary of their key findings:

✔ **Most center-based day care is mediocre.** A group of researchers from the University of Colorado made headline news when they announced the result of their national study of day-care centers in the mid-1990s. Their key finding? The quality of childcare in most day-care centers in the United States was poor to mediocre. The researchers concluded that one out of every eight centers provided care that was so poor that children's health, safety, and development were put at risk. Only one out of every seven day-care centers made the grade, in their opinion.

✔ **Infants receive the poorest quality of care.** The same group of University of Colorado researchers had even more damning things to say about the quality of day care provided to infants. They concluded that 40 percent of infant rooms in day-care centers across the country were guilty of providing substandard care. Only one in twelve infant rooms measured up to nationally recognized standards of quality, according to their research.

✔ **The situation in family day cares is equally alarming.** A national study of family day cares conducted by the Families and Work Institute at around the same time found that more than one-third of family day-care programs were of such poor quality that they were harmful to the development of the children in their care. Only one in eight of the homes evaluated in the study managed to provide care that actually enhanced the growth and development of the children being cared for in that home.

The bottom line: You can't count on anyone else to guarantee your child's health, safety, and well-being in a particular child-care setting. Like it or not, the buck stops with you. That's why you owe it to yourself and your child to read books like this one that show you how to be a smart and savvy day-care consumer. So give yourself a huge amount of credit for facing up to the problem rather than trying to bury your head in the sand. As with anything else in life, recognizing that there's a problem is more than half the battle.

The child-care crunch is everybody's problem

Even though it's been a generation since the June Cleavers of the world traded in their aprons for briefcases en masse, we're still trying to wrap our heads around the fact that the dual income family is now officially the norm. The result? The demand for child-care spaces constantly exceeds the supply. And if you do a bit of number crunching, you'll see that the demand is huge.

According to the National Center for Education Statistics, approximately 13 million children under the age of six spend some or all of their day being cared for by someone other than their parents.

Of course, you don't have to be employed outside the home to be in the market for childcare. Approximately one in three children under the age of six whose mothers are not in the paid labor force are enrolled in some sort of child-care or early education program, according to the National Center for Education Statistics.

So don't let anyone try to tell you that the child-care shortage is just a problem for working families. It's everybody's problem.

Part-time childcare, full-time headache

Finding standard, no-frills childcare (full-time daytime childcare from Monday to Friday) is hard enough. If you're looking for something a little out of the ordinary, such as half-day or every-other-day childcare, you could find yourself out of luck unless, of course, you're willing to pay for a full-time child-care space, even though you only need it part-time.

The administrator of the local day-care center or the home day-care provider isn't looking to make your life miserable, by the way, by refusing to accept part-timers. Because facilities are limited as to how many kids they can accept, they *have* to make every space they've got count. So unless you're willing to find another parent who's willing to sublet your day-care space, you may be stuck footing the bill for full-time care even if you use it only part-time or continuing to pound the pavement until you find a day care that welcomes part-timers.

Because the quest for childcare can quickly turn into a full-time job if your working hours are anything but nine-to-five, I devote an entire chapter to this topic (Chapter 13). If you want to get a handle on the types of child-care options that have worked particularly well for other families requiring part-time childcare, you may want to skip ahead to this chapter.

The affordability crisis

Of course, finding a suitable child-care arrangement is one thing. Being able to afford it is quite another. According to the Children's Defense Fund, full-time childcare can cost anywhere from $4,000 to $10,000 per child per year, which makes it the second or third biggest expenditure in the budgets of families with children between the ages of 3 and 5.

According to the Annie E. Casey Foundation, millions of children who could benefit from high-quality child-care and early education programs are denied those opportunities because their parents simply aren't able to afford them. Ironically, although parents pick up the tab for roughly only 23 percent of the cost of a public college education (government and the private sector pay the rest), they're on the hook for 60 percent of child-care costs (local, state, and federal governments pay 39 percent of the costs, and business and philanthropic interests contribute the other 1 percent). Is it any wonder that families with children in childcare are feeling the pinch? (See Chapter 4 for more on the financial aspects of childcare.)

When Plan A fails: Finding backup care

Something else that can make the search for childcare tremendously frustrating is the need to think like an emergency services coordinator. Having one child-care plan (call it Plan A) isn't enough. You also have to be thinking about Plan B and Plan C. Now before you jump to the conclusion that I'm a card-carrying member of the International Order of Worrywarts, allow me to give you a concrete example of why a little bit of paranoia can take you a long way in the often unpredictable world of childcare.

Assume that your main child-care plan (Plan A) involves having your husband's mother come into your home each weekday to take care of her beloved grandchildren. (If you're thinking of asking family members to help you out in this capacity, head over to Chapter 10 where I discuss this topic in more detail.) Also assume that Granny — who's never even requested so much as a single week of vacation time because she so loves being with her grandkids — wins big at bingo one night and walks away with the grand prize: six weeks' use of a mobile home. Well, Granny's never been one to look a gift horse in the mouth, and before you can even ask her when she's leaving, she's backing out of the driveway, blowing kisses, and promising to send postcards.

So much for Plan A.

Fortunately, you once read a brilliantly written book about childcare (I'm blushing — you just confessed it was this book!), and the author stressed the importance of having a backup plan. So you came up with Plan B a long, long time ago. Plan B involves asking your neighbor, Jane, to pinch-hit in the event that Granny's suddenly unavailable. But wait! Jane is due to give birth to her eighth and ninth children any day now (yep, she's expecting twins!).

There goes Plan B.

So that leaves you with Plan C — hitting the panic button. (Just kidding! I wouldn't leave you in the lurch.) Because this is my book and I love happy endings, I'm going to give this story just that: a picture-perfect happy ending. Let's just say that the old adage about necessity being the mother of invention pans out, and you're suddenly struck with a brilliant thought while you're pacing the floor at 3:00 in the morning: Why not convince *your* mother to come and visit for the six weeks when your husband's mother is away?

As it turns out, Plan C is a hit with all concerned. The kids are thrilled, your husband's thrilled, you're relieved, and as for your mom — well, she's euphoric. As luck would have it, she's been trying to come up with a reason to hop on a plane and come visit her grandchildren, and now, you've given her the perfect reason. She couldn't be happier or more grateful — and neither could you.

As this heartwarming, three-tissue story indicates, you can never have enough child-care backup plans in place because you never know when life is going to toss another child-care curveball your way. All you can count on is that another curveball *will* be coming, so you'd better be prepared. And if you have a job that really does require that you make it to work as often as possible — for example, you're a brain surgeon, and you can't exactly ask your secretary to fill in for you in the operating room — you may want to move beyond Plan C. Heck, you may want to extend your backup plans all the way to Plan Z.

If you want the lowdown on how other families handle the need for backup care, you can find plenty of ideas and inspiration in Chapter 12.

When you and your partner don't see eye to eye

People tend to have strong, even passionate, feelings about childcare, so it's not unusual to run into conflicts with your child's other parent over child-care-related issues — something that only adds to the stress and frustration of searching for childcare.

There's no easy way to resolve these kinds of child-care conflicts, but you may find it helpful to try to understand the other person's point of view. If, for example, you have your heart set on a family day care around the corner, but your partner is totally sold on the highly regarded day-care center on the other side of town, you'll want to ensure that you've each had a chance to check out both facilities. Otherwise, you risk getting married to your own option just because it's, well, *yours!*

If you're still at an impasse at this point, you may have to resort to the child-care world's equivalent of flipping a coin: letting the parent who will be most actively involved in your child's day-to-day day-care life (the parent responsible for drop-off and pick-up most days) have the final say.

If a deep-rooted philosophical debate is what's causing your partner to get hung up on a particular child-care option, you may find that a little bit of information-sharing can take you a long way. Chapter 2 provides a concise run-through of your various child-care options. Who knows? Maybe you'll decide that center-based childcare and family day cares aren't what your family needs at all: Maybe a nanny is the answer to your prayers!

And the Search Begins: Making the Process Less Stressful

Your odds of eliminating all the stress from your child-care search are pretty much slim-to-none, but you can take some steps to make the process a little less stressful: starting your search early, tapping into your network of contacts, finding out about the application process at day-care centers and some family day cares, and deciding how to work around waiting lists and other hurdles.

Starting your search early

Landing a space at the best day-care center in town can be even more of a challenge than getting a table at that hot new restaurant everyone is talking about. At least tables at the restaurant turn over every couple of hours; child-care spaces tend to turn over only every couple of years! And just as you'd better plan to call early in the week if you want to book a table for Friday or Saturday night, you'd better get your name on the day-care center waiting list as soon as you're clear about your family's needs.

Of course, just how early you should start your search largely depends on the type of childcare you're considering:

✔ If you're considering a day-care center (an option I discuss in Chapter 6), you'll want to start your search as much as a year in advance and get your name on as many waiting lists as possible, particularly if you're looking for childcare for an infant or toddler. Infant spaces are hard to come by and are typically reserved for families who already have children enrolled at the day-care center, so they can be in particularly short supply.

You can do everything right — call a year ahead and get your names on the waiting lists of every day-care center in town — and still come up empty. I know because it's happened to me. When I found out that I was pregnant with my youngest child, one of the first things I did was call the local day-care center to put my name on the waiting list. Believe it or not, it still wasn't soon enough! Despite the fact that the day-care center director found out about my pregnancy before my husband did (I called her within minutes of getting the pregnancy test results!), she wasn't able to find me an infant space when it came time for me to go back to work.

✔ If you're thinking of placing your child in a family day care (an option I discuss in Chapter 7), you can afford to be a little bit more laid back. For one thing, family day cares have a lot more spaces than day-care centers, and for another, it's impossible for an owner of a family day care to predict a year in advance whether she's likely to have any spaces in her program. You also can't expect a family day-care provider to hold a space in her day care for months and months, just so that it'll be available when you need it — unless, of course, you're willing to start paying for the space ahead of time to reserve it. That's why most parents hold off on the search for a home day-care space until approximately six to eight weeks before they need it. That's usually more than enough lead time to conduct a thorough search.

✔ If you're thinking of enrolling your child in a part-time preschool program (an option I discuss in Chapter 8), plan to sign your child up in the winter or the spring if you want to secure a space in the program for the fall. Of course, if the preschool in your community is in hot demand, you may have to sign up a year or two in advance. Believe it or not, getting into some preschools is as hard as getting into Harvard!

✔ If you're thinking of hiring an in-home child-care provider (an option I discuss in Chapter 9), you'll need to bank on a similar timeline (six to eight weeks). You can't conduct a search for an in-home child-care provider too far in advance because you can't realistically expect her to tread water for six months while she's waiting for you to finally be in need of her services. However, these things can be negotiated from time to time, so don't let the nanny of your dreams slip through your fingers just because you found her a little too soon. If the position you're offering her is sufficiently attractive, she may be willing to do some temporary, fill-in work for another family — perhaps pinch-hitting for their regular child-care provider while she's off on maternity leave — until you have need for her services.

Tapping into your network of contacts

"It's not what you know; it's who you know." Those words of wisdom have no doubt served you well over the course of your career. Come on, 'fess up. You didn't get your first summer job at the local hamburger joint because of your great personal charm and your extraordinary burger-flipping abilities. You got it because the guy who owned the burger joint was an old football pal of your father's!

Well, now's the time to start flipping through your address book to see if you know anyone who might be able to help you hit pay dirt on the child-care front. (And, no, you don't have to know Mary Poppins personally to make a flip through your address book worthwhile.) Friends and family members can be an excellent source of leads on childcare. Here's why:

✔ **They may be tapped into the local child-care grapevine.** Count yourself lucky if you have friends and family members raising young children in the same neck of the woods as you because they can act as your eyes and ears on the street. If they happen to hear that a home day-care provider in the neighborhood has had an infant space open up, they can pass along that news to you. They can also help to steer you clear of child-care arrangements that may be less than ideal. It's amazing how quickly bad news travels when a group of moms gets together at the playground!

✔ **They can launch an informal child-care advertising campaign on your behalf.** Remember that 1970s hair commercial that talked about how quickly news can be spread "if you tell two friends and so on, and so on, and so on"? Well, your friends and family members can start this same kind of mouth-to-mouth advertising campaign on your behalf by letting the people in their circle of friends know that you're in the market for childcare. And if these same friends happen to be online, they can get that same e-mail message out to dozens and dozens of people with the click of a mouse. Hey, ain't technology grand?!!

Of course, you don't have to limit your child-care search to your immediate circle of contacts. You increase your odds of tracking down some leads if you cast your childcare net far and wide. Here are some resources you'll want to tap into as you embark on your child-care search:

✔ **Your local Child Care Resource and Referral Center:** One of the first calls you make should be to your local *Child Care Resource and Referral Center (CCR&R)*. The staff of your CCR&R can provide you with referrals to local child-care providers, give you the lowdown on state licensing requirements, make you aware of child-care subsidies that you may be eligible for, and help to guide you through the process of choosing childcare. They're basically information central when it comes to finding childcare in your community. You can track down the number of your local CCR&R by checking out your phone book, by calling Child Care Aware at 1-800-424-2246, or by visiting the Child Care Aware Web site at www.childcareaware.org.

✔ **The "nanny network":** If you're in the market for an in-home child-care provider, ask friends with nannies or full-time child-care providers if they know of anyone else looking for work. They may be able to put you in touch with someone who's new to the area and trying to find suitable employment. If that particular strategy doesn't pan out for you and you're in the market for a bona fide nanny (a graduate of an accredited nanny school; see Chapter 9), you may want to get in touch with the National Association of Nannies at 800-344-6266 to see whether their members are aware of any nannies in your area who are looking for work.

✔ **The local family day-care network:** Although you won't find a family day-care network in every community, they can be an absolute gold mine to a parent who's looking for childcare. Basically, a family day-care network is a group of family day-care providers who've banded together to offer one another support, exchange information, and explore opportunities for ongoing professional development. Because the day-care providers in the network are in regular contact with one another, members of the network generally have a pretty clear idea about who does and doesn't have spaces opening up.

✔ **The pediatrician's office:** Ask your pediatrician and the members of her staff if they know of any child-care vacancies in your community. And the next time your child is in for his checkup, scan the bulletin board in the waiting room. You may stumble across an advertisement from a home day-care provider who's just about to open up shop in your neighborhood. Obviously, because you'll be dealing with a complete stranger, you'll want to scrutinize the family day-care arrangement and the family day-care provider particularly carefully. Don't assume that your pediatrician endorses this caregiver just because you found the advertisement on her bulletin board.

✔ **Other family hot spots:** And while I'm talking bulletin boards, get in the habit of scanning the bulletin board at every family-friendly venue you visit: the library, local elementary schools, the community center, the laundromat, the consignment store — even your favorite family restaurant. You never know what you'll find plastered on the bulletin board, so be sure to keep your eyes wide open.

✔ **Newspapers, magazines, newsletters, and community directories:** Pick up every community publication you can get your hands on. Day-care centers and family day-care providers routinely advertise their services in these types of publications. Or, if you prefer, take the bull by the horns and place an advertisement yourself. You can find practical tips on wording your advertisement in Chapter 11.

✔ **Local people in the know:** Real estate agents, business development consultants, and others whose business it is to know your community inside out can also be a source of child-care leads. Ditto for people who work with families on a regular basis, like doctors, teachers, nurses, psychologists, and those who work for organizations that provide parent education. Ask them to keep their ear to the ground for you.

✔ **The Internet:** The Internet is overflowing with information on every conceivable topic, and childcare is no exception. If you're wondering exactly what the Internet has to offer in terms of child-care resources, check out Chapter 18, where I give you the scoop on the crème de la crème of Web sites.

✔ **The career placement center of your local college or university:** Your local college or university may be able to provide you with leads on graduates who are either looking for employment as in-home caregivers or thinking about opening up their own family day-care businesses or day-care centers. And if you're in the market for part-time or occasional childcare, they may even be able to hook you up with an early-childhood development student who's looking to get some hands-on experience working with young children and who's eager to earn a few extra dollars at the same time. I've used this recruiting method time and time again over the years, and I've consistently hit pay dirt. I hope that you'll be equally lucky if you decide to give it a shot.

✔ **Your human resources department at work:** Find out what assistance may be available to you through your human resources department at work. Some companies hire work and family consultants to assist employees with their child-care search; others purchase spaces in day-care centers and make them available to employees at a reduced rate. You won't know what kind of perks are available to you unless you ask, so plan to set up an appointment to talk to your human resources manager before you do a lot of legwork on your own.

With any luck, all this pavement pounding will generate tons of great leads. After you come up with a short list of possibilities, you'll want to do some initial pre-screening by phone and then arrange some onsite visits to day-care centers (see Chapter 6) or family day cares (see Chapter 7), and/or to set up some interviews with potential in-home caregivers (see Chapter 9) — your first step in determining which child-care arrangement is likely to be your best bet.

The application process: What to expect

If you decide to go the day-care center route, odds are you'll be asked to fill out an application form at some stage of the game — either at the time your child's name goes on the waiting list or later on when they call to notify you of an available spot. (Don't assume, by the way, that you'll be off the hook in terms of paperwork if you happen to go the family day-care route. Some family day-care providers ask parents to fill out a less detailed version of the basic day-care center application form.)

After you've finished filling out the application form, you have one more tiny piece of paper to fill out — the check for your application fee. Although most fees are relatively small (typically $25 to $50), they can really add up if you're hedging your bets by putting in application forms at every day-care center in town. See Chapter 6 for further details about the application procedure.

Waiting lists and other hurdles

After you hand over your application form and your application fee, the waiting game begins. Your name gets placed on a waiting list, and you receive a call whenever your name finds its way to the top of the list. That could be a matter of days, weeks, months, or even years. Phoning the day-care center every once in a while to double-check that your name is still on the list isn't a bad idea. You'd hate to find out a year or two after the fact that your day-care application was misfiled!

If a spot in the day care comes up before you're ready for it (perhaps you indicated that you wanted to start your child in the center in April, but they call you in February to let you know that a space has come available), you'll have to decide whether you're willing to take the space a little bit early or allow the center to offer the space to someone else.

The first thing you'll want to find out, of course, is what happens if you turn down the space. Some centers keep your name at the top of the list and offer you the next spot that becomes available. Others bump you back down to the bottom of the list, and you find yourself right back at square one.

Rather than missing out on what might be your one-and-only chance at a spot, you may want to think about taking the spot early, even if you don't actually intend to use it until after your originally scheduled return to work. Going this route may cost you a couple of hundred dollars in extra child-care costs, but, sometimes, knowing that your child-care problem has been solved is worth the extra money.

Figuring out what to do if the opposite problem occurs isn't quite as easy: You're due to return to work in a couple weeks' time, and you still haven't heard a peep from the day-care center. Obviously, you have two basic choices in this situation:

- ✔ Come up with a temporary child-care solution and hope that the day-care center will find a space for your child sooner rather than later
- ✔ Abandon your plans to enroll your child in this particular day-care center and start looking for a different long-term child-care arrangement

Neither alternative is likely to feel particularly satisfying if you had your heart set on placing your child in this particular day-care center, but given that that's simply not an option, you have little choice but to move on to Plan B.

Taking Out-of-Home Facilities into Consideration

As you may imagine, out-of-home childcare is childcare that takes place somewhere other than the child's own home — in a day-care center or in a family day-care home, for example. Most parents who choose an out-of-home day-care arrangement do so for one of the following three reasons:

- Out-of-home childcare tends to be less expensive than in-home childcare.
- Out-of-home child-care arrangements may provide for greater socialization opportunities.
- You don't have to worry about sharing your home with a stranger on a full- or part-time basis.

Where out-of-home child-care loses out to in-home childcare is in the convenience department: You have to drive somewhere every morning and you may have to arrange for backup childcare if your child is too sick to go to his regular out-of-home day-care arrangement. (See Chapters 2, 6, and 7 for more on the pros and cons of out-of-home childcare.)

Looking into In-Home Options

Although the majority of American parents choose to have their children cared for in out-of-home child-care arrangements, that's not to say that an out-of-home child-care arrangement is necessarily the best bet for your family. When families decide to hire a nanny or other child-care provider to care for their child in their own home they often do so because

- They want to take a bit of the rush out of the morning rush hour.
- They want to ensure that the same person will be taking care of their child day after day (not always possible in a busy day-care center).
- They want to minimize the number of colds and flus their child is exposed to (the more kids, the more viruses!).
- They're looking for maximum flexibility when it comes to scheduling.

Of course, in-home childcare isn't without its drawbacks: It's more expensive, provides children with fewer opportunities for socialization, requires that you assume total responsibility for monitoring the quality of your child's child-care arrangement, and forces you to come up with your own backup arrangements in the event that your nanny calls in sick. (See Chapters 2, 9, and 11 for more on the pros and cons of in-home childcare.)

Red tape unlimited: Hiring a domestic worker

Of course, there's another major drawback to going the in-home child-care route that many parents don't even stop to consider: all the hidden work in being an employer. You see, the moment that you decide to hire someone to care for your child in your home, you find yourself saddled with the responsibilities that go along with being that person's boss. That means dealing with reels and reels of government red tape.

Here's a quick overview of what's involved from a government standpoint after you decide to hire a domestic worker (the government's term for any person employed in your home). You need to

✔ Verify that the child-care provider is legally entitled to work in the United States

✔ Obtain an employer identification number

✔ Fill out the necessary paperwork so that you can start withholding Social Security, Medicare taxes, Federal Unemployment Tax (FUTA), and (if both you and she agree that this tax will be withheld at source) federal income tax from her wages

✔ Find out if you're required to pay state unemployment taxes on her wages

✔ Ensure that you're meeting all your record-keeping and tax reporting responsibilities

If you're notorious for filing your own personal tax return late, you may want to think seriously about hiring a bookkeeper to handle some of the paperwork for you. It may cost you a bit of money, but chances are it'll be cheaper in the long-run than the penalties you could rack up for getting on the wrong side of the IRS. This is heavy duty stuff, I know, which is why I devote an entire chapter (Chapter 11) to the ins and outs of employing an in-home child-care provider.

And nanny makes three: Privacy concerns

If you're thinking about hiring a live-in child-care provider, you have another issue to grapple with: the whole issue of privacy — yours and hers. Here are a few examples of how adding a child-care provider to your household can really cramp your style.

✔ Your partner and you are having a heated discussion in the kitchen one evening. You're about to give him an earful when you suddenly remember that the child-care provider is sitting in the other room. So much for getting this particular argument resolved anytime soon.

✔ The argument has long since blown over, and now, you're getting ready to celebrate your anniversary. You and your partner are going to have to abandon your long-standing tradition of taking the day off work to spend the day in bed! It just doesn't seem right to be getting romantic when your nanny is playing blocks with your toddler in the next room.

✔ Your partner's in the habit of sleeping in the buff. Now that a strange woman is sleeping under the same roof, he's thinking that he's going to have to invest in his first-ever pair of pajamas.

Although none of these problems is insurmountable, they may require a little bit of creativity and/or compromise. As you no doubt found out when you first became a parent, you can't expect to add another person to your household without experiencing at least a few growing pains.

If you're feeling uncertain about how to handle these types of sticky situations, relax. You can find all kinds of practical tips on dealing with privacy issues and a whole lot more in Chapter 9.

Chapter 2

What's on the Menu? Understanding Your Child-Care Options

. . . .

In This Chapter

▶ Zeroing in on out-of-home child-care options

▶ Focusing on in-home child-care options

. . . .

*A*lthough checking out a new restaurant for the very first time is always fun, deciphering the menu can be more than a little bit overwhelming — particularly if you're sampling a new kind of cuisine for the very first time. I don't know about you, but I often find myself wishing that I'd had the foresight to tote along a dictionary so that I could figure out what some of those exotic-sounding ingredients on the menu actually are. After all, it's pretty hard to feel confident that you're going to like what you ordered if you aren't exactly sure what it is. It's enough to give you heavy-duty flashbacks to Aunt Mildred's much feared "mystery casserole"!

You may get the same feeling when choosing childcare for the first time. It's hard to feel confident that you've made the right decision if you aren't quite clear exactly what it is that you've decided to order off the child-care menu. Well, you've come to the right place. This chapter explains your child-care options so that you can feel more confident about making your choices. After all, nothing's worse than figuring out after the fact that triple chocolate soufflé was on the menu, but you missed it . . . .

Considering Out-of-Home Child-Care Options

Most of the time, when people talk about "out-of-home" childcare, they're talking about two basic things: day-care centers and family day cares. However, this term is sometimes used to describe a third type of care — preschool programs — so I briefly touch upon that kind of care in this section, too.

But first things first: Just so you know exactly what I'm talking about when I start bouncing these three terms around, let me take a moment to define them.

- *Day-care centers* are facilities that provide care to a large number of children (usually more than 20). The children in these centers are cared for in small groups. (Some daycare centers group children by age, and others allow children to be cared for in mixed-aged groups, which allows children from the same family to spend their days together.)

- *Family day cares* are home-based businesses that provide care to a relatively small number of children in the child-care provider's home. Some states allow family day cares to hire additional staff and to increase the number of children that they care for accordingly, but even the largest family day-care operation is typically smaller than the smallest day-care center.

- *Preschools* (less commonly called nursery schools) are early education programs designed to prepare children for kindergarten entry. The majority of these programs follow the school year (they run from September to June), and they tend to operate on a half-day rather than a full-day basis. (This is starting to change, however. It's becoming increasingly common for preschools to offer full-day rather than half-day programs.)

Where the boys (and girls) are . . . .

Wondering where America's youngest children spend their days? According to the Urban Institute's *1999 National Survey of America's Families* (NSAF)

- 28% of children under age 5 are cared for in day cares and preschools.

- 14% of children under age 5 are cared for in family day cares.

- 27% of children under age 5 are cared for by their parents.

- 27% of children under age 5 are cared for by relatives other than their parents.

- 4% are cared for in their own homes by nannies or other child-care providers.

Although day-care centers, family day cares, and preschools all happen to fall under the out-of-home child-care umbrella, each of the three types of care has something slightly different to offer. To help you decide if any of these options seems like a good bet for your family, I want to walk you through the pros and cons of each.

Ol' reliable: Day-care centers

Day-care centers are the child-care method of choice for the majority of American families. However, that doesn't necessarily mean that they're automatically the right choice for yours.

Before I get into the pros and cons of going the day-care center route, a quick terminology note. A number of child-care centers refer to themselves as early care and education centers and make a point of offering preschool programming to the children in their care. So sometimes a day-care center can be a bit like a preschool — and vice versa. It's an important point to keep in mind.

Pros

Day-care centers have a lot to offer you and your child. Here's the lowdown on some of the key advantages.

- ✔ State child-care standards may not be anything to write home about, but they at least guarantee a basic standard of quality — assuming, of course, that the day-care center in question is covered by the relevant state legislation. (As I explain in Chapter 5, not all day-care centers are.) Still, knowing that someone else other than you is monitoring the quality of your child's care can be a huge relief. Sometimes, it's nice to have Big Brother on your side!

- ✔ Day-care center staff is generally required to have at least some basic training in child development — something that tends to improve the quality of the care they provide. Of course, this standard is by no means universal, so inquiring about staff credentials when you're evaluating a particular day-care center is always a good idea. (See Chapter 6 for more on the ins and outs of checking out a day-care center.)

- ✔ You don't have to worry if the child-care provider is ill or otherwise unavailable. If the child-care provider who's responsible for your child happens to be away, the center director will arrange for someone else to replace him or her. You don't have to worry about working the phone at 7 a.m.

- ✔ Day-care centers provide young children with the opportunity to play with other children — something that can be particularly valuable to your child if you don't happen to have any other children living at home and he's had limited opportunity to work on his budding social skills.

Cons

Of course, day-care centers aren't without their drawbacks. Here's what you need to know if you're considering this type of care.

- ✔ Children who are cared for in day-care centers tend to get sick more often than kids who are cared for in either an in-home or family day-care setting. And you don't have to be an MD to figure out why this is the case: More kids equals more germs.

- ✔ Most day-care centers don't offer particularly flexible hours. If you work rotating shifts, evenings, or weekends, odds are you'll have to consider a different type of care. (See Chapter 13 for tips on finding creative solutions to your need for childcare during offbeat hours.)

- ✔ Your child may be required to adjust her eating and sleeping schedule in order to fit into the center's routine. Although the truly crème de la crème of day-care centers go out of their way to try to accommodate the individual schedules of the children in their care, in reality, it's only possible to accommodate individual needs to a certain degree when you're dealing with a large number of children. Just ask any mother of six!

- ✔ Center-based childcare is the most expensive option when it comes to out-of-home day care. If you require childcare for more than one child, the combined fees may be more than your budget can swing. (Before you give up in total despair, however, be sure to take a quick flip to Chapter 4, where you can find out how to get the maximum bang for your child-care buck.)

You can find out more particulars about day-care centers in Chapter 6.

Parents' top day-care worries

What do parents fear more than anything about enrolling their child in a day-care center? Abuse. A recent study conducted by the nonprofit think tank Public Agenda found that 63 percent of parents with children under the age of 5 believe that abuse can and does occur in a typical day-care environment — despite the fact that only 1 percent of child abuse cases reported to the U.S. Department of Health and Human Services in 2000 were actually perpetrated by day-care staff. (Federal statistics show, in fact, that a child is 75 times more likely to be abused by his own parent as he is to be abused by a day-care worker.)

Parents aren't just worried about the possibility of abuse in day-care centers, however. They also worry about neglect (62%), poor supervision (62%), and the possibility that their child might not receive enough personalized attention (55%). And a final worry identified by 52% of parents is one of those concerns that pretty much dates back to the caveman days: concern that their kids might pick up bad habits from other kids.

You can tap into Public Agenda's extensive research on childcare and other related issues by visiting the Public Agenda Web site at www.publicagenda.org.

A more intimate setting: Family day cares

The second most popular type of out-of-home childcare is family day care —
childcare that takes place in someone else's home.

Pros

Parents who decide to go the family day-care route typically do so for one of
the following reasons.

- Family day care is both the least expensive kind of childcare and the easiest to find. If you ask around, you'll probably find at least a couple of
family day cares up and running in your neighborhood. Whether they
actually have vacancies is another issue entirely, but it just goes to
show how popular this particular child-care option has become.

- Many parents are drawn to the family-like atmosphere and the small
group size that a typical family day care has to offer.

- Your child's eating and sleeping schedule may be more easily accommo-
dated in a family day-care setting than in a large institutional setting,
such as a day-care center.

- If you have more than one child and you're able to find spaces for
them in the same family day care, they'll be together during the day.
They wouldn't necessarily be able to play together if you were to place
them in a day-care center because children in day-care centers are
often grouped according to age. Some day-care centers offer mixed-age
groups, however, so make sure that you have all the facts before you
make your decision.

Cons

Family day cares don't work for every family, however. Here are some of the
key reasons that you may choose to steer clear of this particular type of care.

- Family day-care providers are less likely than day-care staff to have
received specialized training in child development. That's not to say that
they're any less qualified to care for children, however: Many family day-
care providers have years of round-the-clock experience in raising their
own children. But in terms of having a tangible credential, such as a
diploma in child development, you're less likely to find one listed on
the resume of a family day-care provider than you are of someone
who's working full-time in a day-care center.

- Not all family day-care operations are in full compliance with state regulations. As a day-care consumer, you're responsible for determining
whether or not the standards are being met. This means educating yourself about the standards in your state. (**Hint:** If you put in a call to your
local Child Care Resource & Referral Agency, they can tell you everything
you need to know about family day-care standards in your neck of the

woods. You can track down the number of your local CCR&R by looking in your phone book, by calling Child Care Aware at 1-800-424-2246, or by visiting the Child Care Aware Web site at www.childcareaware.org.) See Chapter 5 for more about finding quality childcare.

✔ You'll probably have to arrange for your own backup if the family day-care provider needs time off due to illness or a family emergency. Although some family day-care providers make a point of arranging for backup care, these folks tend to be the exception rather than the rule. And even if the family day-care provider does do some of the legwork for you, you'll still want to check out the backup caregiver for yourself anyway. (This is one of the key differences between having your child cared for in a family day care as opposed to day-care center setting: If your child is enrolled in a day-care center, the center director is the one who has to worry about arranging for backup care. If you're a family day-care parent, more often than not, you have to take on that role.)

✔ A family day care may lack some of the equipment and facilities found in large day-care centers: high-priced educational toys, institutional-quality playground equipment, and so on. I'm certainly not suggesting that you should pick your child's care arrangement solely on the basis of the great stuff your kid would have a chance to play with (and ignore such factors as the quality of the overall program and whether or not he "clicks" with the child-care provider in question), but it's just one more factor to keep in mind when you're making your child-care decision.

✔ If you require childcare for more than one child, you may have to do a bit of searching before you find a family day-care provider who has enough vacancies to accommodate all your children. State child-care laws are quite specific about the number and ages of children that can be cared for in any one home, so if someone has only one infant space available and you require day care for your 6-month-old twins, you're out of luck.

Read more about going the family day-care route in Chapter 7.

The scholarly route: Preschools

Preschools typically fall under the early education umbrella rather than the child-care umbrella, but because some parents use preschools to address their child-care needs, and that care happens in an out-of-home setting, including preschools in this part of the chapter only makes sense.

Pros

Some parents feel quite strongly that they want their child to attend preschool rather than day care per se even though, as I note earlier in this chapter, the lines between day care and preschool can sometimes be quite blurry. Parents who choose to enroll their children in preschool typically do so for one of the following reasons.

Is out-of-home childcare the best bet for your family?

Unsure whether out-of-home childcare is the best bet for your family? This quick, five-question quiz should help you to decide. The more "yes," answers you get, the more confident you can feel that out-of-home childcare will work well for you and your child.

1. **Do you work a standard 40-hour work week?** Finding out-of-home childcare that accommodates your schedule can be a major challenge if you happen to work evenings, weekends, rotating shifts, or other offbeat hours. Many parents who work non-standard hours find that in-home childcare works better for their families. (See Chapter 13 for a more detailed discussion of this issue.)

2. **Is it important to you that your child spend his days in the company of other kids the same age?** If it's important to you that your child hangs out with other kids his age while he's in childcare, you've pretty much eliminated out-of home childcare as an option — unless, of course, you happen to be the parent of twins! One of the key drawbacks to out-of-home childcare is the fact that your child could end up being home alone all day with an adult child-care provider. You can solve the problem by arranging play dates or enrolling your child in a preschool for a few hours a day, but nothing beats the convenience of having "built in" playmates.

3. **Are you willing to put up with the fact that your child is likely to pick up a fair number of colds and flus from day care?** Children don't just bring home armfuls of artwork from day care: They also tend to bring home colds and flus. Enrolling your child in a group day-care situation means agreeing to put up with the virus *du jour.* Fortunately, the situation will improve over time as your child's immune system gets a little feistier — small solace in the meantime, I know, if you're walking around with a permanently red nose!

4. **Are you willing to head out the door a little earlier and arrive home a little later each day?** Even if the family day care or child-care center is just around the corner from your house, finding a parking spot and getting your child in and out the door takes time. You can count on running the day-care marathon more than 200 times each year, so make sure that you have the requisite patience and stamina!

5. **Is your family's budget already stretched to the max?** Out-of-home childcare is a much more affordable option than in-home childcare, particularly if you need childcare for only one child, so if you need to get maximum bang for your child-care buck, this is the way to go. You can pick up some great dollar-stretching tips in Chapter 4.

✔ Preschool programs can provide young children with opportunities for early learning and socialization in a highly *child-centered environment.* (Child-centered simply means that it's a child rather than an adult who's in the driver's seat when it comes to determining how learning happens.)

✔ Preschool programs can help to promote a lifelong love of learning and to ease the adjustment from home to school. What they can't guarantee, however, is that Little Johnny will be a shoe-in for a Harvard scholarship 20 years down the road. So don't kid yourself or allow any preschool director try to tell you otherwise!

✔ Preschool programs can afford the opportunity for enrichment and stim-ulation. A high-energy child who seems to be bored at home or in the family day-care environment may benefit from a preschool program. Of course, you'll want to make sure that the preschool program that you're considering delivers the goods when it comes to offering a lively and stimulating program for young children. Otherwise, there's no point in signing your child up.

Cons

However, preschool programs do have their disadvantages. For example:

✔ Preschool programs are typically offered on a half-day basis (although some programs are offered on a full-day basis), and they tend to follow the school year (which means they're closed during the summer months) — something that makes them less appealing to parents who work full-time. That's not to say that you have to rule out preschool as an option entirely: If you're committed to providing this opportunity to your child, you'll find a way to make it happen. One mom I know used to spend her lunch hours shuttling her child from preschool to her after-noon child-care arrangement. So where there's a will, there's a way . . . .

✔ Preschool isn't an option if you have a baby or young toddler. Most preschools are licensed to accept only two- to five-year olds. (If you have a younger child and you want to enroll him in preschool someday, you may want to get his name on the waiting list sooner rather than later. The waiting lists at some of the more popular preschools are astoundingly long!)

✔ You may end up paying for more childcare than you need. If you work full-time and you send your child to a part-time preschool program, you're still going to have to arrange childcare for the other half of his day. If, for example, you have your child enrolled in a mornings-only preschool pro-gram, and he spends the rest of his day at family day care, odds are you'll end up paying for approximately one-and-a-half day-care spaces — a half-time space at preschool and a full-time space at family day care.

✔ Many preschools accept only children who are toilet-trained — something that can really put pressure on parents to get their kids out of diapers before they (the kids!) are fully ready. If you have a child who's not exactly eager to bid farewell to diapers, you may want to give serious thought to coming up with an alternative child-care arrangement — one that's a little more diaper-friendly!

You can find out more about preschools by reading Chapter 8.

Mulling Over In-Home Child-Care Options

The term "in-home" childcare describes any childcare that takes place in the child's own home, whether that care is provided by a professional nanny, an au pair, a relative (see Chapter 10 for a detailed discussion of how that can play out, for better and for worse!), or another in-home child-care provider (also known as "a baby sitter"). Because each of these terms describes something entirely different, I just want to take a moment to go over the lingo.

- **Professional nannies:** Even though parents in some parts of the country like to use the term *nanny* to refer to any in-home child-care provider, that's not entirely accurate. (It's kind of like referring to anything with four wheels as a Porsche.) A true nanny (a professional nanny) is someone who's graduated from an accredited nanny school. That's why real nannies — the Mary Poppins of the world — have started tacking the word "professional" in front of the word "nanny." They're trying to distinguish themselves from all the nanny wannabes. Remember that a nanny by any other name is definitely not a nanny!

- **Au pair:** An *au pair* is a young person — typically from a foreign country — who exchanges child-care services for the chance to live and study in the United States. Fans of the au pair program describe it as a highly successful cultural exchange; critics describe it as an abysmal failure that puts the lives of America's youngest and most vulnerable citizens at risk by leaving them in the care of young girls who may have little training and even less inclination to care for young children. Who knew that childcare could be so controversial?

- **Baby sitters and other in-home caregivers:** Although the term *baby sitter* has not yet gone the way of the dinosaur, it's well on its way. These days, it's increasingly being used to describe the teenager who pops over for an hour or two so that you and your partner can enjoy a kid-free night out as opposed to an adult who comes into your home on a daily basis to care for your kids while you go to work.

Because each of these three types of in-home caregivers brings something very different to the child-care table, I consider the pros and cons of each arrangement separately, starting with nanny care.

Professional nannies

According to the International Nanny Association, the number of nannies working in America grew by 25 percent between 1996 and 2001, and that still wasn't enough to meet demand for their services. Clearly, nannies continue to be a huge hit with families. Still, they're not necessarily the right choice for everyone.

Pros

If you choose to go the nanny route, it will likely be for one of the following reasons.

- ✔ Professional nannies are thoroughly trained in all aspects of early childhood education and, therefore, are capable of developing an early education program that's uniquely tailored to your child's needs and stage of development.

- ✔ Although no Good Housekeeping Seal of Approval exists in the world of childcare, a diploma from an accredited nanny school is pretty much the next best thing. (But, as with any form of childcare, it's no substitute for a genuine love of children. You can find a nanny with all the right credentials who is truly dreadful at her job.)

Cons

Nannies aren't necessarily the right choice for every family. Here are some reasons that you may decide to take a pass on Mary Poppins.

- ✔ Professional nannies don't come cheap. In fact, hiring a professional nanny is the most expensive child-care option — something that puts nanny care out of the reach of all but the most affluent of families. You can find out more about nanny salaries in Chapters 9 and 11.

- ✔ Professional nannies are in short supply. In fact, you may have to put your name on a waiting list to get one. Figure on at least three months' lead time if you're hiring a domestic nanny, and even longer than that if you're planning to recruit from overseas.

- ✔ Don't be snowed by fancy credentials: A diploma from even the very best nanny school is no substitute for common sense. Some supposedly "unqualified" baby sitters have far more hands-on experience with young children than people who have the word "nanny" stamped on their business cards.

- ✔ You have to do your homework to ensure that the prospective nanny's credentials are up to snuff. If you're not sure whether the nanny school that's listed on her resume is a bona fide nanny school or one that advertises on the covers of matchbooks, put a call into the American Council of Nanny Schools (517-686-9417) to find out for sure. The last thing you want is to inadvertently hire a grad of Matchbook U!

Au pairs

Over the past 20 years, more than 100,000 au pairs have taken part in the U.S. State Department's highly popular (and highly controversial) au pair program.

Pros

If you're sold on the idea of hiring an au pair, odds are it's for one of the following reasons.

✔ The au pair program allows you to open your home to someone from a different culture — something that could prove to be both fun and enlightening for you and your kids.

✔ The childcare provided by an au pair is extremely affordable. Under the terms of the Au Pair In America program (call 800-727-2437 or visit the Au Pair in America Web site at www.aupairinamerica.com to find out more) you can expect to pay approximately $240 per week for 45 hours of childcare. This salary includes the au pair's pocket money, insurance, visa, orientation, and flight. (**Note:** You're also required to pay an education allowance, an application fee, and to pick up the tab for a few other incidentals, so make sure that you have a thorough understanding of your financial responsibilities before you sign on the dotted line.)

Cons

If, on the other hand, you're dead set against this form of care, it's likely to be for one of these reasons.

✔ A huge backlash has occurred against au pairs in recent years following a high-profile au pair murder trial, with a number of people in the childcare profession pointing out that many young au pairs arrive in America anticipating a good time, not the hard work that goes along with caring for children. Criticism of the program was so heated in the late 1990s that the International Nanny Association launched a campaign urging the House Committee on International Relations to discontinue the au pair program.

✔ Because the program is aimed at young people between the ages of 18 to 26, many au pairs have little, if any, previous experience in caring for young children.

✔ Not every au pair-host family match works out. In approximately 15 to 20 percent of cases, the au pair asks to be moved to another family or to be put on the next plane home. So you could go to all the trouble of planning for your au pair's visit, only to have her bail on you at the eleventh hour.

✔ You may be just as eager to bid a not-so-fond farewell to the au pair as she is to wave goodbye to you. The strain of sharing a home with a teenager or young adult combined with the resultant loss of privacy can be simply too much for some host parents.

✔ The au pair program lasts for only one year, so you'll have to look for a new child-care arrangement at the end of that time — an important point to bear in mind because caregiver consistency has been proven to be extremely important for young children. (And do you really want to have to go back to the child-care drawing board again in a year's time?)

Baby sitters and other in-home caregivers

The vast majority of child-care providers fall into the "other" category; they're neither professional nannies nor au pairs. Here's a quick rundown of the pros and cons of going with this type of in-home childcare.

Pros

If you're thinking of hiring an in-home caregiver, odds are you're leaning toward this form of care for one of the following reasons.

- ✔ A standard in-home caregiver won't cost you as much as a professional nanny. Although the going rate for childcare varies considerably from community to community, professional nannies are almost always able to command more money than their less formally trained counterparts.

- ✔ You'll have an easier time recruiting a standard in-home caregiver than you will a nanny or an au pair because you have a much larger pool of candidates to draw from.

Cons

In-home childcare isn't necessarily right for every family. Here are some reasons that you may not be particularly keen on this option.

- ✔ Because the amount of training and experience that in-home caregivers bring to the table varies considerably from caregiver to caregiver, you'll need to assess the caregiver's credentials carefully and monitor her performance on an ongoing basis. (You have to do this with any child-care arrangement, of course, but you'll want to be especially vigilant if the child-care provider in question isn't being supervised by anyone but you.)

- ✔ A high rate of turnover exists among in-home caregivers, both because the profession tends to be quite stressful and isolating and because pay rates are rock bottom. You simply have no way of knowing upfront whether or not this particular Mary Poppins is going to be prepared to stick around.

You can discover more about hiring an in-home caregiver by reading Chapters 9 and 11.

Is in-home childcare the best bet for your family?

Unsure whether in-home childcare is the best bet for your family? This quick, five-question quiz should help you to decide. The more "yes," answers you get, the more confident you can feel that in-home childcare will work well for you and your child.

1. **Can you actually afford to pay for in-home childcare?** Chances are you'll be hard-pressed to find a nanny or other in-home child-care provider who's willing to work for less than $400 to $500 a week, so you're likely looking at a child-care bill of $20,000 to $26,000 per year — considerably more than the $4,000 to $10,000 per year that it costs for a full-time child-care space. (Of course, if you have an exceptionally large family or day-care costs are higher than average in your community, in-home childcare may be more affordable than you think. So before you make up your mind either way, you'll want to do the necessary number crunching. See Chapter 4 for a quick crash course in the economics of childcare.)

2. **Do you work something other than standard business hours?** If your work hours are anything other than 9-to-5, you may find yourself scrambling to locate an out-of-home child-care provider willing to meet your family's child-care needs. Unless you have a friend or relative who's willing to provide weekend or after-hours care in your home, or you can find a day-care center or family day care that provides extended hours, in-home childcare may be your only option.

3. **Is it absolutely critical that you make it into work each and every day?** If you have the kind of job that requires close to 100 percent attendance (for instance, you're an attorney who's required to make courtroom appearances on behalf of clients or a heart surgeon with a very busy medical practice), you need a child-care arrangement that's as reliable as possible — one that won't get pre-empted every time your child comes down with a case of the sniffles. Because some child-care centers and family day cares tend to err on the side of caution when it comes to allowing even mildly ill children to participate in their programs, you may find your

head cold-prone toddler being "benched" on a regular basis. An in-home child-care arrangement would be a much better bet as long as the child-care provider isn't prone to taking a lot of sick days herself. If she tends to get sick more often than your child, you'll find yourself in even more dire straits!

4. **Do you have the time, energy, and skills required to be someone's employer?** A quick flip to Chapter 11 should be all that's required to convince you that having an employee isn't exactly a walk in the park. Not only do you have to deal with government red tape galore, you also have to deal with professional development issues, vacation requests, employer-employee conflicts, and all the other sticky issues that go along with being someone's boss. Add to that the fact that you have to assume sole responsibility for ensuring that your child is receiving the quality of care that she deserves, and you can see that being the caregiver's boss is a job in itself.

5. **Does your child find it difficult to handle disruptions to her daily routine?** If your child is easily thrown by life's little curve balls (she's the kind of child who'd be positively destroyed if another child were to put on her rubber boots by mistake), she may be more comfortable with an in-home child-care arrangement than an out-of-home day-care arrangement. After all, the more children you toss into a particular environment, the more unpredictable life can get! (Of course, some folks would argue that group child-care settings managed by skilled and sensitive child-care providers can provide such children with a tremendous opportunity to learn the ins and outs of getting along with others. Because you know your child best, you're in the perfect position to decide whether she'd find the experiencing enriching or overwhelming.)

Chapter 3

Ages and Stages: Making Childcare Work for Your Child and Your Family

In This Chapter

▶ Focusing on your child's needs

▶ Keeping in mind your family's needs

*Y*ou wouldn't dream of hitting the local automotive showroom without having at least a rough idea of what you're looking for in a vehicle. After all, you need to know upfront whether you're in the market for a sporty two-seater or a minivan that positively screams family. Otherwise, you run the risk of making a huge mistake — like falling head-over-heels in love with some sexy little red sports car and realizing after the fact that you've just spent $40,000 on a vehicle that doesn't have enough seats for your kids. (Just try to explain *that one* to your better half!)

The same principle applies to choosing childcare: You need to be clear about your needs right from the start. That's what this chapter is all about: getting a clearer picture of your child's needs by considering such factors as your child's age and temperament, as well as your family's needs. Thinking about all these important issues now means that you likely won't end up with the child-care world's equivalent of that little red sports car — an arrangement that may look good in the showroom but that isn't going to do the job over the long term.

Zeroing In on Your Child's Needs

When you're sizing up your child-care needs, you should first look at the needs of your child. Basically, you want to zero in on three key factors:

- Your child's age
- Age-specific worries and concerns
- Your child's temperament

Factoring in your child's age

Children change dramatically during their first few years of life. They evolve from tiny, helpless human beings into fully verbal, fully mobile little people. So, not surprisingly, their child-care needs change by leaps and bounds, too. The child-care arrangement that seemed so ideal when your child was a sleepy newborn may not seem quite so perfect by the time he's morphed into an active toddler. So don't forget to keep your child's current and future needs in mind when you're evaluating a particular child-care arrangement. Otherwise, you may find yourself having to switch child-care arrangements simply because your child has outgrown a particular situation.

Two of the most influential things to look for when choosing care for children of all ages are a low caregiver-child ratio and a small group size. Table 3-1 offers the ideal ratios and group sizes for children of various ages, as spelled out in *Caring for Our Children: National Health and Safety Performance Standards for Out-of-Home Childcare Programs* — a joint publication of the American Academy of Pediatrics, the American Public Health Association, and the U.S. Department of Health and Human Services. These ratios are what these three leading health authorities recommend based on research into what leads to the best outcome for children. They're not mandated by law. You'll probably find that the child-care standards in your state are much less rigorous.

Table 3-1	Caregiver Child-Care Ratios	
Age of Child	*Recommended Caregiver-Child Ratio*	*Recommended Group Size (Maximum)*
Birth to age 12 months	1:3	6
13 months to 30 months	1:4	8

Age of Child	Recommended Caregiver-Child Ratio	Recommended Group Size (Maximum)
31 months to 35 months	1:5	10
3-year-olds	1:7	14
4-year-olds	1:8	16
5-year-olds	1:8	16
6- to 8-year-olds	1:10	20
9- to 12-year olds	1:12	24

What follows is a breakdown of what to look for when you're shopping for childcare for children of various ages.

Babies

Researchers have spent years trying to pinpoint the key ingredients in the "recipe" for an ideal child-care arrangement for an infant. Here's a quick summary of their findings to date.

- **Continuity of care:** Infants do best in child-care situations in which they're cared for by the same person day after day. This daily interaction allows them to form strong attachments to their caregivers — something that contributes to their emotional health and well-being.

- **Responsive caregivers:** The responsiveness of the caregiver is another critically important factor in determining whether an infant will do well in a particular child-care setting. In order to feel safe and secure and to develop a sense of trust in his caregiver (to say nothing of the universe as a whole!), a baby's needs must be met promptly and consistently by the person who's responsible for caring for him while he's away from his parents.

- **Lots of affection:** This one is hardly a surprise, but it warrants a mention nonetheless: Babies tend to thrive in settings that provide plenty of opportunities for cuddling, holding, and unhurried care.

- **A program that follows a baby-friendly schedule:** Babies do better in settings in which they're allowed to follow their own eating and sleeping schedules, as opposed to being forced to conform to some predetermined mealtime and naptime schedule.

- **A predictable environment:** Like human beings in general, babies are creatures of habit. Consequently, they tend to feel more comfortable and secure in situations that have some sort of predictable routine.

✔ **A safe yet stimulating environment:** Babies need to have access to a safe yet stimulating environment — one that's designed to provide them with plenty of opportunities for learning, but that's been suitably child-proofed for babies at every stage of development from creepers to crawlers to walkers.

✔ **Plenty of opportunity for communication between parents and care-givers:** Parents and caregivers should share information on a regular basis — daily if possible. Such communication can happen informally at pickup and drop-off times via written notes in a notebook that travels back and forth to day-care each day.

Toddlers

Wondering what you should be looking for when you're shopping for a child-care arrangement for your toddler? Research has shown that children between the ages of 18 and 30 months of age benefit most from child-care arrangements that meet the following criteria:

✔ **Continuity of care:** Like babies, toddlers do best in child-care situations in which they're cared for by the same person from one day to the next. They're creatures of habit who thrive on routine, and part of that routine involves having the same smiling face greet them at the door each morning.

✔ **Patient and energetic caregivers:** Not every child-care provider has the patience and energy to deal with toddlers, so when you're checking out a particular child-care arrangement, you want to determine whether the child-care provider in question has a knack for dealing with toddlers.

✔ **Lots of affection:** Toddlers may not need to be cuddled and held as much as babies — they're much too squirmy for that! — but they do need to know that the adults in their lives (caregivers included) think they're really special.

✔ **Predictable routines:** Toddlers like to know what's coming next, whether it's snacktime, storytime, naptime, or outdoor playtime. And the only way they can master the rhythms of the day-care day is if those rhythms are routine and predictable. If you're tempted to underestimate the importance of rituals to a typical toddler, just stop and consider how your child reacted the last time you asked her to put her pajamas on before brushing her teeth (as opposed to performing these tasks in their usual order) or otherwise broke one of the "rules" of her universe!

✔ **A safe yet stimulating environment:** Providing an environment that's simultaneously safe and stimulating for toddlers is a challenge, but that's exactly what's required for children of this particular age group. After all, they have an abundance of energy but not a lot of commonsense!

✔ **Plenty of opportunity for communication between parents and care-givers.** Communicating with your child's caregiver can be a major challenge when your child's competing for your attention, so if you haven't done so already, you may want to add the logbook method of communication during the toddler years. It's an excellent way to share important information back and forth — communications that may otherwise get missed in the midst of the chaos at drop-off and pickup times.

Preschoolers

Research has shown that *preschoolers* — children between the ages of 3 and 6 — also have specific child-care needs. Following is a quick summary of what the research has shown to be of benefit to preschoolers.

✔ **Continuity of care:** Continuity of care continues to be important during the preschool years. Although preschoolers may have an easier time adjusting to teacher changes than babies or toddlers do, they still find it reassuring to see a familiar face waiting for them each morning when they arrive at day care.

✔ **Caring and attentive teachers:** Preschoolers benefit from having caring, attentive teachers who are interested in talking with them and playing with them, and who adapt their teaching style to the needs of each individual child so that each child's needs are met.

✔ **Lots of affection:** Preschoolers need to be on the receiving end of a steady stream of affection from the important adults in their lives, teachers included.

✔ **A predictable environment:** Like toddlers, preschoolers thrive on routine. Knowing what to expect over the course of the day-care day helps them to feel in control of their world.

✔ **A preschooler-friendly environment:** Preschoolers need to have access to age-appropriate activities and equipment, so if your preschooler is grouped in with younger children, make sure that the environment includes plenty of materials that will be of interest to a preschooler.

✔ **Plenty of opportunity for communication between parents and teachers:** As soon as your preschooler starts talking up a storm, getting a word in edgewise can be next to impossible, but keeping the lines of communication open between yourself and your child's child-care provider is still as important as ever. If you don't have time to say everything that needs to be said during the daily drop-off and pickup, write the child-care provider a note, or better yet, use a daily logbook so that you'll both be able to communicate back and forth.

School-aged children

After children start school, their child-care needs change dramatically. Not only do the hours for which they need care change now that they're in school on a part-time or full-time basis, but the nature of that care changes, too. Here's what to look for when you're searching for an after-school child-care arrangement for your school-aged child.

✔ **A program that provides suitable hours of care:** The key challenge that parents of school-aged children face is in finding a program that provides care exactly when they need it — typically before school, after school, and, in the case of kindergarten students, for certain hours during the day. You don't want to waste a lot of time considering programs that won't meet your child's scheduling needs, so find out about the hours of care before you get too far into the evaluation process.

✔ **A program that your child can get to each day:** Although you no doubt assumed full responsibility for shuttling your child to and from day care during his younger years, school-aged children often assume responsibility for getting themselves to after-school child-care programs, assuming, of course, that the child-care program in question is within safe walking distance of the school or that the school bus is willing to drop off your child at the program after school. (If you're counting on your child's school bus to provide him with transportation to an after-school program, be sure to check with the school bus company about your plans before you sign your child up. Most school bus companies have very strict drop-off policies. The fact that the school bus drives right by the after-school program is no guarantee that the driver will actually be willing to drop off your child.)

✔ **Appropriate age groupings:** What fifth grader is going to want to spend his after-school hours hanging out with a bunch of first-graders? None that I can think of! That's why it's important to ensure that the after-school child-care program you're considering groups children by age. You also want to consider whether your child is at the upper end or lower end of that age grouping and whether that's likely to be problematic for your particular child.

✔ **Staff who understand the unique challenges of caring for school-aged children:** The children who show up at an after-school child-care program may be tired after spending a full day in school, or they may be full of pent-up energy and ready to burn off some steam. Clearly, child-care providers need to be up to the challenge of meeting the needs of both types of children: those who want to do something quiet while they recharge their batteries and those who are ready for a pickup game of basketball.

✔ **Staff who make an effort to coordinate their curriculums with the school communities they serve.** The staff of after-school programs should be aware of what the children in their care are doing in school so that they avoid repeating a lot of the same activities in the after-school program. Carving a pumpkin is fun, but it tends to lose some of its thrill if you just finished carving a pumpkin at school two hours earlier!

✔ **A program that's designed to meet the needs of older children:** An after-school program that's designed to meet the needs of older school-aged children should include a quiet place where children can get a head start on their homework. It's also important that program staff include activities that will appeal to older children and that they make a point of encouraging older children to be involved in planning some of their own activities.

✔ **Opportunities for communication between home, school, and the child-care environment.** After-school child-care programs are better able to meet the needs of the children they serve when there's plenty of communication between home, school, and childcare. If your child is having difficulty with a group of bullies at school, for example, you'll want to make the school and child-care staff are aware of the problem so that they can ensure that your child is safe at all times.

FRIDGE NOTES

The benefits of after-school child-care programs

Although after-school programs are still in relatively short supply (only 67 percent of schools nationwide offered onsite after-school programs in 2001), according to the National Institute on Out-of-School Time, children who participate in such programs are likely to reap some significant benefits. Studies have shown that children who participate in after-school programs are more likely to

✔ Attend school regularly

✔ Do their homework

✔ Have a better attitude toward school work in general

✔ Do well in school

✔ Attend college

✔ Have strong interpersonal skills and a solid work ethic

✔ Steer clear of drug use and avoid unplanned pregnancies during their teen years

You can find out more about the benefits of after-school child-care programs by contacting the National Institute on Out-of-School Time at the Center for Research on Women (www.wellesley.edu/WCW/CRW/SAC or 781-283-2547).

Academics sometimes use the term *out-of-school time* to describe the care that school-aged children receive during their nonschool hours, so don't be surprised if you see that term being bounced around if you do further reading on the child-care needs of school-aged children.

Considering age-specific worries and concerns

The items that find their way to the top of your worry list when your child is a baby tend to be quite different from those issues that have you hitting the panic button during the toddler and preschool years. So it only makes sense to factor in some of these age-specific worries and concerns when you embark on your child-care search. Here's the scoop on four issues that may show up on your parental radar screen, depending on the age of your child.

Finding a breastfeeding-friendly child-care provider

If you're intending to breastfeed after you return to work, you want to add an additional item to your list of things to look for in a child-care arrangement: a breastfeeding-friendly child-care provider. Here are the key questions to ask when you're trying to determine how supportive a particular child-care provider is likely to be of your decision to breastfeed your baby and how well she understands her role in supporting your breastfeeding decision.

✔ **Have you had experience in caring for breastfed babies?** Keeping a breastfed baby happy can be a challenge if that baby is used to nursing for comfort as well as for food, so try to find a child-care provider who's had some experience in caring for breastfed babies. A period of adjustment may be involved for both the baby and the child-care provider until the baby learns other ways of soothing himself while mom's breasts are out of range. Make sure that the child-care provider in question understands how your baby may react when he can't get what he wants and that she's willing to work with you to devise some alternative strategies for soothing your baby.

✔ **What techniques do you use to comfort breastfed babies who are used to nursing for comfort?** What you're looking for here is evidence that the child-care provider understands that she may end up spending a lot of time rocking your baby or otherwise trying to soothe him if he happens to become fussy while you're at work. She may find that something as simple as putting the baby in a baby carrier, "wearing" the baby while she goes about her day, is all that is required. Or she may find that your pint-sized town crier requires an endless repertoire of baby-soothing techniques in order to encourage him to (momentarily) focus on something other than the fact that he wants to nurse!

✔ **How many other breastfed babies are currently in your care? What are their ages?** Because breastfed babies may demand a little extra time and attention than their bottle-fed counterparts, find out the number and ages of any other breastfed babies who are being cared for by the same child-care provider. The age question is relevant because breastfed babies become much less demanding as they get a little older. Not only do they find ways to sooth themselves, but they also start taking a much greater interest in the world around them — something that generally leads to a much more contented baby. Add to that the fact that they typically start eating solid foods sometime between 4 and 6 months of age, and you can see why caring for older breastfed babies is a whole lot less demanding than caring for a much younger baby who's solely breastfed. If the child-care provider clearly has her hands full caring for a couple of very young (and very demanding) breastfed babies, you may want to consider an alternate child-care arrangement.

✔ **Would you mind if I dropped by at lunchtime to breastfeed my baby?** If you'd rather spend your lunchtime hooked up to a real baby than a breast pump and your child-care provider happens to be situated with a block or two of your workplace, you may want to talk to your child-care provider about how she'd feel about having you "do lunch" with her and your baby on a regular basis. Some child-care providers will support your decision to work in a midday feeding, but others worry about the disruption that this pop-in may cause to the day-care day, so make sure that you know where the child-care provider stands if this midday rendezvous is an important part of your breastfeeding game plan.

✔ **Do you support extended breastfeeding?** If you believe in a child-led form of weaning (the baby rather than the mother decides when weaning should occur), discuss the weaning issue with the child-care provider upfront. Otherwise, this issue could become a source of conflict down the road.

FRIDGE NOTES

Don't hit the bottle after returning to work

Although switching from breastfeeding to formula feeding after you return to work may be easier, your baby could miss out on some significant health benefits if you make the decision to wean too soon. The U.S. Department of Health and Human Services' *Blueprint for Action on Breastfeeding* recommends that children be breastfed exclusively for the first six months of life and that breastfeeding continue for at least the first year of life.

Research has shown that children who've been breastfed

✔ Score higher on cognitive, IQ, and vision tests

✔ Are less likely to succumb to *Sudden Infant Death Syndrome* (SIDS)

(continued)

(continued)

- ✔ Are less likely to suffer from infectious illnesses and their symptoms (diarrhea, ear infections, respiratory tract infections, meningitis)

- ✔ Face a lower risk of developing Crohn's disease and ulcerative colitis — the two most common inflammatory bowel diseases

- ✔ Suffer less often from certain forms of cancer, including both childhood leukemia and Hodgkin's disease

- ✔ Are less likely to develop juvenile onset diabetes (in cases where the family has a history of the disease, and the children have been breastfed exclusively for at least four months)

- ✔ Are less likely to develop asthma and eczema (when they're at risk of developing an allergic disorder and when they've been breastfed exclusively for at least four months)

- ✔ May be less likely to become obese during childhood and adolescence

- ✔ May have fewer cavities

- ✔ May be less likely to require orthodontic treatment

You can find out more about the benefits of breastfeeding by visiting the United States Breastfeeding Committee Web site at www.usbreastfeeding.org.

Potty time! Avoiding toilet-training problems

When you're shopping around for a suitable child-care arrangement for a toddler, another issue to think about is how the child-care provider you're considering handles toilet-training issues. Here are some questions that you'll want to ask upfront.

- ✔ **What are your philosophies and strategies when it comes to toilet training?** The child-care provider's answer to this question should provide you with a pretty clear indication of where she stands on the whole potty-training issue. If she notes rather matter-of-factly that most of the children in her care are trained sometime between age two-and-a-half and age three-and-a-half, you can figure that she's taking a pretty child-centered approach to toilet training, letting the child take the lead. But if she declares with tremendous pride that she's yet to have a child still in diapers on his second birthday (despite the fact that only 4 percent of two-year-olds nationwide can make the same claim), you can bet the family diaper money that she's operating some sort of toilet training boot camp for toddlers.

- ✔ **How do you typically coordinate toilet training with the parents of the children in your care?** Nothing can cause a toddler to flunk out of Potty Training U more quickly than being flipped between underwear at home and diapers at day care — or vice versa! — so you want to find a child-care provider who understands the importance of working cooperatively. And while you're talking toilet-training strategy, you also want to get a handle on what techniques she typically uses to train the children in her care. Learning to use the potty is tough enough for most kids without being subjected to two entirely different training methods, so you want to be sure that you're likely to be in synch when it comes to toilet-training techniques.

✔ **How do you go about encouraging success?** Research shows that praising successes and not making a big deal about the accidents are important factors in successful toilet training. Find out if the child-care provider is in the habit of sending children to the timeout chair if they don't quite manage to make it to the toilet in time. That kind of approach to toilet training is not only badly out of date and hard on a child's self-esteem, but it's also completely ineffective. (Imagine how you'd feel if someone sent you to the timeout chair every time you made a mistake when you were trying to master a new skill — like using a new software application? It certainly wouldn't make you want to fire your computer back up anytime soon.)

✔ **Do you have a potty seat and a stool or a free-standing potty on hand so that your toddler won't have to learn to use the big toilet right from day one?** Most toddlers balk at the idea of sitting on the big toilet when they're first mastering the ins and outs of toilet training: Not only is it miles off the ground (at least in their opinion), but it can feel icy cold to a warm little bum! Most toddlers feel much more secure launching their potty training careers by either using a free-standing potty chair or by using a toilet seat ring that attaches to the regular toilet seat. *Note:* If the child-care provider encourages the children in her care to use a toilet seat, she'll need to provide a step-stool as well. Having one's feet dangling when trying to use the potty isn't only scary but can also interfere with a toddler's ability to push out stool.

✔ **What words do you typically use when you're teaching toddlers about bodily functions?** Whether you use the words "pee" and "poop" or something else entirely, find out whether you and the child-care provider speak the same language when it comes to potty training. After all, your toddler is likely to be more than a little mystified if the child-care provider asks him if needs to "wee," but he's never heard anything but "pee." Fortunately, these types of linguistic challenges are easily resolved provided that the child-care provider is willing to follow your lead and use the toilet training vocabulary that your family chooses to adopt.

You can pick up some additional tips on troubleshooting day-care-related toilet-training challenges by reading *Potty Training For Dummies,* by Diane Stafford and Jennifer Shoquist, MD (Wiley).

Preventing food-related problems

Toddlers and preschoolers are notorious for dawdling over their meals and snacks, turning up their noses at foods they supposedly loved the day before, and engaging in all kinds of other food-related behaviors that adults may find totally bewildering. Because sidestepping food-related struggles with kids is so important, you want to ensure that the child-care provider shares your philosophies about feeding young children. Here are some questions that should help you to figure out where the child-care provider stands on food-related issues:

✔ **What is your basic philosophy about kids and foods?** It's important to share your ideas about how you want your child to be fed and address any areas of disagreement. For example, if you believe that it's the adult's job to decide what types of food to serve and when to serve them and that it's the kid's job to decide whether he wants to eat the food and, if so, how much he wants to eat, let the provider know that. If the child-care provider that you're considering announces proudly that all the children in her care belong to "the clean plate club"(they're expected to eat everything on their plates, whether they're hungry or not!), you'll know whether you need to discuss this issue with her and see if she's willing to adapt her approach for your child.

✔ **How do you handle the issue of "good foods" versus "bad foods"?** Our parents may have conned us into eating our veggies by promising us a bowl of chocolate pudding for dessert, but we now know that labeling foods as "good" and "bad" can backfire by teaching kids to value dessert over vegetables. You want to steer clear of any child-care provider who exhibits this kind of outdated thinking.

✔ **How often do you introduce new foods to the children in her care?** Child-care providers can easily fall into a rut when preparing meals and snacks for young children: If everyone happens to like grilled cheese sandwiches, that can quickly become the *menu du jour* day in and day out. Children need to be exposed to a variety of foods, however, both to ensure that they obtain a greater range of nutrients and to help them to acquire a taste for a broader variety of foods.

And don't assume, by the way, that your preschooler will necessarily go on a food strike the moment the child-care provider puts something other than grilled cheese sandwiches on the table. Studies have shown that preschoolers are generally willing to try new foods at day care if they're only asked to try one new food at a time, the new food is accompanied by other foods the preschooler likes, the new food is presented in an appealing way, the toddler sees the other children eating it, and the child-care provider doesn't pressure the child to try the food. Persistence (and a headache tablet or two) may also be required: Research has shown that some children have to be exposed to a new food on as many as 15 different occasions before they're actually willing to eat it!

✔ **How are transitions from activity to mealtime made?** Preschoolers may have a hard time settling down into a meal or snack if they've been involved in particularly active play. That's why experienced child-care providers understand the importance of allowing for some transition time before mealtimes and snacktimes — perhaps scheduling storytime for the half-hour before lunchtime, for example. (The child-care provider's approach to this issue won't merely indicate how she handles food-related issues, by the way; it'll also give you a pretty solid indication of her ability to structure the day-care day in a manner that works well for both herself and the children in her care.)

✔ **How do you go about keeping mealtimes and snacktimes relaxed and stress-free?** Preschoolers are much less likely to dig in their heels on food-related issues if the adults in their lives are able to keep mealtimes and snacktimes relatively relaxed. That means allowing enough time for even the most leisurely of diners to eat their meals and snacks without feeling rushed. After all, it's hard to enjoy your meal if you feel like your plate's going to be snatched away from you at any second, and you're going to be rushed off to the next activity!

Deciding whether your school-age child needs childcare

The National SAFE KIDS Campaign recommends that parents hold off on leaving children alone until they're 12 years of age or older, and state laws make it illegal to leave a child unsupervised before the age of 12 or 13. However, that doesn't necessarily mean that your child's ready to be left on his or her own after he reaches this particular age. The following checklist should help you to decide whether your child has the necessary judgment to be left home alone or not.

✔ **Does your child know his name, address, and phone number (including area code)?** Would she be able to provide this information to rescue personnel in the event of an emergency? Being able to rattle off your personal contact information when no pressure's on you is one thing; retrieving each of these crucial bits of data from your memory vault if the house is on fire or you've just cut yourself badly is quite another. You need to feel confident that your child would be able to convey this all-important information to rescue personnel in the event of an emergency.

✔ **Does your child know what number to call in the event of an emergency?** Make sure that your child knows exactly what to do in the event that disaster strikes — that he'll know enough to dial 911 as opposed to panicking. (Of course, it only makes sense to hedge your bets by programming all the important emergency numbers into your phone and posting them beside the telephone, too. That way, if your child happens to panic momentarily, she'll have an easier time figuring out what to do.)

✔ **Does your child know how to disarm and reactivate the security system?** In addition to teaching him how the security system works, you want to stress the importance of keeping the code secret. After all, your security system isn't nearly so secure if every kid in the seventh grade knows the code needed to disable it!

✔ **Does your child understand how and when to use a fire extinguisher?** Just as important as teaching your child how to use a fire extinguisher is teaching him when *not* to use a fire extinguisher. He shouldn't feel obligated to stick around to fight what started out as a small grease fire on the stove if the fire is clearly getting out of control. He needs to know that his safety is your number one priority. Houses can be replaced; people can't!

✔ **Can you trust your child to be discreet about the fact that he's home alone after school?** If your child is likely to treat the house key on the chain around his neck as a bit of a status symbol and flaunt it to other kids, he's probably not ready for home alone status yet. After all, one of the ground rules of being home alone is being discreet about the fact that you're *sans parent*.

✔ **Does your child know how to answer the telephone appropriately while she's home alone?** Most kids require a bit of coaching on this front because they may not know quite what to say if someone calls and asks them point-blank if their mother or father is home. You may have to give your child explicit permission to tell a little white lie (indicate to the person on the phone that a grownup is at home, but that person can't come to the phone right now) because most kids have been taught to be truthful to grownups.

✔ **Will your child remember to keep the doors locked at all times?** Your child needs to know that some basic safety rules need to be followed, no matter how eager he may be to get through the front door to flip on the TV or fire up his video game system. One of those rules involves locking the front door behind him. You may also want to make it a rule that he's not to unlock the door for any reason unless you've specifically given him permission to do so.

✔ **Are other people on your street home during the hours when your child will be on his own, or is your street pretty much a ghost town at these times of day?** If a couple of neighbors are around during the hours when your child will be responsible for her own care and they're people that your child would feel comfortable approaching for help in the event of an emergency, you may be a bit more willing to let your child stay home on her own. Keep in mind, however, that these people may or may not be available in your child's hour of need, so don't take too much solace in the fact that they *may* be home at the time. If you need to know that someone will be available to your child no matter what, you need to have a more solid child-care plan in place.

✔ **How well has your child coped in the past when he's been left on his own for an hour or so?** If your child has exercised poor judgment in the past when you've left him on his own while you've dashed out to grab a loaf of bread, you may want to think twice about giving him full responsibility of taking care of himself before and after school. I knew that my 12-year-old was anything but ready to be left home alone when he decided to resolve a dispute with a sibling over the family computer by turning off the main power switch to the house. I swear: That particular child may be 30 before he's allowed to stay home alone!

✔ **Does your child have a pretty solid track record when it comes to following rules?** If your child is going to be spending a couple of hours a day taking care of herself, you're going to have to have some clearly defined rules about what is and isn't allowed in your absence. You probably want to spell out some pretty clear policies governing each of the following issues:

- **Visits from friends** (whether all visits from friends are taboo or only certain friends are allowed to come over, whether homework has to be completed before friends are allowed to visit, how many friends are allowed in the house at one time, and so on)

- **TV viewing** (how much TV time is allowed, what programs are considered appropriate, whether homework has to be completed before your child flips on the tube, and so on)

- **Homework** (when homework is to be done, whether it has to be done before your child has any friends over or before he's allowed to leave the house, and so on)

- **Answering the door or phone** (whether you want him to answer the door or the phone while you're out and, if so, what he's to do or say)

- **Playing outside or at friends' houses** (whether he's allowed to play outside or at friends' houses while you're out and, if so, how he's to communicate his whereabouts to you so that you will know where to reach him)

- **Cooking** (whether your child is allowed to do any cooking while you're out, whether he's limited to using certain appliances — the microwave and the toaster versus the stovetop, for example, and what safety checks he needs to do after he's finished cooking)

Bottom line? Although being *Home Alone* may make for a great series of movies, it doesn't necessarily play out that well in real life. Only you can decide whether your child is up for the challenge.

Knowing your child's temperament

You don't have to have a PhD in child psychology to know that children are born with their own unique personalities right from day one. Even siblings growing up with the very same set of parents can be polar opposites when it comes to temperament: One may be extremely easy-going, while the other may give the expression "high-maintenance" a whole new meaning!

Although every child psychologist or medical doctor who's ever authored a parenting book has relied on a slightly different list of terms to describe children's temperaments, linguistic nuances aside, they all boil down to the three basic types of temperaments that psychologists Alexander Thomas and Stella Chess first described back in the 1950s:

✔ The *shy* or *slow-to-warm-up* child. A child who doesn't adapt well to new situations and who needs a bit of extra time to settle in and adjust.

✔ The *spirited* or *difficult* child. A child who reacts intensely to most situations and who tends to have a negative attitude much of the time.

✔ The *easy, flexible* child. A child who's upbeat, adaptable, and generally pretty easy-going about life.

Because your child's temperament can have a major impact on how readily she settles into a particular child-care arrangement, you want to keep her temperament in mind when you're considering various child-care options. Here's a quick rundown of the key characteristics of temperament and what they may mean in terms of your child's day-care experience:

✔ **Energy level:** *Energy level* refers to the amount of energy a child has — whether she's more inclined to sit quietly in the corner building a tower out of a pile of blocks or whether she's the kind of kid who's in perpetual motion. A high-energy kid is likely to thrive in a day-care setting where there's plenty of opportunity for active play. For a child who's less physically active, lots of opportunities for more sedentary exploration with books, puzzles, and so on should be available.

✔ **Regularity of patterns:** *Regularity of patterns* refers to the degree to which a child's basic biological patterns (eating and sleeping, for example) are predictable. Some children have highly regular and predictable patterns and find it relatively easy to settle into highly structured day-care programs. Others have much more erratic rhythms and may benefit from a program that's better able to accommodate their ever-changing needs. (Fitting into the regular day-care center routine can be difficult if you get hungry at 11:30 a.m. one day and 1:30 p.m. the next, or if you want to take two naps on Monday and none on Tuesday.) Obviously, you'll need to weigh the pros and cons of gently encouraging your child to become more flexible and adaptable by choosing a more challenging child-care environment for him versus allowing him to remain in his comfort zone for now.

✔ **Approach and withdrawal:** *Approach and withdrawal* refers to a child's initial reaction to something or someone new. If your child has a hard time coping with new people or new situations, you want to look for a child-care situation that provides a lot of consistency from one day to the next — the same child-care provider, the same group of children, the same child-care room, and so on. Also look for evidence that the child-care provider you're considering gives children a chance to warm up to their surroundings before they're expected to join in a group activity.

✔ **Adaptability:** *Adaptability* refers to your child's ability to adjust to whatever curveballs life may throw his way. If you know that your child is easily freaked out by changes to his routine (his world would be rocked if another child were to sit in his chair at the snack table or to wear his rubber boots home by mistake!), you may want to look for a child-care arrangement where orderliness and routine are emphasized. Obviously kids who are extremely rigid in their thinking need to learn to relax and go with the flow to a certain degree. The question is whether your child is ready to learn that lesson now — or whether he needs a little more time to mature first.

✔ **Intensity:** *Intensity* refers to the amount of emotion a child displays when reacting to life's ups and downs. A highly intense child may react with tremendous exuberance or throw a massive temper tantrum — or do both within a matter of minutes. If you have a very intense child, look for a child-care provider who'll respect your child's feelings while helping her learn how to express them in a more controlled way. On the other hand, if you have a child who's much less intense, you want to find a child-care provider who'll take steps to engage your child in activities and ensure that his needs don't get overlooked simply because he's less demanding than the other children.

✔ **Mood:** *Mood* refers to the overall feeling that a child transmits to the world on a consistent basis, be it positive or negative. Some children are naturally happy and upbeat, while others are more reserved or even negative. If your child falls into the latter category, make sure that the child-care provider in question has the patience required to deal with a child who consistently sees the glass as half empty rather than half full.

✔ **Attention span and distractibility:** *Attention span and distractibility* refers to a child's ability to stick with a task without becoming distracted. If you have a highly distractible toddler or preschooler, you may find that a small group or in-home child-care arrangement presents fewer distractions than a large-group setting.

✔ **Sensory threshold:** Sensory threshold refers to the amount of stimulation that a child requires in order to respond. Some children have a very low sensory threshold and become distressed by relatively low noise thresholds, while others are able to tune out an amazing amount of background noise and chaos. If you have a child who reacts strongly to sensory stimulation (for example, loud noises) or tries to block out background noise by covering his ears if a lot of people are talking at the same time, a small group or family day care may be a better choice for him.

As you can see, keeping your child's temperament in mind when you're weighing your various child-care options is important. Here are some additional points to keep in mind when you're evaluating child-care options for your shy, spirited, or easy child.

The shy child

A shy child may find the hustle-and-bustle of a child-care center environment to be somewhat overwhelming. (In fact, a recent study found that shy toddlers release considerably higher levels of stress hormones when they're being cared for in a child-care center than when they're being cared for at home.) She may be more comfortable being cared for in a smaller-group setting, perhaps a family day-care setting or an in-home child-care arrangement. You also want to find a child-care provider who'll be patient with your child and find ways to help her to feel comfortable in her new environment. You don't want a child-care provider who's unsympathetic toward or impatient with her feelings of shyness or who'll allow your child to languish on the sidelines while the other children demand and receive the lion's share of her attention.

The spirited child

A spirited child tends to have boundless energy and a high need for stimulation. Consequently, he may be most at home in a child-care setting that offers a stimulating environment and with a child-care provider who has the patience and energy required to deal with his often challenging behavior. Some spirited children thrive in a child-care center setting where a lot of activity is present to entertain them; others do better in a small-group setting or an in-home child-care arrangement where they may benefit from more individualized attention. You just have to weigh the pros and cons of each option and decide which is likely to be the best fit for your child.

The easy child

An easy child tends to thrive in any type of quality child-care arrangement. If you happen to be looking for a child-care arrangement for a child with this kind of temperament, you're likely to find that your child will settle into any type of child-care arrangement with relative ease. Your child may experience a few initial moments of uncertainly, but nothing like the theatrics that the parents of a spirited child can expect to witness. (Hey, they don't call 'em spirited for nothing!)

When your child has special needs

Finding a suitable child-care arrangement can be a challenge for any parent, but it tends to be doubly challenging if you happen to be the parent of a child who has special needs (physical or mental challenges or other exceptionalities). Telephone prescreening can save you a lot of time because it allows you to quickly weed out options that aren't going to meet your child's needs. Here are some questions you may want to ask when you're making initial contact with a family day-care provider or a child-care center:

- Is the child-care facility fully accessible to children with physical disabilities?

- Can therapeutic services, such as occupational therapy, physical therapy, and speech therapy, be worked into the child's day-care program, if necessary?

- Does the program accept children who aren't yet fully walking and/or toilet-trained?

- Has the child-care provider had any previous experience in caring for children with special needs?

- Has the child-care provider received any specialized training in caring for children with special needs?

- Is the child-care provider enthusiastic about working with you and your child?

- Does the child-care provider recognize the fact that your child's disability is secondary to who he is as a person?

- Is the child-care provider willing to work with you to set individual goals for your child and to help him achieve them?

- Is the child-care provider prepared to adapt the child-care program to make it more accessible to your child, given his current level of functioning?

- Does the child-care provider feel comfortable dealing with a child with his particular types of medical conditions and/or developmental challenges? (**Note:** You want to explain the nature of your child's needs in sufficient detail, so that the center director or family day-care provider can have a clear idea of what'll be involved in caring for him.)

FRIDGE NOTES

Now, that's the IDEA . . . .

The *Individuals with Disabilities Education Act* (IDEA) guarantees "free appropriate public education" to children with certain types of mental, physical, or emotional disabilities or chronic medical conditions who, because of the nature of their disability or chronic illness, require special instruction in order to learn.

If your child qualifies for such a program, a plan will be developed by the appropriate state agencies to ensure that your child receives the educational, therapeutic, and health services he needs. The plan is called an *Individualized Family Service Plan* if your child is an infant or a toddler or an *Individual Education Plan* if your child is a preschooler or school-aged child.

You can find out more about IDEA and what it means to you and your child by getting in touch with the Office of Special Education and Rehabilitative Services (OSERS) of the U.S. Department of Education: 202-205-5465 or www.ed.gov/offices/OSERS/.

You may find it better to make your child-care decision based on your child's developmental age as opposed to his chronological age. After all, a 3-year-old with limited self-care and mobility skills needs a lot more hands-on assistance from his child-care provider than a 3-year-old who's relatively self-sufficient.

Meeting Your Family's Needs

The earlier sections of this chapter had you zeroing in on your child's needs. Now, you need to consider your family's needs in terms of finding the right child-care arrangement. That means considering such factors as

- The location of the child-care arrangement you're considering
- Whether or not you're willing to pay a premium for convenience
- How your child-care needs may change if you require childcare for more than one child
- How your long-term child-care needs may differ from your short-term child-care needs
- How your needs for childcare may be affected if you work offbeat hours
- How running a home-based business may impact your child-care needs
- How your child-care situation may change if you become a single parent

Location, location, location

The saying that location is everything is true, especially when you're talking about childcare. The following list brings up some important points to keep in mind when you're considering the location of a particular child-care arrangement.

- **How close the child-care arrangement is to your home:** Although a 15-minute drive out of your way may not seem like much when you're checking out a particular child-care arrangement, if you stop and think about the number of times you're going to make that drive over the course of a week, a month, or a year, you can see why finding childcare in your own neighborhood is a priority for most parents. Finding child-care in your own neck of the woods has an added advantage, of course: It'll be easier for your child to make plans to visit with her friends from day care on evenings and weekends. Who knows? They may even show up on the school bus when she makes that first eventful journey to kindergarten!

✔ **How close the child-care arrangement is to your workplace:** Some parents whose workplaces are situated a considerable distance from their homes prefer to find day-care arrangements that are closer to work than home. The reason: If an emergency arises and the child-care provider calls to ask you to meet her at the closest hospital, being minutes away is much better than being a good hour away. Going this route has another bonus: You and your child can enjoy some guaranteed time together while you do the weekday work and daycare commute. (This time together may not work out quite as well if your child is prone to carsickness or general in-car crabbiness: As with anything else kid-related, your mileage may vary!)

✔ **How close the child-care arrangement is to the school your child will eventually attend:** Imagining the day when your child will head off to kindergarten while he's still a tiny babe-in-arms can be heart-wrenching, but that kind of forethought is definitely in order if you're going to make the best possible child-care decision. If you're lucky enough to find a day-care center or home day-care provider who offers a before- and after-school child-care program or an in-home child-care provider who's willing to stick with your family for the long-term, your child may end up being in the rather enviable position of only requiring a single child-care arrangement during his lifetime. The alternative — yanking your child from the family day-care home he adores because it happens to be in the wrong school district — can be heartbreaking for all concerned and, in a perfect world at least, is a trauma to be avoided at all costs.

Weighing the cost of convenience

Anything you can do to reduce the stress that goes along with being a working parent is going to reap tremendous dividends for you and your kids. That's why it only makes sense to zero in on a convenient form of childcare. For some parents, that may mean in-home childcare (having the childcare provider come into your own home). For other parents, it may mean workplace-based childcare (having your child cared for in a child-care center that's based in the same building as your workplace).

Of course, a hefty price tag usually accompanies convenience. You can expect to pay more for childcare if you decide to opt for the ultimate in convenience and hire an in-home child-care provider to care for your children in your own home. Assuming that in-home care is even an option for you — not everyone's budget can swing it, after all — you'll have to weigh cost versus convenience and decide whether the additional cost is justified. You can get a rough idea of what costs are involved and what you can do to get the maximum bang for your child-care buck by reading Chapter 4.

Finding childcare for more than one child

Your child-care needs change significantly after you start looking for child-care for more than one child. If you've already got two or more children or if you suspect that the stork will be paying you a visit in the very near future, you may want to stop and consider the impact that your growing family is having (or is going to have) on your child-care needs both today and down the road. Here are a couple of points to consider:

- **Economics.** Although out-of-home childcare is a less expensive option if you're purchasing care for one or two children, in-home childcare is more affordable if you require care for three or more children. (See Chapter 4 for a detailed discussion of what you can expect to pay for various types of childcare.)

- **Logistics.** Because you're likely to want to have your children cared for in the same day-care setting — the morning day-care marathon is challenging enough, after all, without having to make pit-stops at two or three different day-care facilities! — you may have to do a lot of searching in order to find a child-care program that has openings for all your children at the same time. You may find yourself facing an even bigger challenge if you're looking for childcare for infants who are multiples. Because child-care spaces for infants tend to be few and far between at the best of times, your odds of finding a day-care center or family day-care home with three infant spaces open at the same time may rival that of winning the lottery!

Although you may luck out and find a family day-care provider who's just opening up shop around the corner or a day-care center that happens to have a couple of vacancies that happen to correspond with the number and ages of your children, you'll have better luck lining up care if you decide to hire an in-home child-care provider to care for your children.

If you've been reluctant to go this route because you're uncertain how to go about hiring an in-home child-care provider or what's involved in being someone's employer, you can find detailed information on both those issues in Chapters 9 and 11.

Judging your short-term needs versus long-term needs

Something else you need to think about when you're considering a particular child-care arrangement is whether or not this particular child-care arrangement is likely to serve your child or your family's needs over the long-term. Here are some questions that you may want to ask yourself before you make your final decision:

✔ **Is my child likely to "outgrow" this particular child-care arrangement?** This type of situation is more common than you may think: The child-care arrangement that seems perfect when your child is a baby turns out to be less than ideal as he enters the toddler or preschool years. Suppose that you arrange for your baby boy to be cared for by a kindly, grandmotherly home day-care provider who's renowned for her love of babies. You may discover a year or two from now that she simply doesn't have the energy required to keep up with an active toddler. Although anticipating all your child's needs ahead of time can be next to impossible, this type of problem can sometimes be avoided if you make a point of asking the right questions when you do your reference checks (see Chapter 5) — like whether the caregiver in question is as skilled at dealing with toddlers as she is with babies.

✔ **Will my child be able to remain in this particular child-care environment until the time she starts school? What about after that?** I know, I know: You'd need a have a state-of-the-art crystal ball in order to be able to answer that particular question definitively, so I guess what I'm asking you do to is to make an educated guess. Given what you know right now about your family's plans and your child-care provider's plans and/or your child-care facility's policies, does it seem likely that your child would be able to remain in this particular child-care environment at least until she starts school? Or would she likely have to change child-care arrangements at least once, and perhaps even more often than that? What will happen after she starts school? Will the child-care facility or child-care provider be able to provide before- and after-school care to your child, or will you find yourself going back at the child-care drawing board?

✔ **What would happen if your employer were to change the nature of your job responsibilities?** Would you be able to stick with the same child-care arrangement if your employer were to significantly change the nature of your job, perhaps promoting you to a position that requires a lot of out-of-town travel or rotating shifts or (gulp!) transferring you to the company's other location on the opposite side of town?

✔ **Would you need to change your child-care arrangement if your family situation were to change dramatically?** No one likes to borrow trouble, but sometimes, you have to sublet it long enough to consider how it may affect your child-care situation. Here are some of the types of doomsday scenarios you may want to play out in your head: How would a sudden change in your family situation affect the child-care arrangement you're considering? Would you have to switch child-care arrangements if your partner were to lose his job? What if you were to find yourself suddenly single?

Finding childcare when you work nights or weekends

According to the U.S. Census Bureau, 19.7 percent of fathers and 12.9 percent of mothers with children under the age of 6 work nonstandard hours. Parents who work rotating shifts face even greater challenges when looking for child-care, due to the shortage of evening and weekend childcare and the fact that their child-care needs are constantly changing.

If you work nonstandard hours, you need to consider one of the following options:

- ✔ Hiring a live-in or live-out in-home child-care provider who can be available to meet your family's ever-changing child-care needs

- ✔ Finding a family day-care provider or day-care center that provides overnight care to children of shift-working parents. (You're more likely to find a day-care center that operates around the clock if the day-care center is operated by a local employer whose employees require around-the-clock childcare.)

- ✔ Using one or more types of childcare so that your child's needs are met from week to week (for example, having your child attend a daytime child-care arrangement in a family day care or child-care center during those weeks when you're working standard day shifts and having a family member stay with your child overnight during those weeks when you're working afternoon or evening shifts).

If you want to find out more about the creative solutions that other shift-working families have come up with in order to meet their needs for child-care, be sure to check out Chapter 13.

Determining child-care options for home-based workers

According to the U.S. Census Bureau, approximately 6.4 million workers in America are home-based. More than half of home-based workers are parents with children under the age of 18.

Although working from home has many advantages, juggling the responsibilities of running a business with the demands of raising a family can push even the most energetic and motivated parent into overload mode. Home-office burnout is even more likely if you're struggling with child-care problems, so if you're serious about operating a business from home, you need to get serious about childcare, too.

Trying to take care of your child while you run a business from home is generally a recipe for disaster — unless, of course, you're willing to limit your working hours to those times of day when your child happens to be taking a nap. If you attempt to entertain your child while attempting to answer e-mails from your clients or otherwise attend to the day-to-day work of running a business, you'll probably find that you end up shortchanging your baby and your business.

Of course, if you happen to be blessed with an exceptionally placid child, you can probably pull it off for a time, but eventually, your luck will run out, just as it did for a friend of mine. She had the perfect home-office baby for the better part of 22 months, but then he morphed into a full-blown toddler!

Over the course of a single day — a day his exhausted mother will never forget, I might add! — this sweet-faced little cherub managed to climb over a railing to play with the wood stove, drag a kitchen chair over to the microwave to turn it on, tip over the dehumidifier, answer the upstairs extension phone (after pole-vaulting out of his crib for the umpteenth time), cover his body with permanent black magic marker, ride down the stairs on his toy train, and remove all the baby-proof hardware that his parents had so painstakingly installed in the kitchen to keep him out of mischief. That was his last day as his mother's home-office sidekick. The very next week, he started day care!

My friend's experience serves to illustrate why childcare is anything but a frill for a home-based worker. If you're planning to run a business from home, you need to give some thought to which of the two basic child-care options is most likely to meet your family's needs:

- ✔ Hiring someone to care for your child elsewhere in your home while you run your business from behind your office door.
- ✔ Sending your child to an out-of-home child-care arrangement, such as a child-care center or family day care during your working day.

You can find out about the pros and cons of each of these solutions and pick up some tips on troubleshooting the most common day-care-related problems faced by home-based workers in Chapter 13.

Flying solo: Childcare and the single parent

Being a single parent can certainly affect your child-care needs. If you happen to be a single parent, you have to keep some additional points in mind when you're shopping around for a suitable child-care arrangement:

✔ **Cost:** Single-income households typically have less disposable income than dual-income households. You may find that your final child-care decision is largely determined by monetary concerns.

✔ **Scheduling considerations:** Depending on your relationship with your ex and what other types of support systems you have in place, you may be the only person who's available to do the day-care pickup and drop-off. If so, you need to zero in whatever child-care arrangements mesh best with your working hours.

✔ **Reliability:** Because you may not be able to rely on your ex to pinch-hit on the child-care front, finding a reliable child-care arrangement is likely to be a top priority for you. Of course, even the most reliable child-care arrangements in the world can and do go up in smoke with little or no warning, so you also need a waterproof backup plan or two. (See Chapter 12 for tips on putting together a backup plan that will eliminate most, if not all, of your child-care-related nightmares.)

Chapter 4

Adding Up Your Dollars and Sense

· ·

· ·

Childcare takes a big bite out of the average family's budget. A huge bite, in fact. According to the National Association for the Education of Young Children, the only things that parents with young children spend more of their income on than childcare are housing and food.

Childcare *is* expensive, but it doesn't have to be the stuff of which nightmares are made — not if you're armed with all the facts about child-care subsidies, tax credits, employer grants, and so on. And that, in a nutshell, is just what this chapter is all about — showing you how to get maximum bang for your child-care buck.

Figuring Out the Costs of Out-of-Home Childcare

If you flipped to this part of the chapter in the hope of enjoying some light bedtime reading before you slip into dreamland, you may want to reach for something a little more cheerful and upbeat — like *War and Peace* or *Wuthering Heights*, for example. Although I wouldn't go so far as to say that this chapter is going to depress the heck out of you or give you nightmares, it certainly isn't going to make it any easier for you to get a good night's sleep. So do yourself a favor and put the book aside until breakfast. Who knows? The child-care expenditure stats may give you such a jolt that you can forgo your usual cup of java!

Putting a positive spin on the latest stats about the cost of out-of-home child-care is simply impossible. The statistics are hair-raising, no matter how you slice 'em and dice 'em. So hold on to your hat. Here's the plain, unvarnished truth about the cost of out-of-home childcare in the U.S.:

✔ Child-care costs typically range from $4,000 to $6,000 per child per year, and in some parts of the U.S., costs can actually top the $10,000 mark, according to the Children's Defense Fund (a nonprofit think-tank that focuses on the welfare of children).

✔ Out-of-home childcare tends to be more expensive in urban areas than in rural areas, but it's still quite high in rural areas. According to the Children's Defense Fund, most parents living in rural areas can expect to pay between $3,000 and $6,000 per year for out-of-home childcare.

✔ An employed family with children under the age of 13 typically spends approximately $303 a month, or 9 percent of its household income on childcare, according to the Urban Institute (a nonprofit think-tank that studies life in U.S. cities).

✔ In more than half the states, the average cost of childcare for an infant in an urban area is more than twice the cost of public college tuition, according to the Children's Defense Fund.

✔ Infant care is the most expensive type of childcare. You can expect to pay approximately $1,100 more per year for infant day care than you would for day care for a 4-year-old, according to the Children's Defense Fund. The cost is higher for infant day care because government regulations limit the number of infants that a single individual can take care of; as a result, day-care providers can charge a premium for available infant spaces. The caregiver-child ratio increases as children get older (see Chapter 3 for more about caregiver-child ratios), so you can expect to pay more for childcare for a toddler than for a preschooler, and more for a preschooler than for a school-aged child.

✔ Even after children start school, childcare is a significant expense. According to the Children's Defense Fund, parents in urban areas of the U.S. can expect to pay $3,500 or more for childcare for their school-aged children each year. Parents in rural areas typically pay between $2,500 and $3,000 per year.

Up until now, I've been speaking in generalities. The next few sections get down to specifics. You find out what you need to know about the costs of the various types of out-of-home childcare.

Day-care centers

Having your child cared for in a day-care center doesn't come cheap. In fact, day-care centers are typically the most expensive out-of-home child-care option. I say typically because there are a few exceptions. In a few parts of the U.S., family day care is more expensive than center-based care. A handful of preschools also charge Harvard-type tuition fees to start a child's private school education before he's even learned his ABCs. But, for the most part, you can assume that center-based care is going to be the most expensive out-of-home child-care option in your community.

You can also assume that you're going to pay more for center-based care if you live in an urban area as opposed to a rural area. A child-care survey conducted by the Children's Defense Fund in 2000 reached the following conclusions:

- In one-third of states, the annual cost for an infant space in a day-care center in an urban area averaged $6,750 or higher and ranged from a low of $3,900 in Arkansas to a high of $12,978 in Massachusetts.

- In one-third of states, the annual cost for an infant space in a day-care center in a rural area averaged $5,000 and ranged from a low of $3,380 in Arkansas, North Carolina, and South Carolina to a high of $7,475 in Alaska.

Family day cares

As a rule, you can expect to pay a few hundred dollars less for a space in a family day care than you would for a comparable space in a day-care center. (This rule doesn't apply in all cases, but it seems to be the way things work in most communities.)

The rule about paying more for infant care in urban areas than in rural areas also holds true for family day cares. The Children's Defense Fund child-care survey found that

- In one-third of states, the annual cost for an infant space in a family day care in an urban area averaged $5,500 or higher and ranged from a low of $3,380 in Idaho to a high of $7,935 in New York.

- In one-quarter of states, the annual cost for an infant space in a family day care in a rural area averaged $4,500 and ranged from a low of $2,990 in Missouri to a high of $7,475 in Alaska.

Preschools

When it comes to preschool programs, expect to pay about what you'd pay for care in a day-care center if you were purchasing a comparable number of hours of care. Because most preschool programs provide care on a less than full-time basis (a typical child attending preschool attends for only 26 hours per week), you can count on paying roughly two-thirds of the going rate for childcare in your community for the weeks of the year that the preschool is open. (Most preschools follow the school calendar and close up shop for the summer months.) This means that you can expect to pay roughly $2,800 to $3,700 per academic year or $280 to $370 per month for each month that the program is running.

Of course, spending considerably more than that is possible. Some families choose to pay $15,000 to $20,000 per year to send their children to what can only be described as Ivy League preschools — schools that promise to give their child that intoxicating mix of educational advantage and social contacts right from day one. Despite the hefty price tags, competition to get into these schools can be fierce. Some families go so far as to hire consultants to help them fill out preschool applications to increase Junior's chances of making it into the right school — perhaps fudging his sandbox aptitude test or putting the most positive spin possible on his lackluster cut-and-paste skills. ("But don't you see? He's taking a deconstructionist approach to cut-and-paste. Can't you see that he's gifted?")

How to make out-of-home childcare more affordable

Not a lot of wheeling and dealing can be done when negotiating the cost of childcare. For one thing, most parts of the country have a chronic shortage of childcare — something that tends to keep the cost of childcare high. Also, most day-care options operate on a very small profit margin, if, in fact, they actually make money at all — something that leaves them very little room for cost cutting when setting day-care fees. That's not to say that there aren't any bargains to be had, but they are few and far between. That said, leave no stone unturned when looking for child-care discounts.

Here are a few questions you'll want to ask when checking out a particular day-care center or family day care. (A family day care is much less likely to offer these sorts of perks. You're more likely to hit pay dirt if you're digging for discounts at the local day-care center.)

✔ **Do you offer a discount to parents with two or more children enrolled in the program?** Some day-care centers offer a discount to parents who have more than one child enrolled in that particular center. In most cases, the discount is fairly small (typically 10 percent), but some centers offer more sizeable discounts (sometimes as high as 30 percent for the third child enrolled in a particular center).

✔ **Do you offer discounts to members of any local community organizations?** Some day-care centers offer discounts to members of certain community organizations. If your day-care center is affiliated with the local YMCA, for example, your membership at the local gym can be your ticket to considerable savings on day care.

✔ **Do you offer discounts to employees of any local companies?** Some employers negotiate discounts with local day-care centers on behalf of their employees. Making a quick pit stop in your company's human resources department is always a good idea when you first embark on your child-care search: you never know what kind of special deals they may have negotiated on your behalf. (See the more detailed discussion of workplace benefits in the section, "It's a Living: Getting Your Employer on Board" later in this chapter.)

✔ **Do you offer any subsidies?** Sometimes day-care centers have subsidies available to eligible families. In certain cases, these subsidies are made available by local philanthropists or foundations that are eager to do their part to help make childcare a little more affordable for working families.

✔ **Do you offer a sliding scale?** Some day-care centers try to make their fees more affordable to lower-income families by offering a sliding scale of fees. Basically, your day-care fees are determined by what you can afford to pay. A sliding scale fee plan can be a real lifesaver if you make too much money to qualify for a child-care subsidy program, but you don't make enough to afford the center's going rate.

Estimating the Price Tag of In-Home Childcare

Of course, out-of-home childcare is downright affordable when compared to in-home childcare. Here's what you can expect to pay if you decide to hire a professional nanny or another type of in-home child-care provider.

Professional nannies

Hiring a professional nanny (someone who has graduated from an accredited nanny school) is the most expensive child-care option. But what you can expect to pay a nanny can vary tremendously from year to year and from region to region.

The fortunes of professional nannies tend to rise and fall with the United States' economic fortunes. During the economic boom of the mid-1990s, nannies in large urban areas like New York City commanded salaries in the range of $1,500 per week. But within the last few years, the downturn in the economic fortunes of most Americans has sent many nannies' salaries nosediving to the $400- to $600-per-week range.

What a particular nanny ends up being able to command on the salary front is determined by a number of factors, including

✔ The number and ages of the children requiring care

✔ The nature of her job responsibilities

✔ How much training she has received

✔ How many years of experience she has

✔ Whether she will be living in or living out (live-out nannies tend to command a higher salary than live-in nannies because room and board is factored into a live-in nanny's salary).

Of course, hiring a nanny involves a lot of invisible costs — things like the increase in your car insurance premiums when you add an extra driver, the fact that you're responsible for all the so-called nanny taxes, and the fact that you're likely to want to offer her some basic employee benefits such as health insurance. (You can find the lowdown on negotiating your nanny's salary in Chapter 9, and you can get a blow-by-blow description of your responsibilities as an employer in Chapter 11.)

Bear in mind that huge regional variations occur in pay rates for nannies. You can't simply pick up the phone and ask your best friend in another state what she's paying her nanny and assume that it's fair to offer your nanny the same rate. Call some local employment agencies to inquire about the going rate for nannies and other in-home child-care providers in your community or monitor the want ads in your local newspaper to see what nannies are asking for and receiving in the salary department.

Although not a lot of research has been done on the salaries nannies are paid, in 2001, the International Nanny Association conducted a detailed salary survey. Here are a few of its key findings:

✔ The average gross hourly wage paid to both live-in and live-out nannies nation-wide was $10.25. Given that the average work week for a nanny was found to be 45.5 hours, this brings the average cost of employing a nanny to just under $470 per week.

✔ Some noteworthy regional differences exist when it comes to salaries. The best paid nannies in the U.S. are those who work in the northeast. Live-in nannies in that part of the U.S. earn an average of $516 per week, while their live-out counterparts typically earn $545 per week. The worst paid nannies in the U.S. work in the southeast. Live-in nannies there typically earn $385 per week, while live-out nannies typically earn $445 per week. (See Table 4-1 for a summary of other key data by region.)

Table 4-1	Average Pay Rates for Nannies in Various Parts of the Country	
Region	*Live-in Nanny*	*Live-out Nanny*
East Coast (North East)	$516	$545
East Coast (South East)	$385	$445
Midwest	$418	$510
Western U.S. (excluding California)	$400	$420
California	$497	$465

Source: 2001 International Nanny Association Salary Survey

Other in-home child-care providers

Pay rates for other in-home child-care providers (baby sitters and family members, for example) also vary tremendously. According to the U.S. Department of Labor's Bureau of Labor Statistics, a typical child-care worker providing in-home child-care services earned $8.71 per hour in 2000. The lowest 10 percent of child-care workers earned less than $5.68 per hour that year, and the highest 10 percent earned more than $10.71 per hour.

Although these wages certainly aren't anything to write home about from the child-care worker's perspective, the majority of parents find it a struggle to pay $5.68 an hour (or $227.20 a week) to an in-home child-care provider. These wages work out to $11,814 a year — more than even the most expensive day-care centers.

How to cut in-home child-care costs

If you like the idea of hiring an in-home child-care provider to care for your child (see Chapter 2 for the reasons why you may find in-home childcare appealing), but you don't have the necessary dollars in your budget to hire a full-time child-care provider on your own, you may consider sharing a nanny with another family.

Perhaps a family on your street is also in the market for childcare; you may consider approaching them to see whether they are interested in sharing a nanny. Basically, the two families split the costs of hiring the nanny, and the nanny assumes responsibility for caring for both sets of children. To prevent this situation from causing you tons of grief after the fact, you want to make sure of a few things:

✔ The nanny is up to the challenge of caring for both families' children. (Offering her additional money to make it worth her while may not be a bad idea.)

✔ The children are reasonably compatible. Forcing a group of kids who hate each other to spend 40 hours a week together is pretty much a recipe for disaster.

✔ Both families are in agreement about the child-care location. (Some families pick one home as the child-care home, and others prefer to have the nanny move from one home to the other from week to week.)

✔ You're clear about who is responsible for doing all the necessary paperwork for having an employee as well as ensuring that all the necessary nanny taxes are remitted to the government on time. (See Chapter 11 if you're not quite clear about what you're getting yourself in for!)

✔ The other family is willing to stick with the arrangement for the long-term or pay for their half of the nanny's salary until you're able to sublet their half to someone else. Otherwise, you can find yourself on the hook for a huge — and unbudgeted for — expense.

Looking into Child-Care Subsidies, Tax Credits, Employer Grants, and More

Your chances of having a long-lost relative show up out of the blue and offer to pick up the tab for your child-care bills may be pretty much slim-to-none, but some kindly strangers may be willing to lend you a helping hand. Believe it or not, some of them even work for the tax department!

Child-care subsidies, tax credits, and employer grants are pretty much the next best thing to a doting and cash-flush relative. Here's what you need to know about each.

Child-care subsidies

Child-care subsidies are funds that are set aside by the federal or state governments (or, in some cases, by private organizations) to help families pay for some or all of their child-care costs. To find out what child-care subsidies may be available to you, do the following:

✔ Get in touch with your local Child Care Resource and Referral Agency (call Childcare Aware at 1-800-424-2246 or visit the Childcare Aware Web site at www.childcareaware.org for referrals to your nearest Childcare Resource and Referral Agency).

✔ Contact your state child-care administration (you can find the contact information for your state child-care licensing authority in your phone book or obtain this information from your local Childcare Resource and Referral Agency).

✔ Check with your human resources department at work and ask your partner to check with his human resources department, too.

✔ Check with your college or university child-care center if either you or your partner is a student or a graduate of that institution. (A number of educational institutions make child-care subsidies available to needy students and alumni.)

✔ Find out whether any community groups or charitable foundations in your community offer child-care subsidies (your local Childcare Resource and Referral Agency can give you the lowdown on these types of subsidies).

Red tape unlimited

Although child-care subsidies are a great idea in principle — after all, we're talking free money here! — they're not without problems. Some parents who apply for child-care subsidies find that the rules governing the programs don't always make a lot of sense. Some families are barely scraping by on an income below the official poverty line, and they still don't qualify for a child-care subsidy. Families who find themselves caught in this administrative catch-22 can't afford childcare on their own, but they're too well off to qualify for child-care subsidies, at least in the eyes of some pencil-pushing bureaucrats.

How subsidies work

The rules governing each child-care subsidy program vary somewhat, but the basic application process is relatively standard. You can expect to fill out a detailed application form and to supply some supporting documentation (typically pay stubs or your most recent tax return) to substantiate your claim.

After your child-care subsidy application is approved, you still have a few more hoops to jump through. Namely, you need to

✔ **Have your child-care arrangement approved by the administrator of the child-care subsidy program.** Most child-care subsidy programs allow parents to make their own child-care arrangements; so after you've made the necessary plans, you need to obtain official approval for the child-care arrangement you've lined up. You can expect the subsidy-granting body to scrutinize your child-care arrangement to ensure that the child-care provider in question is meeting all state health and safety requirements and she's declaring her child-care income on her tax return.

✔ **Provide the center director or family day-care provider with the voucher or certificate that's issued to you after your application is approved.** After your application is approved, you receive a voucher or certificate indicating that your child is eligible for subsidized childcare. This voucher contains detailed information about the arrangements that have been approved: the hours of care that are required and the portion of the fee that is covered by the subsidy and by you personally. (Your portion of the fee is typically referred to as the *parent co-payment.*)

✔ **Keep in touch with the child-care subsidy program staff on an ongoing basis.** Your case is reviewed on a regular basis (at least every six months, and more often than that if your work or family situation changes significantly) to determine whether you're still eligible for a child-care subsidy. Most child-care subsidy agreements require that you notify the program administrator immediately if you

- Stop working

- Go on medical, maternity, sick, or personal leaves

- Change jobs

- Change your hours of employment

- Return to school

- Have another baby, lose custody of one of your children, or otherwise experience an increase or decrease in your family size

- Change child-care providers

Some critics of child-care subsidy programs complain that obtaining and keeping a child-care subsidy can become a full-time job itself, particularly if you have to take time off work to go to the child-care subsidy office to report every change to your work or family situation. Imagine how this may play out if your boss is in the habit of changing your work hours every week or two. You may be tempted to tell your boss where to go — right to the child-care subsidy office! — the next time he hands you a shift change notice.

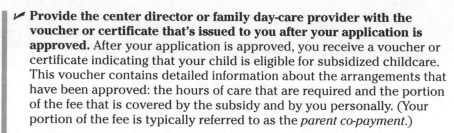

When subsidy demand outweighs supply

The biggest problem with federal and state child-care subsidies is that the demand for the subsidies is often much greater than the supply of funds available. According to the National Women's Law Center, only one in seven children eligible for assistance through the federally funded Childcare Development Block Grant program actually receives any assistance through the program.

State child-care subsidies

The federal government provides each state with money to assist low-income families in paying for childcare. Some states choose to top off this federal money with some additional funds of their own to increase the pool of money that's available to potential applicants.

Although the federal government sets some basic guidelines governing the use of federal child-care funds, the states come up with their own sets of rules about who qualifies for child-care assistance. Consequently, the amount of money that you're eligible for — and whether you're eligible for any assistance at all — can vary tremendously depending on where you live. Most states that offer child-care subsidies have rules spelling out

✔ How much money you can make and still be eligible for a child-care subsidy

✔ How much the state is willing to pay a child-care provider (You can pretty much forget about trying to send Junior to that Ivy League preschool on the state's dime!)

✔ The amount you're expected to contribute to your family's child-care costs (your co-payment)

Tax credits

One of the most lucrative sources of child-care payola is none other than Uncle Sam. You want to make sure you're taking full advantage of the five biggest tax breaks available to parents before you pop your tax return in the mail. These tax breaks include the

✔ Dependent Care Tax Credit

✔ State child-care tax credits and deductions

✔ Child Tax Credit

✔ Earned Income Credit

✔ Dependent Care Assistance Program

Before getting into the nitty-gritty about these tax breaks, I have to momentarily switch to disclaimer mode and remind you that you can't take what I'm about to say at absolute face value. Tax laws change on a regular basis, so you need to check on the child-care tax rules each year to see whether the rules have changed and to find out whether the friendly folks at the tax department have introduced any new goodies for parents. (Yes, I'm a card-carrying optimist!) You can get in touch with the Internal Revenue Service by calling 1-800-TAX-1040 or by visiting the IRS Web site at www.irs.gov.

With a little help from my friends

According to the Urban Institute, at least 28 percent of all employed families with children under the age of 13 receive some sort of help in paying their child-care bills, whether that help comes from relatives, businesses, nonprofit organizations, or good old Uncle Sam. In 20 percent of cases, the person or institution extending the help picks up the entire child-care tab. In 8 percent of cases, the help is partial: The child's parents are responsible for paying part of the child-care expenses.

The Child and Dependent Care Tax Credit

The Child and Dependent Care Tax Credit offered by the federal government provides up to $3,000 in tax relief per person, to a maximum of $6,000 per family for families who have to pay for the care of a child or other dependent in order to hold down a job or look for work. To qualify for the credit, you must meet the following criteria:

- You must have *earned income* from wages, salaries, tips, or other compensation that you have received through your employment.

- If you're married, both you and your spouse must have earned income unless one of you was either a full-time student or was physically or mentally incapacitated.

- Your filing status must be one of the following:

    • Single

    • Head of household

    • Qualifying widow(er) with a dependent child

    • Married, filing jointly

- Your child-care payments weren't made to anyone that you're claiming as a dependent on your return or to any child under the age of 19.

- The childcare must have been provided for one or more qualifying persons as identified on the Child and Dependent Care Credit form. (To meet the definition of a qualifying person, a child must be under the age of 13 at the time that care was provided, unless he was mentally or physically incapacitated, which has no age restriction.)

- You (and, if you're married, your spouse) must share your home with the child you're claiming the child-care expenses for.

✔ In order to claim the credit, you have to provide the IRS with information about the child-care provider who was responsible for caring for your child, namely the provider's name, address, and taxpayer identification. If the child-care provider is a business, you need the business' employer identification number. If the child-care provider is an individual, you need her Social Security number. This is the IRS's way of making sure that the child-care provider is declaring her income as opposed to running her business under the table.

As a rule, the lower your income and the higher your child-care expenses, the larger your credit will be. Of course, if you don't actually owe any taxes, you can't take advantage of the tax credit because this particular tax credit is non-refundable. So, don't subject yourself to all the pain and suffering associated with filling out all the necessary paperwork only to find out that you can't get any money back anyway. Tax season is depressing enough as it is!

State child-care tax credits and deductions

Some states offer child-care deductions that allow families to deduct some or all of their child-care expenses from their taxable income. Others offer child-care tax credits, which tend to be set at either

✔ A flat percentage or a sliding-scale percentage of the federal child-care credit amount

✔ A flat percentage or a sliding-scale percentage of the actual expenses

State credits can be refundable or non-refundable. Obviously, a refundable tax credit is worth a lot more to the average family than a non-refundable tax credit, so hopefully you're lucky enough to live in a state that puts its money where its mouth is (literally!) when it comes to childcare.

Child Tax Credit

The Child Tax Credit allows you to reduce any federal tax you owe by up to $1,000 for each qualifying child under the age of 17. The IRS's definition of a qualifying child in this situation is someone who meets all of the following criteria:

✔ The child is claimed as your dependent on your tax return.

✔ The child was under the age of 17 at the end of the tax year.

✔ The child is your son, daughter, adopted child, grandchild, stepchild, or eligible foster child.

✔ The child is a U.S. citizen or resident.

If your *modified adjusted gross income* (adjusted gross income represents your total income reduced by certain deductions known as *adjustments* before you take your itemized deduction or standard deduction and before you take the deduction for your exemptions) is above a certain amount ($110,000 if you're married and filing jointly, $55,000 if you're married and filing separately, or $75,000 in any other situation, according to the 2003 rules), the IRS reduces the Child Tax Credit by $50 for every $1,000 that your adjusted gross income exceeds the magic number.

If you file regular Form 1040 or Form 1040A, adjusted gross income is the last number at the bottom of page 1 (and the first number at the top of page 2). On Form 1040EZ, adjusted gross income appears on line 4.

Like the Child and Dependent Care Credit, the Child Tax Credit only works to your advantage if you owe the government money. If you don't actually owe any taxes, you can't take advantage of the tax credit because this particular tax credit is non-refundable. (Don't you just hate that word non-refundable?)

Earned Income Credit

The Earned Income Credit may not have the word childcare slapped next to it, but because it's designed to put money back in the pockets of parents with young children, I think it warrants a quick mention, too.

Although the exact cutoffs that determine who's eligible for the Earned Income Credit change from year to year, you can get a rough idea of whether you qualify for a tax credit under the program by considering the rules that were in place for the 2002 tax year. Here's the lowdown:

- If you (and your spouse, if you're married) had earned income and an adjusted gross income of up to $33,178 ($34,178, if you're married) and have two or more qualifying children, you'd be eligible for an earned income credit of up to $4,140.

- If you (and your spouse, if you're married) had earned income and an adjusted gross income of up to $29,201 ($30,201, if you're married) and have one qualifying child, you'd be eligible for an earned income tax credit of up to $2,506.

- If you (and your spouse, if you're married) had earned income and an adjusted gross income of up to $11,060 ($12,060, if you're married) and you or your spouse have no qualifying children, you'd be eligible for an earned income credit of up to $376.

One bit of fine print you need to know about the Earned Income Credit: If you or your spouse claimed investment income of over $2,550 in tax year 2002, you lost your eligibility for the Earned Income Credit. (What the taxman giveth, the taxman can taketh away.)

You're no doubt wondering what constitutes a qualifying child in the eyes of the IRS. According to the friendly folks at the tax department, a qualifying child is a child who meets all of the following criteria:

✔ The child is your son, daughter, adopted child, grandchild, stepchild, foster child; brother, sister, stepbrother, stepsister, or a descendant of your brother, sister, stepbrother, or stepsister that you cared for as if he were your own child.

✔ By the end of the tax year, the child is under the age of 19, or is under the age of 24 and is a full-time student, or is any age and is permanently and totally disabled.

✔ The child lived with you in the U.S. for more than half of the year.

If you expect to have a qualifying child during the next tax year, you may be eligible to get part of the following year's Earned Income Credit advanced as part of your pay. You can find out how this works by asking your employer for details or by contacting your local tax office.

If you want to find out more about these tax credits, you can download a copy of *Credit Where Credit is Due: Using Tax Breaks to Help Pay for Child and Dependent Care* from the National Women's Law Center Web site: www.nwlc.org. This free booklet demystifies the Dependent Care Tax Credit, the Child Tax Credit, the Earned Income Tax Credit, and the Dependent Care Assistance Program (something I discuss in the following section). If you don't have access to the Internet, you can order a copy by calling 202-588-5180. Single copies are free of charge.

Dependent Care Assistance Program

The Dependent Care Assistance Program is a federally sanctioned tax break that allows employers to provide up to $5,000 in tax-free income to their employees to help pay for child- and dependent-care services. This income is exempt from federal income and payroll taxes and may be exempt from state income taxes, depending on where you live. Your employer can give you this income in addition to your current salary, or you can agree to accept it in lieu of part of your current salary. Either way, you're likely to come out ahead, as long as you actually use the funds. After the money is deposited into your Dependent Care Assistance Program account, you can't get it back. You either use it or you lose it.

Assuming you have access to a Dependent Care Assistance Program in your workplace (they're offered by only a very small number of employers), you're eligible to participate if you have a child, stepchild, foster child, or other relative under the age of 13 who was living with you during the tax year and who you're entitled to claim as a dependent on that year's tax return. (If your child is physically or mentally disabled, the age restriction is waived.)

If you decide to participate in a Dependent Care Assistance Program, don't forget to subtract the amount of assistance you receive through the program from the child-care expenses that may be claimed under the Dependent Care Tax Credit on your tax return. Otherwise, you're essentially asking for the same tax break twice — something that can get you into plenty of hot water with the feds.

Employer grants

Believe it or not, Uncle Sam isn't merely reaching into his pocket to help you on the child-care front. He's also trying to help your employer help you through the State Employer Tax Credits for Child Care program.

The program, which is currently running in 28 states, provides employers with tax credits for investing in child-care-related services to benefit their employees. Although each state's rules are slightly different, most states consider the following types of activities eligible for funding:

- Constructing a child-care facility
- Operating a child-care facility
- Purchasing child-care spaces in facilities operated by third parties
- Providing subsidies to employees to help offset the high costs of childcare
- Providing employees with access to child-care referral services to take some of the worry out of finding quality childcare

Although the tax credit program looks great on paper, it hasn't worked out terribly well in real life. According to the National Women's Law Center, in 16 of the 20 states for which data is available, five or fewer corporations claimed the tax credit.

The problem is that the majority of state corporate tax filers either have no state tax liability or insufficient tax liability to allow them to take full advantage of the tax credits. Unfortunately, the money allocated for these programs is tied up for this specific purpose and is unavailable for other child-care programs, like the Child Care and Development Block Grant program that has proven to be more effective in getting child-care dollars in the hands of the people who need them most — parents with young children.

It's a Living: Getting Your Employer on Board

Studies have shown that child-care problems can have a huge impact on an employers' bottom line. A 1997 report prepared by the National Conference of State Legislatures concluded that absenteeism due to poor quality child-care costs American businesses more than $3 billion each year.

That's not the only price that employers can expect to pay when their employees are forced to go AWOL because the nanny called in sick or the day-care provider quit without notice. Child-care problems can lead to

- ✔ Lower productivity
- ✔ Poor job performance
- ✔ Poor morale
- ✔ Reduced commitment
- ✔ Increased turnover
- ✔ Increased training and recruitment costs

A growing number of employers are seeing the advantages of introducing child-care-related benefits as well as other family-friendly policies that make it easier for employees to contend with any child-care curveballs that come their way. Here's a rundown of what child-care benefits employees are asking for and getting, as well as some tips on how to sell these programs to your boss.

Onsite day-care centers

Onsite day-care centers are the crème de la crème of child-care benefits. Only a small number of employees have access to them, but they can act as a huge carrot at recruiting time. One study showed that one-third of American workers were willing to hop jobs and sacrifice salary and benefits to have access to an onsite company day-care program.

Onsite day-care programs are a hit with parents because they have a lot to offer. Here are some of the key benefits:

✔ You can expect your child to receive top-quality care because your employer's reputation is on the line. (Joining forces with a bad day-care center is a really bad public relations move!)

✔ You're likely to have first crack at any spaces that open up in the day-care center because your employer has a vested interest in finding spaces for employees first. (Only after employees' child-care needs have been met are open child-care spaces typically made available to members of the local community.)

✔ You're less likely to pay full market value for your spot. Your employer is likely to pick up part — or all — of the tab for you.

✔ Your commute time in the morning and evening is reduced because you have one less stop to make.

✔ You may find it easier to concentrate on your work knowing that your child is being cared for nearby.

✔ You may be able to visit with your child during your lunch hour or breastfeed your baby during your work day — arguably the best workplace perk ever!

Emergency child-care services

Studies show that working parents miss an average of eight days a year due to child-care problems and an additional six days a year because their child is ill. The resulting cost to businesses is high, which explains why some employers are choosing to make emergency child-care services available to their employees.

Employers may choose to pre-purchase blocks of spaces in day-care centers (ideally one spot for every 350 to 500 employees) or to arrange care through a child-care agency that supplies in-home child-care providers who are available to care for a sick child in the employee's own home.

Employees are typically allowed to make use of a company's emergency child-care plan a certain number of times every year. Some companies choose to cover the costs of such services fully; others ask employees to pay a small co-payment. You may not necessarily feel comfortable making use of this particular benefit, however. It's tough enough leaving your child in the care of a total stranger, let alone when she is ill. (See Chapter 12 for other tips on arranging backup childcare when your child is too sick to go to her regular child-care arrangement.)

Overnight childcare

A growing number of companies are offering to pick up the tab for overnight childcare for employees who are required to travel frequently for work-related reasons. This option can be a major perk for single parents who may otherwise be scrambling to arrange and pay for costly overnight care.

Child-care subsidy programs

Sometimes employers are reluctant to get into the child-care business because of the amount of administrative red tape and financial overhead that can be involved. Instead, businesses may choose to offer a cash subsidy to cover part or all of their employees' child-care costs. Sometimes employers are able to obtain a discount on the cost of spaces in a particular day-care facility by buying in bulk, which allows them to pass this savings on to their employees.

Child-care referral programs

Employers who don't have a lot of money to invest in a benefits program but want to show their support for their employees' child-care struggles often provide their employees with access to a child-care referral service. Typically, a company contracts the services of a work and family consultant who specializes in researching child-care options. Depending on the type of arrangement the employer has made with the child-care referral service, the referral service may help a particular employee to identify child-care vacancies in their community and to schedule some onsite visits — something that can prove to be a huge timesaver for an overloaded working parent.

Flextime

According to a study by the New York-based research firm Catalyst, flextime (the ability to set your own working hours) tops the wish lists of many American workers. Flextime can be a lifesaver to parents who find themselves dealing with an unexpected child-care curveball — like the nanny's mid-morning dental appointment. Working parents can also use their flextime to time-shift so that they minimize the number of hours of childcare they require — something that helps cut down on your family's child-care expenditures.

Getting a life

The Families and Work Institute's *1998 Business Work-Life Study* found that:

✔ 68 percent of employers allow employees to periodically alter their starting and quitting times

✔ 24 percent of employers allow employees to alter their starting and quitting times on a daily basis (flextime)

✔ 55 percent of employers allow employees to work from home occasionally

✔ 33 percent of employers allow employees to work from home on a regular basis

By the way, the Family and Work Institute is a research institute that specializes in researching work-life issues. You can find out more about its current research projects by visiting the Institute's Web site at www.families andwork.org.

Making the case to your boss

Eager to sell your boss on the benefits of introducing some family-friendly child-care policies to your workplace? Your pitch is more likely to be met with success if you keep these important pointers in mind:

✔ **Make her an offer she can't refuse.** Ask your boss whether she wants you to research what's involved in implementing various types of child-care programs and offer to do the necessary legwork on your own time.

✔ **Tackle the cost factor head-on.** Admit to your boss that child-care programs require some upfront investment, but then dazzle her with some statistics on how much money the company stands to save down the road as a result of reduced absenteeism and turnover, improved productivity and job performance, and so on. (See the Child Care and Early Childhood Education page of the Action Alliance for Children Web site for facts and figures galore: www.4children.org/chcare.htm. And download a copy of a report entitled "The Real Savings from Employer-Sponsored Child Care" from the Bright Horizons Web site if you really want to dazzle your boss with your child-care cost-benefit analysis: http://www.bfamsolutionsonline.com/pdf/InvestmentImpact.FINAL.pdf.)

✔ **Sell her on a pilot project.** Ask your employer whether she's willing to introduce a particular program on a trial basis. She may be more willing to give it a shot knowing she can get out of it if it's a disaster from the company's point of view.

Chapter 5

Playing Day-Care Detective: Investigating the Quality of Care

· ·

· ·

Have you had a burning desire to play Sherlock Holmes since way back when? I have great news for you: You're finally going to get your chance to put your detective skills to use by trying your hand at cracking your first big case — the Great Child-Care Mystery!

This chapter is designed to help you polish your day-care detective skills in a manner that would do even Sherlock Holmes proud. I show you how to tap into the child-care grapevine — a sleuth-worthy way of finding clues about any child-care openings in your neighborhood. You get the lowdown on common terminology used to identify child-care facilities and find out how national child-care accreditation standards make your job as a day-care detective a whole lot easier. In addition, you find out some insider tips for conducting reference and background checks. After you've had a chance to get fully in touch with your inner sleuth, I share some tips on making the best possible child-care decision.

Tapping into the Child-Care Grapevine

Your best friend's nanny quits in a huff on a Friday afternoon. By Monday morning, she has a new nanny lined up to take care of her kids. You can't help but wonder if she has some sort of child-care fairy godmother on the case. Because child-care fairy godmothers tend to be in chronically short supply, odds are she's had to settle for the next best thing: tapping into the child-care grapevine in her neighborhood.

Tapping into the neighborhood child-care grapevine is a smart strategy — one that's used with great success by most parents in the know. Not only does asking other people for leads and referrals often allow you to come up with child-care leads quickly, but it also increases the quality of the leads and referrals because these recommendations are being made by someone you know. Here's what you need to know in order to put the power of the child-care grapevine to work for you.

Getting the inside scoop on what's available

You already know how to get the lowdown on what's *really* going on in your neighborhood: Just talk to your nosy neighbor — the one who *just happens* to be looking out her window every time you pull into your driveway. Although you may question the value of the information that you receive from this person, sometimes the nosy neighbors of the world are worth their weight in gold. What better way to find out about child-care openings in your neck of the woods than by checking in with your one-person news bureau? By going to your gal in the street for the lowdown on child-care openings, you're guaranteed a healthy side dish of editorial comment served up with your main dish of hard news.

You may not necessarily trust your nosy neighbor's judgment on everything kid-related, however — especially if he appears to be completely clueless when it comes to grasping what makes a suitable child-care arrangement. Unless he's spent a lot of time around children or he's had children of his own in the not-too-distant past, he may not be qualified to play Watson to your Sherlock Holmes.

Obtaining referrals from other parents

Picking up leads on child-care arrangements from other parents with young children is a good idea because they often have a sense of what makes for a suitable child-care arrangement and are already in tune with the child-care grapevine. They can spread the word on your behalf, letting everyone in their circle of friends know that you're in the market for a quality child-care arrangement. This type of networking can really pay off when you're beating the bushes for leads. (See Chapter 1 for more on the benefits of getting other people actively involved in your search for childcare.)

Finding other sources of child-care referrals

If you don't hit pay dirt by asking people you know for referrals, you may have to go back to the drawing board. A few other sources of referrals that you may want to consider are community agencies that work with families or your local Child Care Resource and Referral Agency. See its Web site, www.naccrra.org for further information.

Just one quick word of caution if you don't personally know the people providing the child-care leads: Inspect their recommendations more carefully than any recommendations coming from friends and neighbors. Considering the reliability of the source is part of the day-care detective job description.

Knowing the Lingo of Quality Childcare

If you've done much research about out-of-home childcare, you've no doubt heard the terms *licensed* and *accredited* being bounced around. Although many parents use the terms interchangeably, they actually have two very different meanings. So before you start pounding the pavement in search of the child-care arrangement of your dreams, take a moment for a crash course in child-care lingo.

Licensed childcare isn't anything to write home about

Having a child-care license sounds exciting — and, I suppose, if you're a day-care center operator who spent months preparing to open her doors, a certain thrill is probably involved in hanging that piece of paper on your wall. But from the point of view of a day-care consumer, a child-care license really isn't anything to write home about.

Licensed childcare is simply childcare that measures up to whatever regulations your state has established for day-care centers. Licensing sets some very basic health and safety standards for day-care centers.

The United States doesn't have a universal child-care system. For whatever reason, each state has chosen to reinvent the child-care wheel for itself. Some states set the bar fairly high when it comes to child-care licensing requirements, while others are much less demanding. You can find out everything you need to know about child-care regulations in your state by contacting Child Care Aware at 800-424-2246. Child Care Aware can put you in touch with your state's child-care licensing authority. Or, if you have Internet access and prefer to research online, surf to the National Resource Center for Health and Safety in Childcare Web site, which features links to the relevant child-care legislation for each state. Access this site at `http://nrc.uchsc.edu/ states.html`.

Accreditation is actually worth getting excited about

Programs that have achieved *accreditation* have managed to distinguish themselves in the child-care field by overshooting what state licensing requirements require them to deliver, in terms of the quality of their programs.

Regardless of which accreditation program a child-care center or family day care commits to, by putting the time and effort into becoming accredited, a child-care program shows its community that it's strongly committed to providing the children in its care with the most stimulating and nurturing day-care experience possible. So count yourself lucky if you can find your child a space in an accredited day-care center or family day care in your community. An accredited day care is like having a Good Housekeeping Seal of Approval in the world of childcare.

Getting the Facts on Child-Care Accreditation

The four major child-care accreditation programs in the U.S. are

- ✓ The National Association for the Education of Young Children's accreditation program
- ✓ The National Association for Family Child Care's accreditation program
- ✓ The National School Age Care Alliance's accreditation program
- ✓ The National Early Childhood Program Accreditation

National Association for the Education of Young Children (NAEYC)'s accreditation program

If you've only heard of one child-care accreditation program, chances are it's the accreditation program operated by the National Association for the Education of Young Children (NAEYC). The NAEYC is the program that typically gets the most press. Its accreditation program is a voluntary program that encourages child-care administrators, staff, and parents to work together to achieve certain quality standards. To be eligible for NAEYC accreditation, an early childhood program must meet the following quality standards:

- ✔ Have been in operation for at least one year

- ✔ Be licensed or exempt from licensing (in which case, proof of exemption must be shown as part of the accreditation process)

- ✔ Provide care to at least ten children in a part- or full-day group program, where at least two adults are present

- ✔ Meet all accreditation criteria for the age groups that it serves (in other words, a center that provides care to infants, toddlers, and school-aged children must meet the criteria for all three age groups)

Family day-care providers can also seek accreditation through this program. The NAEYC defines early childhood programs as "any part- or full-day group programs in centers, homes, or schools that are purposefully designed to promote children's development and knowledge in the areas of intellectual, social, emotional, language and communication, and physical development."

NAEYC accreditation is awarded to the truly crème de la crème of early childhood education programs — programs that promote the physical, social, emotional, and cognitive development of the children as well as the parents, staff, and administrators. The accreditation process considers all the factors that go into creating an early childhood education program, namely the following:

- ✔ **The quality of the interactions between the staff and the children:** The staff is warm and caring toward the children and respectful of individual differences.

- ✔ **The interactions between the staff and the parents:** Parents feel like partners in their children's child-care experience and feel supported and welcomed by day-care staff.

- ✔ **The qualifications of the staff and the extent of their commitment to ongoing training and development:** All staff directly involved in working with the children have had some specialized training in early childhood education.

✔ **The physical environment:** The indoor and outdoor environments are comfortable, well organized, and promote growth and development by encouraging learning and exploration.

✔ **How much attention is paid to health and safety:** The indoor and outdoor environments are designed with safety in mind and are in full compliance with all health and safety standards; a written health record is maintained for every child; children are supervised at all times; any suspected cases of child abuse are reported promptly to the appropriate child protection authorities.

✔ **The caliber of the nutrition and food service:** Meals and snacks meet the nutritional guidelines set by the Child Care Food Program of the U.S. Department of Agriculture; families are provided with written menus so they know what their children have eaten each day; and mealtimes are treated as a pleasant and social learning experience for children.

✔ **The quality of the curriculum:** The program has a clearly defined educational philosophy as well as specific curriculum goals, and those philosophies and goals take into account the individual needs, interests, and abilities of the children being cared for in that particular environment.

✔ **How well the child-care program functions administratively:** The program has written policies and procedures covering fee schedules, sick and holiday policies, and so on. Written job descriptions for both board and staff members are available, and full-time staff members receive an adequate benefits package that covers paid leave, medical insurance, and retirement.

✔ **Whether the program is evaluated on an ongoing basis:** At least once a year, administrators, staff, parents, and school-aged children are involved in evaluating the program to ensure that quality care and education are being provided and to identify areas for further improvement and innovation.

✔ **Whether the program complies with NAEYC recommendations concerning caregiver-child ratios:** Table 5-1 shows what the caregiver-child ratios are.

Table 5-1	Caregiver-Child Ratios, as Recommended by the National Association for the Education of Young Children	
Age of Child	*Maximum Group Size*	*Ratios*
Infants (birth to 12 months)	8	1:4
Toddlers (12 to 24 months)	12	1:4
	10	1:5
2-year-olds (24 to 30 months)	12	1:6

Age of Child	Maximum Group Size	Ratios
2½-year-olds	14	1:7
3-year-olds	20	1:10
4-year-olds	20	1:10
5-year-olds	20	1:10
Kindergartners	24	1:12
6-to-8-year-olds	30	1:15
9-to-12-year-olds	30	1:15

And speaking of improvement and innovation, the NAEYC is in the process of giving its accreditation program an overhaul. The organization hopes to launch its new and improved accreditation program in 2005. You can find out more about the current program guidelines and participate in the redesign of the program by visiting the NAEYC Web site at www.naeyc.org. (If you're interested in finding out about the NAEYC but don't have Web access, you can call the organization toll-free at 800-424-2460.)

National Association for Family Child Care (NAFCC)'s accreditation program

The National Association for Family Child Care (NAFCC) is a national organization that works with more than 400 state and local family child-care associations across the U.S., whose members collectively provide care to more than 4 million children. (I've chosen to use the term *family day care* in this book because that's the term most moms and dads use when describing childcare that occurs in the child-care provider's own home, but *family childcare* means the same thing.)

Why you don't want to send your child to the sardine day-care center

How much space does a kid need in order to have enough room to play? A lot, according to the National Association for the Education of Young Children. The NAEYC recommends that child-care programs allow a minimum of 35 square feet of usable playroom floor space per child for indoor play and a minimum of 75 square feet of play space per child for outdoor play. If opportunities for movement are limited, the quality of play tends to suffer.

The NAFCC first introduced an accreditation system in 1988. The association completely overhauled its accreditation system during the 1990s, however, and formally launched its new accreditation system in 1999. The new NAFCC accreditation standards evaluate the quality of a particular child-care arrangement based on the following criteria:

- **Relationships:** The quality of the relationships that the family day-care provider builds with the children and the parents she works with.

- **Environment:** The environment the family day-care provider creates for the children in her care — the physical setting, the equipment, the play materials, and so on.

- **Activities:** The role the family day-care provider plays in encouraging children to initiate their own play activities and looking for opportunities to help them expand their ideas without dominating or taking over the children's play.

- **Developmental learning goals:** The family day-care provider's ability to set individual and group goals in areas such as physical development, cognition and language, math development, and creative development.

- **Safety:** The family day-care provider's ability to create a safe environment and provide adequate supervision.

- **Health:** The family day-care provider's ability to safeguard the health of the children in her care.

- **Professional practices:** The family day-care provider respects the confidentiality of the families and children in her care and is up-to-date with developments in the early childhood education field.

- **Business practices:** The family day-care provider conducts herself in a business-like manner, obeying all rules governing the operation of family day-care operations and providing the parents of the children in her care with a signed child-care contract that summarizes her key policies and procedures.

To apply for NAFCC accreditation, a family day-care provider must

- Be at least 21 years of age
- Have obtained a high school diploma or GED (some exceptions are permitted)
- Have completed at least 65 hours of documented training

Family day-care providers are required to design their own professional development plan, which addresses any areas that need to be improved upon in order to meet NAFCC accreditation standards. Depending on what training opportunities are available to a child-care provider in your community, she may choose to sign up for a class, form a study group with other family day-care providers, or seek the services of a mentor or advisor.

You can find out more about NAFCC accreditation and search for NAFCC-accredited family day-care providers in your community by visiting the NAFCC Web site at www.nafcc.org/accred/accred.html. You can also find out more about the association and its work by calling 801-269-9338.

The National School-Age Care Alliance accreditation program

Because school-aged children (children between the ages of 5 and 14) have very different child-care needs than younger children, the National School-Age Care Alliance (NSACA) joined forces with the National Institute on Out-of-School Time (NIOST) to come up with some national accreditation standards for before- and after-school child-care programs (also known as *out-of-school child-care programs*).

They chose to zero in on six key areas that tend to determine the quality of out-of-school child-care programs:

- **Human relationships:** Whether the staff relates to the children and youth in their care well; how well the children and youth relate to one another; how well the families and staff relate to one another.

- **Indoor environment:** Whether the indoor environment encourages children and youth to initiate and explore.

- **Outdoor environment:** Whether the outdoor environment encourages children and youth to be independent and creative.

- **Activities:** Whether a variety of activities are available to the children and youth in the program.

- **Safety:** Whether the safety and security of the children and youth are safeguarded appropriately.

- **Health and nutrition:** Whether the foods and drinks served in the program meet the needs of the children and youth.

- **Administration:** Whether staff-child ratios and group sizes are appropriate; whether appropriate policies and procedures are in place to govern the operation of the program; whether a training plan is in place for each staff member.

You can find out more about the NSACA accreditation process by visiting the NSACA Web site at www.nsaca.org or by calling the NSACA at 617-298-5012. The accreditation section of the Web site provides a 36-point checklist for child-care programs that are considering accreditation through the NSACA — the checklist also doubles as a very handy checklist for parents in the market for an after-school child-care program.

National Early Childhood Program Accreditation (NECPA)

The National Child Care Association created the National Early Childhood Program Accreditation program to raise standards for early childhood education programs in the U.S. In order to qualify for accreditation through the NECPA, a program must have operated for at least one year and be in compliance with state-licensing requirements for early childhood education programs. The accreditation program emphasizes the following criteria in assessing the quality of a particular early childhood education program:

- **Administration and general operations:** How efficiently the program operates and whether appropriate policies and procedures are in place.

- **Professional development and work environment:** Whether the staff is provided with opportunities for ongoing professional development and whether the working environment is a positive one.

- **Indoor environment:** Whether the indoor play environment is suitable for young children.

- **Outdoor environment:** Whether the outdoor play environment is suitable for young children.

- **Developmental programs:** Whether programs the staff delivers are developmentally appropriate to the children in their care.

- **Parent and community involvement:** Whether the staff forges links between the program and the child's family, and the program and the community.

- **Formal school linkages:** Whether the staff forges links between the program and the school communities it serves.

- **Health and safety:** Whether the staff creates a safe and healthy environment for the children in their care.

You can find out more about the NECPA by visiting the organization's Web site at www.necpa.net or by calling 800-505-9878.

Playing Sherlock Holmes to Check It Out

Two of the most powerful tools at your disposal as a day-care detective are the reference check and background check. Of course, you may *not* necessarily be in a position to order these checks. You're likely to leave the checking to someone else if you're in one of the following situations:

✔ **You're considering a day-care center.** If you're planning to place your child in a day-care center, the center director has already conducted the appropriate reference checks and police checks on the center's staff — or, at least she should have. Be sure to ask for verification that these checks are, in fact, routinely conducted on all adults working at the day-care center.

And don't be afraid to ask if you can speak to parents whose children are currently enrolled at the center or whose children were recently cared for at the center but have since moved on to full-time school. You generally get a more honest appraisal of a day-care center's strengths and weaknesses from parents whose children are no longer enrolled at the center, because parents whose children are currently enrolled at the center have a vested interest in seeing the center in the best possible light.

✔ **You're using the services of a nanny agency.** If you're hiring a nanny through a nanny agency, the agency likely conducts these checks on your behalf. Naturally, you want to ask for verification that these checks were done, and in the case of the reference checks, you may want to reserve the right to recheck some of the references yourself. Parents are sometimes more upfront and honest when speaking to another parent than when dealing with an employee of a nanny agency.

If you're planning to hire a nanny or other in-home child-care provider or are considering placing your child in a family day care, you should insist on reference checks and background checks. In the case of a family day-care operation, also request a police check on any other adults living in the home. You don't want to find out later that the family day-care provider's boyfriend or adult son is a convicted pedophile.

Conducting reference checks

Tread carefully when conducting reference checks to ensure that you're obtaining reliable information and keeping yourself out of legal trouble.

Some important points to keep in mind are

✔ **Let the child-care provider know upfront that you consider reference checks an important part of the child-care decision-making process.** In the case of a nanny, you may let her know that you reserve the right to contact any of her former employers to discuss her employment performance in detail instead of just sticking to the list of names on her official reference list. This encourages any nannies with poor employment histories or otherwise shady pasts to drop out of the running sooner rather than later — something that can dramatically improve the caliber of candidates you have to choose from.

For obvious reasons, don't contact the child-care provider's current employer without her explicit permission. In most cases, it's simply not possible to obtain a reference from the child-care provider's current employer without putting her job at risk, so you have to settle for contacting her former employers. You can, however, make your employment offer conditional upon obtaining a positive reference from her current employer. Or you can hire the child-care provider and then check the reference with her current employer while she's still completing her probationary period as a new employee. (You can find out more about the ins and outs of the hiring process in Chapter 11.)

✔ **Don't settle for any less than three references and make sure that these references are all employment-related.** Character references (a reference from someone the child-care provider knows through a religious organization or volunteer work, for example) can be useful but should be treated as gravy rather than meat and potatoes. After all, it's easy to come across as charming and personable during the eight hours you work with someone on a charity fundraising campaign. But when you're working with someone day in and day out, coming up smelling like roses isn't so easy.

✔ **Make a point of verifying the educational information that the child-care provider has provided on her résumé.** Ask to see a copy of her graduation diploma, official college transcripts, or some other official document that proves her educational credentials are legitimate. Although it's unlikely that résumé fraud is as rampant in nanny circles as it is in Silicon Valley (one study found that 80 percent of high-tech workers padded their resumes!), you're naïve to assume that every child-care worker measures up to a truth-in-advertising code of ethics!

✔ **If you're responsible for interviewing the child-care provider, have your partner or another family member check the references on your behalf.** The person who interviewed the child-care provider can't be as objective as someone who hasn't actually met the candidate. Human resource departments often take care of reference checking instead of the managers who were involved with the interview for the same reason: the end results are better.

Obtaining permission to explore the child-care provider's background

Attempting to check the child-care provider's references without her explicit permission can land you in legal hot water, so obtaining a signed release form is the smart thing to do. Besides, you may find that her former employers aren't willing to spill the beans about her work performance unless you provide them with a copy of a signed release form anyway. So you may as well have her sign on the dotted line sooner rather than later.

You also want to do some credit and background checks as part of the standard employment work-up. You might as well cover all these background checks on one form and get her signed permission for all these checks at once. See Figure 5-1 for an example of a sample reference-check release form for a child-care provider who's seeking employment with your family.

I, _____, agree to allow _____ to conduct reference and background checks to verify the information that I have provided on my application for employment as a child-care provider and/or to use the services of an outside agency to conduct reference and background checks to verify the information that I have provided on my application for employment. I understand that such reference and background checks will be conducted thoroughly and within the confines of all applicable state and federal laws, and that such checks will be confined to a

___ Criminal-history check

___ Department of Motor Vehicle History check

___ Certification and licensing check (if applicable)

___ Educational-credentials check (if applicable)

___ Employment-eligibility check (including Social Security number verification)

___ Employment checks (to verify the details about past employment)

___ Personal reference checks

I authorize all persons who may have information that might be helpful to _____ in this research to disclose such information to him/her, and I thereby release all persons from liability on account of true and accurate disclosure. I hereby also declare that a photocopy of this document may be given the same legal validity as the original. Should there be any questions about the validity of this release, you may contact me as indicated below.

Finally, in consideration of _____'s review of my application for employment, I hereby release _____ from all claims or liabilities that may result from the inquiry into or disclosure of such information, including claims under any federal, state, or local civil rights laws and any claims for defamation or invasion of privacy.

_____ (Applicant's signature) _____ (Date)

_____ (Full name, printed)

Figure 5-1: _____ Driver's License number and state
Reference
check _____ Social Security number
release
form. _____ Mailing address

_____ Phone number

A simple letter authorizing you to do a reference check and the appropriate background checks should be sufficient if you're checking references for a family day-care provider because in this case, she's an independent business person and you're contracting to purchase services from her — something that allows you to sidestep a lot of the complexities of the employer-employment relationship. However, if you're more comfortable having a signed release form on file, you can modify the release form provided in Figure 5-1 to suit your purposes.

Getting a clue: How to interview references

Stick to a careful script when you're checking references by phone. Making up the questions as you go doesn't just reduce the likelihood that you'll remember to ask all the right questions; it also increases the odds that you'll ask a question that can get you or the child-care provider's former employer in serious hot water. See Chapter 9 for a list of must-ask questions when interviewing a nanny.

As a rule, you want to stick to asking the following types of questions:

- ✔ Fact-based questions designed to help you verify the details of employment (dates of employment, the child-care provider's job title, the nature of her job responsibilities, and so on)

- ✔ Behavior-based questions designed to encourage the person providing the reference to offer specific examples of the child-care provider's past behaviors in specific situations (for example, "Can you tell me about a time when one of the children was sick or injured and Mary had to make an important judgment call?")

Another important reason for sticking to a reference-checking script is if you're checking references for more than one child-care provider, and you ask each person's references entirely different questions, you're stuck comparing apples to oranges — something that makes your final child-care decision ten times more difficult than it needs to be. So do yourself and the child-care providers you're considering a favor and save your improv talents for some local charity's talent night.

When it comes to lying, the (big) eyes have it

Better not rely on gut instinct alone when you're trying to decide whether a particular child-care candidate is all that she seems to be. A study at Colgate University found that adults have only a 50/50 chance of telling if someone is lying or telling the truth. Even worse, adults are more likely to be conned by someone with large eyes, long lashes, smooth skin, or other baby-face traits — so you want to be doubly cautious if the nanny in question is a Drew Barrymore look-alike!

Here are a few other things to remember when checking references:

- **Take detailed notes while checking references:** Otherwise, the information you find out about the various child-care providers you're considering can start to blur together. If you think of a follow-up question in a day or two, having some written notes to refer to can be helpful.

- **Adopt a friendly and conversational style when communicating with the person providing the reference check:** Being friendly and conversational encourages the person to open up more than he would if you adopted a more formal style.

- **Pay attention to what the person providing the reference isn't saying as well as to what she is saying:** Most people are reluctant to admit that they made a truly dreadful child-care choice. But you can assume that the person providing the reference was less-than-enthralled with the child-care provider in question if you're subjected to 30 seconds of deafening silence when you ask about the child-care provider's strengths. Be prepared to read between the lines if the person providing the reference seems lukewarm about the child-care provider, answers in vague generalities, or seems afraid to speak the truth. All are indications of a possible problem.

- **Some employers have a policy of only providing reference checks in writing, so don't be surprised if the person you contact asks you to fax or mail a reference-check form to their attention:** They're just being prudent in the age of lawsuits. (See Figure 5-2 for a sample reference-check request form.)

- **Be on the lookout for phony references:** They're more common than you may think. A common ploy is having a friend or relative pose as a former employer. You can protect yourself against this type of reference fraud by asking the family day-care provider or nanny to tell you as much as possible about her relationship with the person providing the reference (for example, when she worked for this particular family, the number and ages of their children at the time, what her duties involved, and so on). Then, when you call the person providing the reference, make some deliberate errors to see whether she corrects you. If the person providing the reference doesn't appear to notice that her three sons have mysteriously morphed into three daughters or that the nanny worked for her family in 1993 rather than 1998, odds are she's a phony.

Another smart way to protect yourself is by conducting some of the reference checks in person. If someone claims to have 5-year-old twins, but not a single piece of kid-related paraphernalia is in sight when you drop by to do the reference check, you may wonder if the twins were made up for the sake of providing his best friend or family member with a solid reference check. One final tip on the bogus reference front: If the person providing the reference calls you, ask for a number so you can call him back. If he's reluctant to give you his name and phone number, it may be because the reference he's planning to provide is anything but above board.

Date

Your name and address

Name and address of person providing reference

Subject: Reference for Mary Poppins

Dear _____:

Mary Poppins has applied for a nanny position with our family and has provided your name as a reference. We are eager to learn as much as we can about Ms. Poppins' previous work history so we can decide whether, in fact, she would be the best person to care for our three children, ages 5, 3, and 2.

Ms. Poppins has signed a release form permitting you to provide us with the information that we are requesting. A copy of that permission form is attached. Any information you provide to us will be kept in the strictest of confidence.

We are hoping to make our hiring decision at some point during the next two weeks, so we would greatly appreciate it if you would return your completed reference to us at your earliest convenience. You can either mail it to me in the enclosed envelope with the pre-paid postage provided or fax it to our attention at 555-555-5555.

If you have any questions or concerns, please feel free to contact us at 555-555-5556. Thank you again for your assistance with this important matter.

Sincerely,

Your names

Questions:

* When was Ms. Poppins first employed by your family?

    _____

* How long was she employed by your family?

    _____

* What was her reason for leaving?

    _____

* What were the numbers and ages of your children at that time?

    _____

* What was Ms. Poppins' initial rate of pay?

    _____

* What was Ms. Poppins' final rate of pay?

    _____

* Did you find Ms. Poppins to be reliable?

    _____

* Did she exercise good judgment in dealing with the children?

    _____

* What would you describe as Ms. Poppins' greatest strengths as a nanny?

    _____

* Were there any areas of concern?

    _____

* Would you hire Ms. Poppins again, if given the opportunity?

    _____

* Is there anything else you think we should know about Ms. Poppins in making our hiring decision?

    _____

Figure 5-2:
Sample reference-check request form.

Doing background checks

If you've gotten the reference checks out of the way, you need to decide which types of background checks to run on the family day-care provider or nanny.

Although you may feel like a big creep requesting these types of background checks of someone who's likely a wonderful human being, you shouldn't feel embarrassed or awkward at all. You're just doing your job as a parent. Besides, you're not asking any more of a prospective employee than the guy who operates the local burger joint asks of any new worker — and all he's entrusting to that person is what's in his cash register, not the health and well-being of his nearest and dearest! Plus, you're not alone in your decision to do this. The number of criminal reference checks performed on child-care workers skyrocketed between 1973 and 2000: seven times as many checks were performed in 2000 as were three decades earlier.

Any child-care provider who's genuinely concerned about your family's well-being understands why you need to do these checks, both for the sake of your child as well as your own peace of mind. If the child-care provider in question gives you a hard time about any of this, she's done you a huge favor by proving without a doubt that she's *not* the right person to care for your child.

What follows is a list of some of the specific types of background checks you may want to request. Some of these checks can be ordered by the child-care provider for a nominal fee, and others are more readily conducted by a third party, such as a detective agency or security firm. (As a goodwill gesture, you should offer to pick up the tab for any out-of-pocket expenses the child-care provider incurs on your behalf. Asking the child-care provider to cover these fees out of her own pocket isn't fair.)

✔ **Criminal-record check:** Contrary to popular belief, doing a nationwide criminal-record check isn't possible — unless, of course, you happen to be in the FBI. Even private investigators have to conduct record checks on a statewide or countywide basis, which can get quite involved if the child-care provider you're considering has lived and worked in a number of different jurisdictions.

Some states forbid statewide searches, and others require fingerprints to process a search request. Some states are so slow processing requests that your child can be looking for childcare for her own kids before you find out whether the child-care provider in question is legitimate. These are the unfortunate facts when attempting criminal-record checks. Assuming it's possible and practical to conduct one, you can either ask the child-care provider to supply you with a copy of a criminal-record check obtained through the local police department (it costs about $20), or you can hire a private detective or security firm to do the necessary digging on your behalf.

✔ **Court-record checks:** Criminal history information and civil records are public information. You can access this information, provided you know where to look and can go to the courthouse or state repository in person. A private detective can help simplify this process for you, but if you already have some serious inklings that the child-care provider in question may have a dubious past, looking for a more suitable candidate may be simpler and cheaper.

✔ **Department of Motor Vehicles check:** Although you may pick up bits and pieces of information about the child-care provider's driving record by doing a criminal-record check, if you want the true lowdown on her driving record, you need to hit up the Department of Motor Vehicles for information. Policies, procedures, and fees vary from state to state, but you can expect to fork over a nominal fee — usually in the $5 to $15 range. Once again, you want to make a phone call or two to find out about the rules in your particular state.

Although you may be tempted to skip the driving-record check if you don't intend to have the child-care provider drive your children anywhere, bear in mind that a driving-record check can reveal other important informant about a child-care provider, such as a string of drunk driving convictions. Some states automatically notify the child-care provider that you've requested a copy of her driving record, so you want to be upfront with her about your intentions.

✔ **Credit-report check:** A credit-report check can give you a solid indication of how mature and reliable a person is. After all, if the child-care provider you're considering has had repeated difficulties remembering to pay her rent or her mortgage, she may be equally irresponsible in other areas of her life. If you decide you want to see a credit report, you can either ask the child-care provider to authorize you to order the credit report on her behalf or you can ask her to provide you with the report herself. It's a fairly inexpensive proposition and shouldn't cost you more than about $35.

✔ **Social Security Number trace:** A Social Security Number trace is the worst nightmare of a child-care provider who's attempting to hide parts of her past. The trace allows you to find out where she's lived for the past seven years — information that can be invaluable in turning up any inconsistencies in her employment history. A Social Security Number trace can be conducted on your behalf by private detectives and the growing number of online search firms offering people-search services. You don't need the child-care provider's permission to conduct this particular search, and some online firms do it for under $20.

✔ **Workers' compensation check:** Want to find out whether the child-care provider in question has made a career out of making fraudulent workers' compensation claims? You should! Otherwise, you can be setting yourself up to be her next victim. In most states, after an employee's claim makes it through the state system or Workers' Compensation Appeals Board, the case becomes a matter of public record. Be careful not to hold the fact that the child-care provider in question has made any legitimate workers' compensation claims against her: That's against the law.

✔ **Health-record check:** If you want an assurance that the child-care provider in question is physically and mentally fit to care for your child, ask her to undergo a medical exam (at your expense) or to provide you with a letter verifying that she's in good health.

The Envelope, Please: Making Your Decision

When the fact-finding phase of your mission is complete, you must make your decision. In this section, I give you some advice on how to make a decision you can live with.

Weighing your alternatives

Assuming that you've had the luxury of choice — in other words, you've been frantically gathering data on more than one child-care option — your next logical step is to come to a decision. You should review the data that you collected while conducting your reference and background checks, factoring in what you've found out about quality child-care programs. (That's where all the accreditation criteria fits in.)

With any luck, one of the options you're considering emerges as the clear front-runner, and your decision is relatively easy. If the decision isn't quite that clear-cut, you may have to go back into day-care detective mode again.

Finalizing your selection

If you're having trouble deciding between two child-care options, you may want to schedule a repeat visit to the two child-care facilities in question or line up a second interview with the two nanny-finalists. You may want to ask a family member or trusted friend to tag along this time so you can ask him for his input, too: This is definitely a situation where two heads are better than one.

If you're still having trouble deciding, try making a list of your top five criteria when finding a suitable child-care arrangement. After you've clearly defined your criteria, go back through your notes and evaluate each child-care option on that basis. Whichever alternative most matches your criteria wins — case closed. (Well done, Holmes!)

Part II
Out-of-Home Childcare: Evaluating the Big Three

The 5th Wave — By Rich Tennant

@RICHTENNANT

"I'd let you bring your dolls over, but I'm only licensed to handle 4 dolls, 2 ponies, and 1 teddy bear."

In this part . . .

If you're considering an out-of-home child-care arrangement, the next few chapters of the book are for you. You'll find chapters devoted to "the big three": day-care centers, family day cares, and preschools. In each case, I give you practical advice on what to look for when sizing up each type of child-care arrangement — you know, the real nitty-gritty stuff that you need to consider to make the best possible arrangement for your child. (Hey, getting a good night's sleep is tough enough when you're a parent; I don't want you losing sleep about day-care decisions down the road.)

Chapter 6

Evaluating a Day-Care Center

*Y*ou've spent some time checking out the various child-care options, and you've zeroed in on the day-care center part of the child-care menu. Now all you need to do is figure out which particular type of center-based day care is best suited to your family's needs. After all, saying that you've decided on taking your child to a day-care center is kind of like walking into an automotive dealership and announcing that you've decided to purchase a vehicle. (Odds are, the sales staff will suggest that you be a bit more specific about your wants and needs!)

That, in a nutshell, is what this chapter is designed to do — help you make your way through the day-care center part of the menu, while bringing you up to speed on what's involved in finding top-quality center-based care.

Surveying the Various Types of Day-Care Centers

A day-care center is a day-care center is a day-care center, right? Well, sort of. All forms of center-based care have something important in common — the fact that they're all based in a center. But when you're comparing two particular center-based programs, you're more likely to be struck by their differences than by their similarities.

To go back to the vehicle analogy for a moment, trying to point out the similarities between the day-care center that has been repeatedly singled out for national quality awards and the day-care center that always seems to be in hot water with the state child-care licensing authorities is like trying to spot the similarities between a luxury automobile and the 1980s rust-bucket econobox that may have served as your first car.

And don't forget that day-care centers can be operated by very different types of groups for very different purposes — to make money, to provide childcare for a particular group of employees, a particular school community, or members of a particular religious community. Here's the lowdown on the main categories of day-care centers.

- **For-profit day-care centers:** As the name indicates, for-profit day cares are business ventures that are operated with a goal of turning a profit. (A small profit, mind you: pre-tax profits in this particular sector tend to be very slim — around 4 percent to 5 percent, according to a recent report on *BusinessWeek Online*.) The low profit margins may explain why a lot of the mom-and-pop day-care shops of days gone by have gone belly up over the past few years and why the for-profit day-care sector is increasingly dominated by franchise operators: about half of for-profit day-care centers today are chain operations.

- **Not-for-profit day-care centers:** Not-for-profit day-care centers are designed to operate on a break-even basis. Approximately 10 percent of day-care centers nationwide are operated on a not-for-profit basis. Typically, these centers are operated by churches, synagogues, community centers, or other community groups that have identified a need for childcare in their communities and have applied to the Internal Revenue Service for tax-exempt status.

- **Workplace-based day-care centers:** Workplace-based day-care centers are housed in a particular workplace and operated by a particular employer or group of employers (or by a third party on behalf of an employer or group of employers) to meet the child-care needs of its employees. Because an employer's corporate reputation is on the line, the quality in workplace day-care centers is usually extremely high. And, for liability reasons, corporations generally pay careful attention to health, safety, and security issues.

  This particular employee benefit can be quite involved for an employer to offer, so some employers instead choose to purchase blocks of child-care spaces in a nearby child-care center and make these spaces available to their employees at an at-cost or subsidized rate. (You can find out more about this and other family-friendly child-care initiatives undertaken by employers in Chapter 4.)

✔ **School-based day-care programs:** School-based day-care programs are housed in elementary schools. Parents love them because they're wonderfully convenient (if you have older children, you can drop them off at school at the same time you're taking your younger child to day care). School-based day-care programs allow for a virtually seamless transition from day care to big-kid school — in most cases, it's just a matter of walking down a different hall or entering the building through a different door. These programs also tend to be very successful at forging powerful links between themselves and the communities they serve — one of the hallmarks of a quality day-care program.

✔ **Day-care programs operated by religious organizations:** A large number of churches, synagogues, and other religious organizations have their hands in the day-care pie, too. Some offer full-time day-care programs that operate in pretty much the same way as any other center-based day-care program; others are part-time programs that operate on a drop-in basis, with parents purchasing care by the hour or by the day.

There's no such thing as a typical day-care program any more than there's such a thing as a typical automobile. If variety is the spice of life, then the world of day-care centers has spice galore!

Putting a Day-Care Center under the Microscope

Checking out a child-care center can be a time-consuming process, but the task will feel a whole lot more manageable if you break it down into these three distinct tasks:

✔ Doing some initial prescreening by phone

✔ Conducting an onsite visit

✔ Comparing notes with other parents whose children have been cared for at this particular day-care center

Starting off with telephone prescreening

Nothing is more frustrating than taking an entire day off work to check out a day-care center, only to discover five minutes into your visit that it's not a viable option for your family. That's why you may want to ask some key questions over the phone before scheduling an onsite visit.

In this section is a list of questions you want to ask when you call the day-care center director. But before I get to that, here are a few important tips to keep in mind when you go to make your call:

- ✔ **Make a list of questions ahead of time so that you don't forget to ask anything important.** Nothing is more frustrating than realizing that you forgot to get an answer to one of your most pressing day-care questions. Make sure you write out a list of questions before making your calls. (You can pick up plenty of pointers about the types of questions to ask in this chapter and on the Cheat Sheet at the front of this book.)

- ✔ **Keep a pen and a pad of paper handy.** That way, you can take detailed notes while you're chatting with the center director. You can save yourself a lot of time (to say nothing of a heavy-duty case of writers' cramp) if you write out your list of questions ahead of time, leaving plenty of room for your answers, and then make a photocopy of your "child-care master list" each time you start evaluating a new childcare facility.

- ✔ **Consider the timing of your call.** The day-care center director is likely to be busy with parents and children during the morning drop-off and afternoon pick-up periods and may not have time to take your call. You probably should avoid the lunch hour period, too, because she may be busy with the staff or the children. So try to make your phone call during one of the less crazy times — perhaps right before or after the morning or afternoon day-care rush hour. After all, the less rushed the day-care center director is when she takes your call, the more willing she is to answer your questions in detail.

What follows are the key questions you want to discuss with the day-care center director when you get her on the phone.

Does the day-care center have spaces available?

If you need childcare soon, this question should be at the top of your list. After all, if the child-care center doesn't have any openings now, going through the rest of your questions may be pointless. I say *may be,* because if the center is highly recommended, you may want to check it out and put your child's name on the waiting list, in the hope that a space will open up down the road. Sometimes that's the only way to secure a space at the more in-demand day-care centers.

If no spaces are available, how long is the waiting list?

Before you fill out an application and pay an application fee (see the section, "Sealing the Deal: Filling Out Your Application" later in this chapter for more on the application process), you want to feel reasonably confident that your child's name is likely to make its way to the top of the list before he starts kindergarten! The waiting lists at some of the better day-care centers can be hair-raisingly long: In some cases, you may be looking at a multi-year wait. Fortunately, most day-care center directors are sensible enough to freeze their waiting lists before the wait gets to this point. Otherwise, people may end up calling to reserve spots in the truly crème de la crème of day-care centers before they even manage to conceive!

Does the day-care center require special criteria for admission?

If you're considering enrolling your child in a workplace-based child-care center and you don't work for the employer who is affiliated with it, find out whether children of non-employees are also welcome to enroll at the center. The employer may prefer to reserve all the day-care spaces for its own employees, even if that means having a few vacancies. Or the employer may open a certain number of spaces for non-employees. You won't know unless you ask.

Where is the day-care center located?

You probably have a rough idea where the center is located, but you need to find out the specifics, such as:

✔ If you're commuting to the center by public transit, find out if it's on a major bus route or in the vicinity of a subway station or commuter train.

✔ If you're driving to the center, find out whether it's situated on a downtown city block with no parking in sight or in a suburban neighborhood with plenty of parking. These kinds of things can make your life as a day-care parent a total dream or an absolute nightmare.

Of course, you also want to determine how long it takes to get to the day-care center from work and home. (For more on the pros and cons of choosing a day-care center that's closer to home versus work or vice versa, see Chapter 3.)

What are the hours of operation?

If the day-care center's hours of operations don't mesh well with your working hours, you can strike that particular center off your list of options. Otherwise, you may waste hours of the day-care director's time and your own, only to find out that the day-care center doesn't even open its doors for business until after you've had your mid-morning coffee break at work!

When you're trying to decide whether the day-care center's hours of operation are going to work for your family, don't just take into account your driving time on the sunniest August day; think about how long it typically takes you to battle traffic during both winter blizzards and summer construction season. If you're overly optimistic with your driving time estimates, you may find yourself second-guessing your child-care decision a few weeks or months down the road — something that can send you right back to the child-care drawing board again. Groan.

Is there a limit to the number of hours a child can spend at the center each day?

Don't assume that you can leave your child at the day-care center 12 hours a day just because it's open from 7 a.m. to 7 p.m. Most child-care centers limit the number of hours a day children can spend in care to nine or ten hours a day. (Of course, if your employer requires you to work 12-hour shifts as part of your job and operates a day-care center to meet the child-care needs of its workers, this particular child-care rule doesn't apply.)

Are part-timers welcome?

You're less likely to find a day-care center that accepts children on a part-time basis than you are to find a home day-care provider who accepts part-timers. But asking if part-time care is an option at this particular day-care center is still worth it. Just don't be surprised if the center director tells you that you either have to share a space with another family with a compatible schedule (for example, your child uses the day-care space on Mondays, Tuesdays, and Wednesdays, and the other family's child uses the space on Thursdays and Fridays) or you have to pay for a full-time space, even though you're only using the space on a part-time basis.

Don't assume that you don't need to ask about the availability of part-time care unless you need this service. Every day-care parent should ask this question, whether she's actually in the market for part-time care, because centers that accept children on a part-time basis are usually a lot more chaotic than those that serve the same group of children every day. In fact, centers that accept children on a part-time basis can be so chaotic that some child-care experts recommend that you avoid them entirely, especially if your child doesn't cope well with disruptions to her usual routine.

And a child who doesn't cope well won't do well in a day-care center that offers drop-in care.

Because parents purchase care on a daily or even hourly basis, the composition of children changes daily in drop-in day-care centers — something that can do a real number on your child if she can barely cope with the fact that her favorite red dress happens to be in the laundry today.

Is the center licensed and accredited?

Although knowing that a child-care center is licensed through the state and accredited through one of the national child-care accreditation programs is no guarantee of quality, such credentials do carry a fair bit of weight. In fact, you may decide to drop some child-care centers off your list of possible contenders right from the start if they don't pass muster in this department. (See Chapter 5 for more on what licensing and accreditation mean in terms of day care quality.)

What's the age range of the children?

Make sure you inquire about the ages of the children that the day-care center services. That way, you know how soon your child is likely to outgrow this particular day-care center. For example, if you're looking for care for your 4-year-old, you want to find a day-care center that provides care to school-age children, too. That way, when you're in the market for school-age childcare in a year, you already have a built-in solution.

Do you group children according to age or do you use mixed-age groupings?

Some day-care centers group children according to age; others use mixed age groups, which are groups made up of children of various ages. Parents who have children of different ages enrolled in the same day-care center typically prefer mixed age groupings because siblings can spend their days together. (The alternative scenario — grouping children according to age — would likely result in your 3-year-old daughter spending her days in the preschool room while her 2-year-old brother spends his days in the toddler room.)

An added advantage of going the mixed-age grouping route is that your child most likely has fewer child-care providers during his day-care career. If you enrolled your child in a program that grouped children according to more traditional age groupings, he would graduate from the baby room to the toddler room, and from the toddler room to the preschool room, and so on, getting a new care provider with each move.

Here's something else to think about: If you enroll your child in a day-care center that relies on age-based groupings, you may want to consider the effect that this turnover may have on the other children in the group. If a child moves up from the baby room to the toddler room and spends a lot of time crying during her first few days in the toddler room because her new caregiver hasn't learned how to meet her needs as quickly or as efficiently as her old caregiver, the other children in the group may become extra whiney or clingy, or start acting out to ensure that they're getting their fair share of the caregiver's attention. Fortunately, most children adjust relatively quickly to a change of caregivers, but those days of transition can be rough for the entire group, not just the caregiver and the new child.

While you're talking about the need to make adjustments, don't forget to factor in your own reaction to this particular child-care curveball. If the child-care provider has taken months to get accustomed to all your child's idiosyncrasies, you may not be thrilled about repeating the entire training process for the new child-care provider. You may also feel sad about having to part with the old child-care provider and hand your child over to someone new. If she did a terrific job of caring for your child, chances are your child isn't the only one who formed a strong attachment to her — odds are you did, too.

Does the child-care center shut down during any times of the year?

Most people have a finite number of vacation days, which is why you need to find out upfront whether the day-care center closes for extended periods of time during the year — say for two weeks in December during the holiday season, for example. When you have an idea how many days of your vacation time are likely to be gobbled up each year by center shut-downs, you can decide whether enrolling your child at this day-care center is even an option for you.

Of course, you want to err on the side of caution when figuring out how you're going to use your vacation days. Unless you have an exceptionally generous sick-leave package that allows you to take time off when your child is ill, you're probably going to need a few of those vacation days to take care of your child when she's battling the latest (but by no means greatest) day-care virus. (I know: some vacation!)

Has the center staff had appropriate training in first aid?

Anyone who's responsible for caring for young children should be trained in basic first aid, including infant and toddler CPR (cardiopulmonary resuscitation — a series of potentially life-saving resuscitation procedures). Young children face a significant risk of choking, so you want to feel confident that the day-care center staff is fully equipped to handle this and other emergencies that can potentially arise while your child is in their care.

According to the *National Health and Safety Performance Standards for Out-of-Home Childcare Programs* developed by the American Academy of Pediatrics, the American Public Health Association, and the U.S. Department of Health and Human Services, all day-care workers should receive first-aid training that will equip them to deal with the following types of pediatric emergency situations:

- Abrasions and lacerations
- Bleeding (including nosebleeds)
- Burns
- Fainting
- Poisoning (including tips on managing poisons that are swallowed, inhaled, or come into contact with the skin)
- Puncture wounds (including splinters)
- Biting wounds (insect, animal, and human)
- Shock
- Convulsions and other types of seizures
- Loss of consciousness
- Electric shock

✔ Drowning

✔ Heat-related injuries, including heat stroke and heat exhaustion

✔ Cold-related injuries, including hypothermia and frostbite

✔ Sprains, fractures, and other types of musculoskeletal injuries

✔ Dental and mouth injuries

✔ Allergic reactions (including information on managing potentially life-threatening allergic reactions)

✔ Eye injuries

✔ Techniques for positioning and moving sick or injured children

✔ Rescue breathing (including strategies for dealing with a blocked airway)

✔ Severe illness

If the center director wows you enough to convince you to schedule an onsite visit, you can grill her further about the center's health and safety procedures. For now, you just want to make sure that the basics are covered — in other words, that any staff member who could be entrusted with the health and well-being of your child has the necessary skills to cope with any emergency situation.

What are the fees?

You may want to make sure you're sitting down when you ask this particular question. Day-care center fees can sometimes come as a bit of a shock, particularly if you're in the market for childcare for two or more children — the proverbial double or triple whammy. But finding out the facts right away is best so that you can quickly decide whether your budget can handle these fees.

As a rule, expect to pay more for childcare for an infant or a toddler, because infants require more hands-on care and because child-care regulations in all states mandate lower caregiver-child ratios for infants and toddlers than for older children — something that increases staffing costs. In day-care centers in New York, for example, a caregiver can provide care to three infants under the age of six weeks, or four infants and toddlers between the ages of six weeks and 18 months, or five toddlers and preschoolers between the ages of 18 to 36 months.

Don't forget to ask what your day-care fees cover and don't cover. Are you expected to supply diapers, wipes, food, and baby equipment, such as a car seat and stroller, or are these included in your basic day-care fee? Obviously these extras can add up to a lot, so you want to know upfront whether they're covered, particularly if you're trying to compare a couple of different day-care centers' fees. (Nothing is more frustrating than trying to compare apples to oranges to kiwis, now is there?)

If you're in the market for childcare for more than one child, find out whether the day-care center offers price breaks to parents who are looking for childcare for two or more children. Don't expect much more than a 5 to 10 percent discount on the fees of your second child: Most day-care centers operate on painfully tight profit margins as it is, and as much as they may like to help cash-strapped parents by slashing fees, most simply can't afford to go that route.

And speaking of your growing family, you want to find out about while you're grilling the day-care center director about fee policies: Whether you're required to pay a reinstatement fee if your older child stops attending day care for a period of weeks or months while you're home on maternity leave with his younger brother or sister. Some centers require that parents go through the entire application process again, including the payment of a second application fee. So make sure you know what you're in for if you decide to keep your older child home with you while on maternity leave. Find out more about day-care fees in Chapter 4, and see Chapter 1 for more on application fees.

Do you offer discounts or scholarships to families on limited incomes?

Some day-care centers give parents on limited budgets a break by setting fees based on a sliding scale geared toward income level or by offering scholarships that offset some or all of the day-care fees. If you think you may qualify for some sort of financial assistance, be sure to inquire about what's available and what's involved in applying for aid. (See Chapter 4 for more about childcare subsidies and other ways of making childcare more affordable.)

Are parents expected to fundraise on behalf of the day-care center?

Many day-care centers rely on fundraising activities as a means of generating additional income for their programs without having to raise fees. If your idea of hell includes hawking frozen muffin batter to your nearest and dearest (or if you work for a company that absolutely prohibits fundraising activities of any type), you may be reluctant to enroll your child in such a center. The reason is obvious: You either have to live with the guilt that goes along with being the only parent in the entire day-care center who managed to come up empty in the frozen muffin batter sales department or spend a small fortune of your hard-earned cash on frozen muffin batter — something that could easily squeeze out all other food groups in your freezer for the foreseeable future.

I don't know about you, but I'd rather bite the bullet (as opposed to the frozen muffin batter!) and fork over a bit extra in day-care fees instead of being nickled and dimed to death by fundraisers down the road. If you feel the same way, you'll definitely want to inquire about fundraising policies when you inquire about the day-care center's fees — and steer clear of centers that expect you to play the role of part-time salesperson.

May I bring my child with me when I conduct my onsite visit?

Most day-care center directors encourage parents to bring their children along when checking out the child-care facility, so don't be afraid to ask the director if this is okay. On the other hand, don't feel obligated to bring your child along if you feel that her presence distracts you from sizing up the day-care center. If you decide to go with this particular day-care center, you can always bring your child back for a visit before her first official day. (See Chapter 15 for tips on making that all-important first week at day care as stress-free as possible for the entire family.)

What kind of information do you require to register my child at the center?

If you decide to schedule an onsite visit, make sure you ask what types of information you need to complete the various application forms. If the application form is relatively brief, you may want to fill it out on the spot. If, however, the form looks like something written by the IRS, you may want to take it home and fill it out at your leisure over a cup of tea and with a couple of headache tablets!

In addition to filling out an application form that gathers information about your child and your family (see the section, "Sealing the Deal: Filling Out Your Application" later in this chapter for more info), you can also expect to complete and sign

- A contract stating your support of the child-care center's no-corporal punishment rule

- A contract stating that you've been advised about the center's legal responsibility to report suspected cases of child abuse

- A contract stating that you're entitled to drop by the center at any time when your child's there and that you'll be admitted immediately (this is more for your benefit than the center's, obviously)

- A written consent form stating that the day-care center has your permission to

  - Transport your child in emergency situations

  - Transport your child on planned field trips

  - Take your child on planned or unplanned trips off-site

  - Release your child into someone else's care when you call to make such arrangements (a so-called *telephone release*)

• Seek medical treatment on your child's behalf and make emergency medical decisions about your child on your behalf, if you're unavailable

• Administer medications to your child (with your prior authorization)

• Release information about your child to agencies, schools, or other service providers

Conducting your onsite visit

Although you can learn a lot about a day-care center by asking the director the right questions by phone, the only way to get a true sense of whether the day-care center is right for your child is to schedule an onsite visit. Here are three key reasons for deciding to go this route:

✔ Meeting the day-care center director and members of her staff to decide if these are people you feel comfortable leaving your child with

✔ Asking further questions about the day-care center's policies and procedures

✔ Checking out the day-care premises for yourself

But what about the timing of your visit? Should you schedule your visit so that you arrive at the day-care center at a relatively quiet time of day when the director is likely to have more time to answer your questions, or should you plan to hit one of the busier times of day so that you can get a true feel for how the day care actually functions on a day-to-day basis?

A few radical thinkers suggest that you drop by the day-care center completely unannounced to get a candid look at the day-care operation. But given the ever-heightening emphasis on security in most day-care settings, your impromptu visit may merely lead to some impromptu questioning by the less-than-impressed security staff!

If you're bound and determined to get an unscripted look at life in the day-care center, you may want to go for a modified approach: Follow the standard protocol by setting up an official visit with the day-care director and then make an unscheduled return visit to the center.

Whether you decide to go for the scheduled visit, the impromptu visit, or the combination approach, what follows are the key questions you want to ask while you're checking out a particular day-care center in person.

Survey says

A study conducted by the National Institute of Child Health and Development found that only one-third of infant child-care providers have received any specialized training in child development, and only 18 percent have received a bachelor's degree or higher in this area.

How do you make families feel welcome?

No one wants to leave her child in a day-care center that exudes all the warmth and charm of a prison. So if you're picking up those kinds of impersonal, institutional vibes, you definitely want to exit stage left. (Or stage right. Whichever is quickest!)

You also want to steer clear of any day-care setting that seems overly neat — the kind of place where cleanliness and tidiness are valued over creativity and exploration, for example. Orderliness may be great for keeping carpets immaculate and walls pristine, but it's not so great for kids' brains!

Here's something else to keep in mind when evaluating the day-care environment: The day-care environment can help to set the tone for the relationship between the caregiver and the parent. If the environment is warm and welcoming, you're more likely to feel encouraged to drop by and to play a more active role in your children's day-care experience. Likewise, if the day care offers a comfortable place where you can breastfeed your baby, you may feel supported in your decision to continue breastfeeding after your return to work.

Is the day-care center designed to be secure?

On the one hand, you want the day-care center to be warm and welcoming. On the other hand, you want it to be every bit as secure as Fort Knox. (We day-care parents don't ask for much, now do we?)

Pay close attention to how security is handled at the day-care center. You want to note in particular

- ✔ **How well access to the day-care facility is controlled.** Is access controlled by a keypad, a security pass, or by walking through a checkpoint manned by a real person?

- ✔ **Whether the day-care center has sign-in procedures.** These procedures are designed to prevent unauthorized personnel from gaining access to the day-care center and to keep track of who is in the center at all times.

With day-care roulette, everybody loses

Continuity of care is particularly important for infants and toddlers. Studies have shown that young children who are repeatedly switched from caregiver to caregiver may eventually find it hard to form new relationships with other people. Some studies have even indicated that frequent changes in caregivers can also lead to poorer language and social skills — an important reason to inquire about a day-care center's turnover rates before you sign on the dotted line.

If you have any reason to doubt that your child will be safe and secure during his day-care day, you may want to call off the center tour at this point. There's no point wasting the center director's time or your own if you know in your heart that you would never feel right about leaving your child in such an unsecure child-care environment.

Is the day-care environment healthy and safe?

You don't have time to do an item-by-item safety check of the entire day-care center unless you plan to camp out for a week or two, so just focus your attention on the following key points:

✔ Check to see if the day-care center has a safe place for babies to sleep. If you have an infant, make sure that the center's director is up-to-speed on safe sleep practices for babies (for example, the importance of not putting babies to sleep in any position but on their backs). The incidence of deaths due to Sudden Infant Death Syndrome (SIDS) is higher in child-care settings than in non-child-care settings.

✔ Are enough cribs or cots available for all the children to take naps? If more than one child uses a cot or crib over the course of a day, are the sheets changed after the first child is finished using the bed? Who's responsible for supplying and washing the sheets?

✔ Are the floors in the day care generally clean, well-maintained, and reasonably clutter-free?

✔ Are dangerous materials such as cleaning supplies, scissors, and knives stored safely out of the children's reach?

✔ Are any environmental hazards in the day-care setting (lead paint, asbestos, radon gas)?

✔ Is the day-care center well-ventilated, well-lit, and kept at a comfortable temperature?

✔ Has the day-care been designed for adequate supervision? Is the child-care provider able to monitor the entire room at one time?

✔ Are the food preparation areas hygienic?

✔ Are infant and toddler toys disinfected on a regular basis?

✔ How often are diapers changed? Does the staff make a point of wearing disposable gloves? Do they make a point of sanitizing the diaper-changing area and washing their hands before they change the next child?

✔ Does the outdoor playground equipment measure up to current safety standards? One study found that 25 percent of day-care playgrounds are either hazardous or very hazardous. If you're unsure what to look for, visit the U.S. Consumer Product Safety Commission Web site at `www.cpsc.gov` or call 800-638-2772 (TTY 800-638-8270) to find out more.

✔ Is the outdoor play area properly fenced?

Does the day-care have some sort of predictable rhythm to the day?

Children do best when there's some sort of predictable daily rhythm to their lives, so you want to make sure that the day-care center staff has endeavored to build some sort of structure into the day-care day. (Of course, overkill can be a bad thing when it comes to routine. No one wants to send her toddler off to a boot camp–like day-care facility — the kind of place where every 2-year-old in the room is expected to put down her juice glass at exactly 9:12 a.m. because the toddler room sergeant — I mean the toddler room *supervisor* — said so.)

What kind of training in working with young children has the day-care staff received?

Because it's likely that your child will be cared for by more than one staff member during her time at the day-care center, it makes more sense to inquire about the credentials of the entire staff than to zero in on the credentials of the child-care provider who will be caring for your child over the short-term.

That's not to say that you shouldn't scrutinize the child-care provider's credentials to the max, too. *Au contraire!* You want to check out the credentials of your child's primary caregiver (the person assigned to provide care to her day in and day out) as well as any secondary caregivers who are likely to also be involved in her care. And because child-care facilities tend to be notorious for their turnover rates, you want to make sure that the day-care center director ensures that all staff members have received adequate training in caring for young children.

According to the American Academy of Pediatrics, the American Public Health Association, and the U.S. Department of Health and Human Services, any day-care center staff member who's directly involved in caring for young children should be properly trained in each of the following areas:

- Child development
- Behavior management strategies
- Common childhood illnesses (including child-care exclusion policies)
- Procedures for preventing the spread of communicable disease
- Immunization requirements
- Injury prevention procedures
- First aid and emergency procedures
- Child-abuse reporting policies
- Health promotion
- Nutrition information
- Medication administration policies and practices
- Information about caring for children with special needs

While you're talking staffing with the center director, also find out how careful she is about doing criminal background checks on all staff and volunteers and about ensuring that all staff members remain up-to-date on their immunizations. Hey, they don't call her the center director for nothing!

What is the staff turnover rate at this particular day-care center?

Staff turnover rates in day-care centers are alarmingly high. A number of different studies have consistently identified turnover rates in the 30 to 40 percent per year range. What this statistic fails to point out, however, is that some day-care centers fare much better — or much worse — than average. Obviously, you want to think twice about enrolling your child in a day-care center where the staff turnover rate is significantly higher than the national average. Not only is it less-than-ideal to subject your child to ongoing care-giver changes (studies have indicated that repeated turnover in caregivers can be harmful to a child's development), the fact that staff members are repeatedly dashing for the door can be indicative of a serious problem.

How long has the primary caregiver who would be assigned to your child been working with young children?

Although academic credentials are important, ideally you also want to find someone with some real-world experience. After all, finding a textbook that teaches you the ins and outs of negotiating a 2-year-old into a snowsuit is pretty hard. Besides, if someone's already been working in this profession for a couple of years, you know that she's highly committed to working with children and their parents. No one goes into this particular line of work for the money!

Of course, you don't want to be totally hung up on the years of experience issue — for example, refusing to have anything to do with a new college grad by sheer virtue of her inexperience. What she lacks in on-the-job training, she may more than make up for in enthusiasm. Besides, you have no way of knowing just how many hours she clocked as a volunteer coach during her high school days. Who knows? Maybe you're not giving her enough credit for time spent in the kiddie trenches!

What are the primary child-care provider's child-care philosophies?

In order to get the answer to this particular question, you want to spend a bit of time with the child-care provider — something the child-care center director should be only too happy to arrange, assuming that the director knows which group and which primary caregiver your child will be assigned to.

Timeout for an update on, well, timeouts!

If you're wondering about the use of *timeouts* (a discipline technique that involves removing the child from the environment for a couple of minutes so that he has a chance to reflect on his behavior) in child-care settings, you may be interested to learn what the American Academy of Pediatrics, the American Public Health Association, and the U.S. Department of Health and Human Services have to say on the matter. Here's a quick summary of the position of these three leading health authorities when it comes to timeouts:

- Timeouts are only appropriate for use with children over the age of three years. They shouldn't be used with infants or toddlers because younger children aren't able to make the link between the misbehavior that led to the timeout and the timeout itself.

- When considering whether a timeout is the most effective means of disciplining a child, the child-care provider needs to consider the child's developmental stage, temperament, and ability to learn from the timeout experience.

- Timeouts should only be used in situations where the child benefits from being able to regain control over his emotions.

- The child-care provider needs to keep the child within visual contact during the entire time when the timeout is being served.

- When timeouts are used, they should be used consistently, for an appropriate length of time (no more than two minutes for very young children and sometimes just long enough for the child to regain his composure), and shouldn't be overused.

Figuring out which group and which primary caregiver your child has is relatively easy for the director if your child is starting at the day-care center next week. It may require some major crystal ball gazing on her part if your child's name goes on a waiting list for the foreseeable future, however. In fact, she's unlikely to even guess in this latter situation: Staff turnover rates and other variables in the day-care environment make it extremely difficult for her to predict who may be assigned to your child down the road.

Assuming the day-care center director knows exactly who will be responsible for your child's primary care and is able to arrange for you to spend some time with this person, you want to use this opportunity to size up the primary caregiver's child-care philosophies. Obviously, you're looking for someone who understands that her job involves much more than merely ensuring that the children in her care don't come to any harm (although that is, of course, important!). You want to find a child-care provider who understands the importance of developing an early childhood program that promotes your child's healthy physical, emotional, intellectual, and social development.

Of course, simply listening to what she has to say or reading whatever statement of philosophy she may have written out to share with you (the truly crème de la crème of child-care providers often have written children philosophy statements available, as do the better day-care centers) isn't enough. Also, pay careful attention to the way she interacts with the children in her care. The child-care provider's body language gives you some pretty clear clues about how she feels about her job at the day-care center and how she feels about the children in her care. If she reacts with embarrassment or discomfort if a highly affectionate 3-year-old tries to give her a hug or her body language tells you that she's becoming extremely frustrated by a 2-month-old baby's fussy behavior, you may want to question the caliber of her skills.

Here are some other clues to watch for when observing the child-care provider's interactions with the children in her group:

- ✔ Whether she sits with the children while they're playing or merely observes them from a distance and how she reacts to the children when they approach her looking for attention. For example, does she greet them with genuine enthusiasm, or does she simply try to meet their needs quickly in the hope that they go back to playing on their own once again?

- ✔ Whether she makes a point of singling out each child for some attention at some point during your visit or whether she only dishes out attention to those children who deliberately seek it from her.

- ✔ Whether she makes a special effort to comfort and reassure any children who are exceptionally frightened or unhappy — even if it means momentarily interrupting her conversation with you to attend to the child's needs.

✔ How she handles any child in the group who happens to exhibit any extra-challenging behaviors, like biting or screaming. Does she treat this child with the same respect as the other children or does she yank him by the arm rather roughly and drag him off to a time-out chair that feels more like a prison camp to you than a place for a child to regain his self-control?

✔ Whether she has a solid sense of when it's appropriate to intervene when a child is attempting to master a new skill and when it's better to back off and allow that child to achieve a healthy amount of frustration so the child experiences the very real sense of accomplishment that goes along with having mastered that challenge on his own.

✔ Whether she's genuinely enthusiastic about the children's achievements or whether she's merely paying lip service to their various accomplishments because she feels that's what she's supposed to do.

Obviously, this is one of those situations where it pays to have exceptionally fine-tuned intuition skills, to say nothing of an ability to read between the lines. You gain some of your most valuable insights by simply paying attention to what's not being said.

Does the child-care provider demonstrate cultural sensitivity?

Although zeroing in on a child-care center that's respectful of cultural beliefs and values is important, the buck ultimately stops with your child's child-care provider, so you'll want to make sure that she demonstrates sufficient sensitivity in this area. Does she assume, for example, that every child in the center will be celebrating Christmas in December, or does she recognize the fact that the children in the center are likely to represent a variety of different faiths and cultural backgrounds and show a willingness to work with parents to incorporate these traditions into the day-care program?

How well does she handle discipline problems?

Although you may like to believe that your child is perfectly well behaved each and every day she toddles off to day care, her odds of making it through her entire day-care career without a single blemish on her day-care rap sheet are pretty much slim to none. After all, a typical day-care day is positively ripe with opportunities for flare-ups. Just think of the number of times a child is asked to share or wait her turn over the course of an average day! And if your child is highly prone to these moments of misdirected passion, you definitely want to know upfront what she — and you — can expect from the child-care provider when it comes to discipline.

What you're looking for is some evidence that the child-care provider understands the following discipline fundamentals:

- ✔ The discipline method is suited to a child's developmental stage and temperament.

- ✔ The discipline method leaves the child feeling good about herself and the caregiver feeling good about herself.

- ✔ The discipline method emphasizes teaching rather than punishing: You want the child to learn something from this incident of misbehavior, not merely be punished for making a mistake.

- ✔ The discipline method helps build on the bond between the child and the child-care provider instead of undermining it.

What are the center's discipline policies?

Having a frank discussion with the day-care center director about what you consider acceptable methods of disciplining a child and what (for your family, at least) is taboo is important. That way, you can be certain that the center's discipline policies are entirely in sync with your own discipline philosophies.

Although discipline policies and procedures vary from day-care center to day-care center, most centers make a point of prohibiting any of the following types of discipline practices because they've been proven harmful to children:

- ✔ Physically punishing a child (for example, beating, hitting, spanking, shaking, pinching, or any other methods that cause a child physical pain)

- ✔ Withdrawing food or threatening to withdraw food

- ✔ Any sort of abusive or profane language or verbal abuse, threats, or derogatory remarks that target either the child or her family

- ✔ Any form of private or public humiliation, including the threat of physical punishment

- ✔ Any type of emotional abuse, including rejecting, ignoring, isolating, or frightening the child

- ✔ Forcible restraint (for example, placing a child in a confined space such as a closet or a locked room)

Most day-care centers have written guidelines governing their policies and procedures (including discipline), so be sure to request a copy while you're conducting your onsite visit. Better yet, see if you can download a copy from the center's Web site ahead of time and review them before your onsite visit. That way, you can come up with a list of questions to ask the day-care center director about any policies and procedures that you're particularly concerned about.

How does the center support parents who are toilet-training their children?

Bet you didn't realize that toilet-training was a team sport. Well, it is — and you definitely want to find out upfront whether you and the day-care staff are likely to end up being on the same team. If you're a firm believer in taking a relatively laid-back approach to toilet-training (for example, you think that allowing toddlers and preschoolers to signal their readiness to enroll at Potty Training U. is best as opposed to parents and caregivers arbitrarily deciding when to enroll them), but the day-care center routinely starts toilet-training all of its children shortly after their second birthdays, you can be headed for trouble.

What you're looking for during your onsite interview with the day-care center director is evidence that the center understands the importance of working with parents when it comes to toilet training: The day-care center staff is there to support you in your efforts to toilet train your child when the moment is right, but not a moment sooner. The last thing you need is daily pressure from some staff member who's got a bee in her bonnet because your kid is still in diapers.

This discussion of potty politics raises an important side issue, by the way — who's likely to call the shots when making parenting decisions concerning your child. Obviously, the person who should be making those decisions is you, but if the child-care provider who's working with your child is highly aggressive, you may find yourself in a bit of a parenting turf war from time to time. Although you may welcome assistance at times, or even solicit her opinion on a particular child-rearing issue, you don't want to feel like the child-care provider has all the answers and you don't. Over time, that can really take its toll on your parenting self-esteem. For more on potty training, check out *Potty Training For Dummies,* by Diane Stafford and Jennifer Shoquist, M.D. (Wiley).

What kinds of meals and snacks are served?

According to the American Dietetic Association, parents need to be on the lookout for evidence of high nutrition standards when evaluating a day-care center. As a rule, you want to find a day-care center that

✔ Provides the children in its care with nutritionally balanced meals and snacks that are consistent with the nutritional practices set out in the Department of Health and Human Service's *Dietary Guidelines for Americans* (see www.health.gov/dietaryguidelines/) and that take into account the age of the child, the number of hours the child is in care, and any cultural or ethnic food habits

✔ Makes age-appropriate and developmentally suitable furniture and eating utensils available to children to promote healthy eating practices

✔ Eats with the children so that a family-style mealtime experience is provided (as opposed to an *Oliver Twist*–style institutional dining experience!)

✔ Teaches children about the link between nutrition and health

✔ Makes parents aware of the types of meals and snacks that their child is fed while at childcare so that the parents can ensure that the meals and snacks served at home complement the foods served at childcare

✔ Ensures that food handling and serving procedures at the child-care center exemplify the best practices when it comes to both food safety and sanitation

Ask the day-care center to show you some sample menus so you get a sense of the types of foods that are served at the center. Time your visit so that you hit mealtime. That way, you find out for yourself whether the meals are varied, nutritious, age-appropriate, pleasant, unhurried, and appropriately supervised. (I know, I know: It's a tall order!)

If you're looking for childcare for an infant, you also want to ask a few additional nutrition-related questions while you've got the day-care center director's ear, namely:

✔ If you continue breastfeeding your baby after you return to work, how will the day-care staff support you in that choice?

✔ Does day-care center staff make a point of holding babies when they're drinking from bottles (as opposed to engaging in the dangerous practice of propping bottles, which can lead to choking)?

✔ Are you expected to supply any of your baby's food or feeding equipment?

What are the day-care center's policies regarding sick children?

Something else you want to find out while talking day-care policy with the day-care center director is how this particular center handles the problem of sick children. Do they refuse to accept any child who has so much as a sniffle (in which case you may as well quit your job now and save yourself a lot of unnecessary aggravation down the road!)? Or is the day-care center a little *too* liberal about allowing parents to send sick children to day care when those kids really don't belong anywhere but home in bed?

Day-care centers have taken a lot of heat from parents and doctors in recent years for being too rigid in their sick kid policies — for refusing to allow even mildly ill children to participate in the program until they're 100 percent sniffle-free and for putting pressure on parents to obtain antibiotics from their doctors in situations when antibiotics are entirely unwarranted.

Because parents need to know how a particular day-care center chooses to handle the issue of illness, the National Association for the Education of Young Children (NAEYC) is now recommending that day-care centers develop written policies that clearly spell out whether they're equipped to only deal with children who are well enough to participate in the regular day-care program or whether some modifications can be made for mildly ill children who may require additional rest and a reduced amount of activity.

According to the NAEYC, this information should be communicated clearly to parents at the time of enrollment or orientation so that they have a clear idea what to expect the first time their child wakes up with a cold or a fever. (Notice I said *when* rather than *if*. That's because the odds of a child who's enrolled in day care picking up a garden-variety illness are fairly overwhelming: Studies have shown that 16 percent of the children attending a particular day care are ill at any given time, and a typical baby enrolled in a day-care center can expect to pick up around ten respiratory illnesses during her first year in care. Now that's nothing to sneeze at!)

Under what circumstances does the day-care center director exclude sick children from day care?

Will the phone in your office start ringing each time your child develops a cough or will the call come only if your child starts vomiting or showing symptoms of a more serious illness?

After you find out how the day-care center director typically handles these situations, compare her policies to the policies of the American Academy of Pediatrics, the American Public Health Association, and the U.S. Department of Health when it comes to excluding sick children from child-care arrangement. Here's a quick summary of their current thinking on this matter. According to these three leading health authorities, it's appropriate for a child-care provider to send a child home from day care if

✔ The child isn't well enough to participate in the regular center routine.

✔ The child's illness poses a threat to the health and well-being of the other children in the day care.

✔ The child has one or more of the following medical conditions:

- An unexplained fever accompanied by changes in the child's behavior or any other symptoms of illness

- An illness characterized by extreme lethargy, uncontrolled coughing, inexplicable irritability, persistent crying, difficulty breathing, wheezing, or any other usual symptoms

- Diarrhea (in particular, watery stools and an increased frequency of passing stools; children with loose stools but who are otherwise well do not need to be excluded from day care)

- Blood in stools that can't be explained by constipation, dietary changes, or medication usage

- Vomiting (two or more episodes of vomiting in the previous 24 hours)

- Persistent abdominal pain (for example, any pain that continues for more than two hours)

- Mouth sores that are accompanied with drooling

- Any sort of rash that's accompanied by a fever or changes in the child's behavior

- Pink eye (conjunctivitis)

- Head lice (pediculosis) (the child can return to day care approximately 24 to 36 hours after the first treatment)

- Scabies (treatment must be completed before a child can return to day care)

- Tuberculosis (the child must have a clean bill of health from the appropriate medical authority before he can return to day care)

- Impetigo (the child can return to day care 24 hours after treatment has been initiated)

- Strep throat or streptococcal infection (the child can return to day care 24 hours after antibiotic treatment begins and her fever disappears)

- Chickenpox (the child can return to day care after all the sores have dried and crusted — typically six days after the first signs of spots)

- Whooping cough (pertussis) (the child can return to day care after approximately 5 days of a 14-day course of antibiotic treatment have been completed)

- Mumps (the child should be excluded from day care until nine days after the onset of swelling)

- Hepatitis A virus (the child should be excluded from day care until one week after the onset of illness, jaundice, or as directed by the health department)

- Measles (the child can return to day care four days after the onset of the rash)

- Rubella (the child can return to day care six days after the onset of the rash)

- Unspecified respiratory tract infection (a child who's exhibiting mild cold-like symptoms without any evidence of a fever) doesn't need to be excluded from the day-care program unless the child isn't well enough to participate in the day-care program or the illness results in a need for more care than what the staff are able to provide without compromising the needs of the other children in the program.

Do parents have to pay for days when their child is absent due to illness?

Something else you want to find out is whether you're required to pay for each day your child misses due to illness. Most day-care centers expect you to pay for your child's space, whether she uses it or not, because the day-care's overhead costs continue, regardless. But some centers give you a break if your child comes down with a more serious illness that requires him to be away from day care for a couple of weeks while he's on the mend.

Does the day-care center charge a fee if parents are late picking up their children?

You know what they say about the best-laid plans of mice and men often going astray? Well, those plans tend to go astray even more often if you happen to be a day-care parent! And sometimes, despite your best intentions, life's little curveballs result in your being a few minutes late in picking up your child from day care.

Although most day-care providers are fairly understanding if you tend to be on time most of the time and you're only running a minute or two behind schedule on this particular occasion, their patience starts to run a little thin if that couple of minutes turns into five or ten minutes or longer — or if this is the third time this week you've been late. The end result? You can find yourself on the hook for some rather hefty late charges — typically $1 for every minute you're past your scheduled pick-up time. (Obviously, you want to find out about these late charges upfront so that you don't find yourself running up a hefty and unexpected tab down the road.)

Comparing notes with other parents

You're probably pretty exhausted by this point of the tour, but you still have one important job ahead of you: Checking the day-care center's references. What you want is a list of names and numbers of parents you can call who are willing to talk about their experiences with the center.

Be sure to ask for the names of both parents of children who are currently enrolled in the center (who may be more in-the-know about current practices at the day-care center) as well as parents of children who are no longer enrolled at the center (who have less of a vested interest in keeping the center director happy and therefore may be willing to be a little more frank). Here's what to ask when you pick up the phone to make that call:

- How long was your child enrolled in this day-care center?
- What was your child's age at the time?
- Did the day-care center meet your expectations?
- Can you give me an example of a situation that was handled particularly well by the day-care center staff?
- Can you give me an example of a situation in which you experienced a conflict or other difficulty with a member of the day-care center staff? Was this situation ultimately resolved to your satisfaction?
- Is there anything else you think that I need to know as I go about making my decision?

You can pick up some additional reference-checking pointers in Chapter 5.

Sealing the Deal: Filling Out Your Application

When you've zeroed in on the child-care center of your dreams, all that stands between you and much-deserved rest is paperwork. Lots and lots of paperwork. You can expect to be asked to supply the following types of information on a standard day-care center application form:

- Your child's legal name
- Your child's preferred name
- Your child's date of birth (or the date when your baby is due if you are pregnant and arranging childcare for your baby-to-be)
- Your preferred starting date
- Whether you require care for any additional children (if you do, you can expect to be asked to fill out an additional application form for each additional child)
- A list of the dates and times when you will require care, including your estimated drop-off and pickup times
- Your name

✔ Your partner's name

✔ Details about your marital situation (for example, whether you're married, separated, or divorced and — in the case of a marital split — what custody arrangements are in place)

✔ Your contact information at work

✔ Your child's other parent's contact information at work

✔ The names and ages of your child's siblings and anyone else living in the household

✔ The names of any family pets

✔ What child-care arrangements, if any, your child has used in the past; the reason for leaving; and, if appropriate, the name and phone number of his previous caregiver

✔ Information that could help to determine your eligibility for childcare subsidies (see Chapter 4 for more about childcare subsidies):

   • Whether you are employed by a particular organization that makes subsidies available to its employees

   • Whether your household income falls below a certain level

   • Whether your child has any special needs that might make him eligible for certain types of child-care subsidies.

After your child has been accepted into the center, most day-care centers will also ask you to fill out a child information sheet that will provide them with some additional background information about your child including

✔ His personality type (Is he quiet and shy or confident and outgoing?)

✔ His energy level (Is he calm or rambunctious?)

✔ His daily routines (especially sleeping, eating, and toileting routines)

✔ What types of things he is afraid of (animals, thunderstorms, and so on)

✔ How he reacts to new and stressful situations and what generally works best in terms of soothing him

✔ Whether or not he's in generally good health

✔ Whether he requires any medication or special medical treatment that the center staff needs to know about

✔ What types of foods he tends to eat over the course of a typical day and whether certain types of foods need to be avoided due to food allergies or intolerances

Although you may feel exhausted by the time you finish getting through all this paperwork, do your best to answer the questions as fully and honestly as possible. After all, the better the quality of the information you provide to the center staff, the better the caliber of care they can provide to your child.

Chapter 7

Sizing Up a Family Day Care

● ●

In This Chapter

▶ Screening a family day-care provider by phone

▶ Assessing a family day care in person

▶ Conducting reference checks

● ●

So you've weighed the pros and cons of your various child-care options and decided that family day care is the best option for your family. (If you haven't gotten that far yet, check out Chapter 2 for the inside scoop on your other options.) But assuming you've decided that family day care is your best bet, you should have clear sailing from this point forward, right? Maybe, maybe not.

Having a picture in your head of what the ideal family day-care arrangement looks like, right down to the captivating whiff of fresh-baked muffins and the cheery smile of the Mary Poppins look-alike who greets you at the door is one thing. Actually finding a family day-care provider who's one part Mary Poppins and one part Betty Crocker — and who happens to live in Mister Rogers' Neighborhood to boot — is something all together different! That's what this chapter is all about: helping you find a family day-care arrangement that you can feel good about from nine to five and beyond.

Evaluating a Family Day Care

Parents are sometimes surprised to discover that evaluating a family day care can be even more challenging than checking out a day-care center. You may find that it feels more than a little awkward to go traipsing through someone's home, passing judgment on everything from her safety standards to her childrearing practices. Don't cut corners just because you feel awkward or embarrassed, however. Remember, you owe it to your child to check out a family day-care arrangement every bit as thoroughly as you would any other type of child-care arrangement. That means:

 ✔ Prescreening family day-care providers by phone

 ✔ Conducting onsite visits

 ✔ Thoroughly checking the family day-care provider's references

Doing telephone prescreening

Because onsite visits take time, you may want to do some initial groundwork by phone first. That way, if the family day-care provider happens to casually mention that her all-time favorite movie was the 1992 hit *The Hand That Rocks the Cradle* (you know, the suspense thriller that starred Rebecca De Mornay as The Nanny from Hell), you can quickly strike that particular family day-care provider from your list!

Chances are you'll have a less dramatic reason for switching to Plan B. You may find that the family day-care provider isn't willing to have children arrive before 8 a.m. — a big problem if your shift at the Acme Widget Factory starts a good hour earlier. Or you may find that she closes up shop for the summer months — bad news again unless you happen to have a most generous vacation benefits package!

You can save yourself plenty of legwork by asking all the key questions over the phone. Then, if the family day-care provider makes it over the initial set of hurdles, you can schedule a home visit.

What follows are some of the key questions you want to discuss with a potential family day-care provider when you first make contact by phone.

Do you have spaces available?

Why waste your time or the family day-care provider's time asking several questions if the day-care is full right now? That's why you should first ask whether the day care has any available spaces. If you find out that she's not able to take on any additional children at this time, you may want to ask if she's willing to notify you of any future vacancies. (Remember, you can never be on too many waiting lists!)

Where's the family day care located?

Assuming the center has potential space for your child, the next thing you want to find out is where the family day care is located. With any luck, it's close to your home or workplace. The morning day care trek is exhausting enough without turning it into an hour-long daily endurance test!

What are the hours of operation?

A family day care's hours of operation tend to be a dealmaker or a dealbreaker for most families. You need a child-care arrangement that meshes well with your working hours. You won't score many points with your employer if you're constantly showing up late for work or cutting out a few minutes early to pick up your child from day care.

Don't forget to factor in bad weather, traffic jams, and other worst-case scenarios when trying to guesstimate whether the center's hours of operation are going to work for your family. Otherwise, you may find yourself having to switch child-care arrangements after only a few short weeks — bad news indeed for all concerned.

Are part-timers welcome?

Asking if part-timers are welcome is important whether or not you're actually in the market for part-time childcare yourself. Confused? Let me explain. Family day cares that take on several part-timers tend to be more chaotic than those day cares that serve the same group of children day after day. In fact, they can be so chaotic that some child-care experts recommend that you steer clear of such arrangements entirely, particularly if you have a highly sensitive child who finds any deviation from the normal routine highly disruptive or upsetting.

And, of course, you want to be particularly leery of a family day-care provider who accepts children on a drop-in basis. Not only is the composition of the day care likely to change dramatically from day to day (after all, the day care may literally have a new crop of kids each day!), she's also likely to end up with scheduling problems that can result in far more children attending the day care on any given day than state laws allow. (This violation is one of the most common types of child-care regulation infractions, by the way.)

What are the ages of the other children?

Inquire about the ages of the other children who the family day-care cares for. After all, your preschooler may be bored to tears if all the other children in the family day care are a good two years younger!

And, your baby would be equally poorly served if she were the only infant in a day care full of toddlers. (Research shows that babies don't fare particularly well if they're cared for in a family day-care setting that's dominated by toddlers. The reason is obvious: Meeting the needs of both non-mobile infants and highly active toddlers simultaneously is no small feat!)

And while you're noting the ages of the other children, stop to do a quick head count. If the family day-care provider is violating state child-care legislation by caring for too many children at one time, you want to know upfront. (You can find out how to track down the specifics on child-care laws in your state in Chapter 5.)

Are you licensed or accredited?

Although it's a mistake to assume that having a state child-care license or achieving accreditation through a national child-care accreditation is any sort of *guarantee* of quality, it's still a good idea to seek out family day cares that have managed to jump through the necessary licensing and accreditation hoops. After all, licensing and accreditation are the closest things to a Good Housekeeping Seal of Approval that the child-care world has to offer. (If you're not quite clear on what I'm talking about when I use the terms *licensing* and *accreditation,* flip to Chapter 5.)

Does the family day care shut down during any times of the year?

Find out upfront whether the family day-care provider closes up shop at certain times of the year. Perhaps she makes a point of taking a week or two off in December while her kids are home for the holidays. Or maybe she hops on a plane for two weeks every July to visit some relatives overseas.

Because her absence is going to have a major impact on your life, you need to have an idea of when you're likely to be hit with these particular curveballs. Otherwise, you may find yourself in scramble mode every time your family day-care provider heads out of town.

Does the family day-care provider have a backup?

Given that they're coughed on, drooled on, and, yes, even vomited on by little kids, it's hardly surprising that family day-care providers manage to get side-swiped by the occasional virus. You have to have a pretty feisty immune system to consider a career in this particular profession! Because hanging out in a germ lab 24-7 means that you're going to occasionally succumb to the illnesses that are going around, you can't reasonably expect that your family day-care provider's going to be up for caring for kids every single day. So, find out if she's lined up a pinch hitter for days when she's feeling too sick to go up to bat herself.

Of course, you may feel quite strongly that you don't want the family day-care provider to have anything to do with lining up a backup provider for your child. If that's the case, then you simply need to come up with a backup plan on your own. (Don't worry, you're not entirely on your own. I give you all kinds of helpful tips in Chapter 12.) But if the family day-care provider is willing to line up backup care for days when she's unavailable, and those arrangements are acceptable to you, her willingness to pitch in and help can save you a lot of time and worry.

Of course, you'll want to find out upfront whether you're expected to continue paying for your child's day-care space even if you have no intention of using the services of the backup family day-care provider. (Perhaps your child's granny is happy to pinch-hit under such circumstances, even if she has no interest in providing childcare on a full-time basis. If you're thinking of asking a family member to be your child-care pinch hitter, be sure to read Chapter 10.)

Should you bring your child with you?

Something you have to decide before heading out the door is whether you should bring your child with you when making your initial onsite visit. Although having your toddler in tow gives you the chance to gauge the chemistry (or lack thereof!) between her and the family day-care provider, you may be so distracted by your toddler's shenanigans that you fail to take note of the toxic waste dump next door. If you feel that having her with you makes it harder for you to get your questions answered and to check out the family day-care operation as thoroughly as you want to, leave her at home for now. If things pan out and you decide to use the services of this particular family day-care provider, you can always arrange a time for her to visit the day care before her official first day. (You can find all kinds of tips on making the first week of day care as stress-free as possible for the entire family in Chapter 15.)

If the family day-care provider intends to arrange her own backup for those times when she's ill or otherwise unavailable, let her know that you want to meet the backup caregiver ahead of time. Then, make a point of conducting the same sorts of reference checks that you would on any other family day-care provider. Yes, it means some additional legwork for you, but it sure beats the alternative: leaving your child with a complete stranger who you know nothing about.

Has the family day-care provider had appropriate training in first aid?

Anyone who's responsible for caring for young children should have received training in basic first aid, including infant and toddler CPR (cardiopulmonary resuscitation — a series of potentially life-saving resuscitation procedures). In fact, most states require it of all licensed family day-care providers. Young children face a significant risk of choking, so you want to feel confident that your family day-care provider is fully equipped to handle all emergencies that can potentially arise while your child is in her care.

If you find a caregiver who has otherwise excellent skills, but who's lacking this all-important first-aid training, you may consider offering to underwrite the cost for her to receive such training and making it a condition of your day-care contract that she completes her training before your child's first day at the day care. If she's not willing to set aside the time to bring her skills up to par, she's not the family day-care provider for you. You simply can't afford to compromise when your child's health and well-being is on the line.

If the family day-care provider makes it through the telephone prescreening process and you schedule an onsite visit, you also want to ask her what other types of childcare-related training she has received. See "Conducting your onsite visit" later in this chapter for more information.

What are the fees?

Ask about the family day-care provider's fees before you schedule an onsite visit. That way, you won't have any nasty surprises down the road.

You can expect to pay a premium for infants and toddlers because they require more hands-on care and because child-care regulations in most states require a lower caregiver-child ratio for infants and toddlers than for older children. In New York, for example, a family day-care provider can care for as many as seven preschoolers in her home, but only four infants at one time.

You also want to find out exactly what the fee does — and doesn't — cover. Are you expected to supply diapers, wipes, food, and baby equipment, such as a car seat or stroller, or are these extras included in the basic day-care fee? Inquiring minds want to know.

And a final point to inquire about, while I'm talking dollars and cents: When are those day-care fees payable? Some family day-care providers accept payment at the end of the week that services were rendered, but, increasingly, family day-care providers are requesting postdated checks in advance.

If you think about it, this kind of arrangement makes a lot of sense and can actually alleviate a lot of stress for both parties if you pay in advance. It prevents the Friday morning checkbook scramble and eliminates the need to make an extra trip to the family day-care provider's house if your child happens to be away the day that the weekly check is due. So don't wait for your family day-care provider to suggest that you hand over a month's worth of postdated checks in advance. Make the suggestion yourself. One of the biggest sources of hard feelings between family day-care providers and parents is the parents' overly casual attitude about paying the caregiver on time ("Oops, I forgot my checkbook. Okay if I pay you next week?"). You'll score yourself tons and tons of brownie points if you show that you're willing to go the extra mile on the payment front.

Want to save yourself the trouble of writing out 52 checks a year? Take advantage of your financial institution's online banking capabilities and arrange to transfer funds electronically from your bank account to your family day-care provider's bank account. Believe it or not, you don't even have to bank at the same financial institution to pull off this bit of financial wizardry nowadays.

Conducting your onsite visit

Up until now, you've been doing all your detective work by phone. Now it's time to take your Sherlock Holmes routine on the road by scheduling an onsite visit.

You want to schedule an onsite visit for three main reasons:

✔ Meeting the family day-care provider you're considering face-to-face to decide whether she's someone you feel comfortable leaving your child with

✔ Gathering more information about the family day-care provider's child-care philosophies and day-care policies and procedures

✔ Inspecting the day-care premises

Two schools of thought exist when it comes to scheduling your onsite visit. Some child-care gurus argue that you should try to time your visit so you arrive at the day care at a relatively quiet time of day so that the family day-care provider is less distracted and better able to show you around and answer your questions. Others say that you get a better sense of how the family day-care provider copes with the day-to-day chaos if you show up during one of the busier times of day — perhaps when she's helping the children settle into the day-care routine during the early-morning drop-off. (If you have the privilege of being a fly on the wall at this time of day, you can note how much attention each child receives, how calm — or harried! — the family day-care provider becomes, how well the family day-care provider relates to the parents, and how comfortable you feel leaving your child in her care.)

Of course, still others argue that you should go for the element of surprise by showing up unannounced. (I know, I know: I told you there were two schools of thought. Well, let's say a third school just opened up on your block!) I'm not a big fan of this third school because I wouldn't like a complete stranger showing up on my doorstep without advance warning. Frankly, I'd be more inclined to call the police than to toss out the welcome mat. So if you're bound and determined to go this route, I'd suggest you try a modified approach. Plan to make two visits: an initial scheduled visit and a follow-up visit that's completely impromptu. You may consider dropping by with your child to see how the family day-care provider reacts to him — and vice versa!

Regardless of whether you decide to hit the family day care during a relative lull or to time your visit to coincide with one of the busier times of day, here are some key questions to keep in mind while checking out the family day care and the family day-care provider:

Does the family day care feel warm and welcoming?

Before you start asking a million and one questions and filling your notebook with semi-legible scribbles, pause to note your initial impressions of the family day care. Does the place feel warm and welcoming? Or do you feel like you've accidentally wandered onto the pages of a home decorating magazine?

If you feel like you've just crash-landed into the pad of the hottest new decorator, chances are your child isn't going to be terribly comfortable here. What you're looking for is an environment that's clean and safe, but not overly neat and tidy. After all, how much fun can a kid have if the family day-care provider is always chasing him around with a broom and a dust pan? Or even worse: If she's constantly reminding the children to put the blue toys on the blue toy shelf and the red toys on the red shelf. Just think of all the years of therapy that may be required to help your kid get over that kind of regimented thinking. Very scary indeed!

Something else to note is whether your child is likely to feel welcome. If the family day-care provider has made a point of creating a special spot for her belongings (perhaps a coat hook and a plastic bin), she's more likely to feel like an invited guest than an unwanted intruder. Ditto if she steps into a child-centered environment: One that features age-appropriate toys and child-sized equipment.

Is the family day-care provider's home child-proof?

Although you don't have time to do an item-by-item safety check of the family day-care provider's home (unless, of course, you're planning to bring a lunch and turn your one- or two-hour visit into an all-day affair!), you want to get a general sense of whether she's conscientious (or clueless) when it comes to child safety. Here are the key things to look for as you give the family day-care safety once-over:

- ✔ Are electrical outlets covered?
- ✔ Are radiators covered?
- ✔ Are portable heaters kept out of the children's reach?
- ✔ Do all windows above the first floor have window guards?
- ✔ Is a safety gate at the top and bottom of each set of stairs?
- ✔ Are smoke detectors and a fire extinguisher present?
- ✔ What's the family day-care provider's fire-escape plan? Does the family day-care provider conduct monthly fire drills to ensure that the children in her care know what to do in the event of a fire?
- ✔ Is an updated list of emergency phone numbers next to the telephone?
- ✔ Does the family day-care provider maintain updated emergency contact and medical information for each child? (Ideally, she should be asking you for updates at least every couple of months.)
- ✔ Are the floors clean, well-maintained, and reasonably clutter-free?
- ✔ Does the changing table have a safety belt on it to keep children from rolling off? Is the family day-care provider in the habit of using it?

✔ Does the family day-care provider have any pets? If so, do they have access to the children in the day care? Do these pets pose any risk to the children?

✔ Are dangerous materials such as cleaning supplies, scissors, and flammable items stored out of the children's reach?

✔ Are there any environmental hazards such as radon, asbestos, or lead paint?

✔ Does the day-care room allow for adequate supervision? Is the family day-care provider able to monitor the entire room at once?

Has the family day-care provider created a healthy environment for the children in her care?

While checking out the house for safety hazards, you also want to look for evidence that the family day-care provider is conscientious about health and hygiene matters, too. Here are the key points to consider:

✔ Are the areas of the home that the children have access to well-ventilated, well-lit, and kept at a comfortable temperature?

✔ Is smoking allowed inside the building (either while the children are at day care or after hours)?

✔ Does the family day care provide enough space for children to crawl, walk, and otherwise enjoy being physically active?

✔ Are the food preparation areas hygienic?

✔ Are infant and toddler toys disinfected when they need it (for example, after they've been mouthed by a child and/or at least a couple of times a week when the toys are in active use)? (Don't worry if the family day-care provider only gets around to disinfecting the preschool toys every now and again. Preschoolers are far less likely to mouth toys than younger children, so their toys don't have to be disinfected as often.)

✔ Are garbage cans, diaper areas, and bathrooms disinfected on a regular basis?

✔ How often are diapers changed?

✔ Does the family day-care provider use disposable gloves when changing diapers? If she doesn't, does she make a point of washing her hands before she changes the next child?

✔ Are the diapering and toilet areas kept clean?

✔ Is a sink next to the diaper-change area so that the family day-care provider can wash her hands?

✔ Does the family day-care provider make a point of sanitizing the diaper-change area after each diaper change?

✔ Are hot running water, soap, and paper towels used after going to the toilet and before every meal and snack?

✔ Does each child have his own crib or cot?

✔ If more than one child uses a cot or a crib over the course of a day, are the sheets changed after the first child is finished? Who's responsible for supplying and washing the sheets?

✔ Are families required to provide proof that their children have received all of the recommended childhood immunizations?

✔ Does the family day-care provider have a rest area where she can temporarily isolate a child who's throwing up or otherwise quite ill?

✔ Is there a first-aid kit?

Is the outdoor play area safe, too?

Something else you need to consider when evaluating this particular family day care is whether the family day-care provider has created a stimulating yet safe backyard play environment for the children in her care. Here are some questions to ask yourself when checking out the family day-care provider's backyard:

✔ Does the playground equipment appear to be safe for young children?

✔ Does the play area have adequate protective surfacing around the playground equipment? (See the sidebar, "Family day-care safety smarts" in this chapter.)

✔ Does the backyard have any other hazards in it?

If the family day-care provider is in the habit of taking the children to a nearby playground or park, you also want to give some thought to some additional safety issues, such as:

✔ Can the family day-care provider and the children walk to and from the park safely?

✔ Is the playground or park located on a busy street?

✔ Is the park or playground fenced?

✔ Is the playground equipment well-maintained?

✔ Does the equipment at the playground measure up to current safety standards?

You can find out about playground safety standards by visiting the U.S. Consumer Product Safety Commission Web site at www.cpsc.gov or by calling the commission at 800-638-2772 (TTY 800-638-8270).

Is there any sort of structure to the day-care day?

Young children are creatures of habit. They positively thrive on routine. So determine whether the day-care day has any sort of predictable structure. You don't want the family day-care provider to go overboard and run things like a military operation — "It's 10:21 a.m.! Please proceed immediately to the snack table!" — but it's reassuring to know that the children can expect one day at day care to bear at least a passing resemblance to the next.

What kind of training has the family day-care provider had in working with young children?

Something else to find out about is what kind of training the family day-care provider has had in caring for young children. According to the American Academy of Pediatrics, the American Public Health Association, and the U.S. Department of Health and Human Services, family day-care providers owe it to themselves and the families that they serve to ensure that they've received proper training in each of the following areas:

- ✔ Child development
- ✔ Behavior management strategies
- ✔ Common childhood illnesses (including child-care exclusion policies)
- ✔ Procedures for preventing the spread of communicable disease
- ✔ Immunization requirements
- ✔ Injury prevention procedures
- ✔ First aid and emergency procedures
- ✔ Child-abuse reporting policies
- ✔ Health promotion
- ✔ Nutrition information
- ✔ Medication administration policies and practices
- ✔ Information about caring for children with special needs

Unfortunately, state legislation governing family day care falls far short of guaranteeing this degree of quality (a problem that's discussed in greater detail in Chapter 2), so the burden is on you to determine whether the family day-care provider you're considering has received the appropriate training. Like it or not, the buck stops with you.

One final point to consider: A family day-care provider should be prepared to invest some time in putting together an ongoing program of professional development for herself. She doesn't have to devote every evening and weekend to taking childcare-related courses (these people are real human beings, not candidates for sainthood, after all!), but she should sign up for at least a couple of workshops per year so that she ensures that she's up to speed on health, safety, and other important topics. Remember: Childcare is a profession. You want to hire someone who recognizes that simple fact and is prepared to conduct herself accordingly.

Are the provider's immunizations up-to-date?

When you're asking the family day-care provider if she's received any training on childhood immunization requirements, be sure to ask her if she's up-to-date with her own shots.

According to the Department of Health and Human Service's Advisory Committee on Immunization Practices, family day-care providers should roll up their sleeves for their annual flu shots and make sure they've had tetanus/diphtheria shots in the past ten years. If the family day-care provider missed out on any of her childhood vaccinations or her vaccination history is unreliable, she needs to consult with her family physician for advice on how to protect her own health as well as the health of the children in her care.

To find out more about adult immunization, call the National Coalition for Adult Immunization at 301-656-0003 or visit the coalition's Web site at www.nfid.org/ncai.

Family day-care safety smarts

U.S. hospital emergency rooms treat approximately 31,000 children age 4 and younger each year for injuries received in child-care and school settings. According to the U.S. Product Safety Commission, parents who are evaluating a particular child-care arrangement should be on the lookout for

✔ Unsafe cribs (cribs that don't conform to current national safety standards or cribs that contain pillows or other soft bedding); visit the U.S. Consumer Product Safety Commission Web site (www.cpsc.gov) for information on current safety standards or call the commission at 800-638-2772 (TTY 800-638-8270)

✔ Unsuitable playground surfaces (playgrounds should have as much as 12 inches of wood chips, mulch, sand, or pea gravel, or mats made of safety-tested rubber or rubber-like materials)

✔ Window blind and curtain cords that pose a strangulation hazard (looped cords are a definite no-no in any day-care setting)

To keep up to speed on these and other important day-care safety issues, sign up for the U.S. Consumer Product Safety Commission's regular product recall bulletins. Simply fax your name and fax number to 301-504-0399 or send an e-mail to listproc@cpsc.gov that says "Join CPSCINFO-L" in the body of the message.

Is the family day-care provider's license current?

If the family day-care provider told you over the phone that her family day care is licensed or accredited, ask for proof. Unless you see a copy of the license or documentation proving that the family day care has been accredited, you'll have no way of knowing whether the family day care has, in fact, actually made the grade. And when you're checking out all the paperwork, be sure to note whether the license or accreditation is current or not. A five-year-old license is about as reassuring as a five-year-old restaurant review!

How long has the family day-care provider been working with young children?

Something else you want to find out is how long the family day-care provider has been working with young children. Although finding someone who's taken courses galore in early childhood education is terrific, there's no substitute for real-world experience. Ideally, you want to find someone who's been working with young children for at least a couple of years, both because of the experience she has picked up during that time and because if she's already been at this for a few years, she's already demonstrated her willingness to stick with a profession that tends to have a pretty high turnover rate.

Of course, you don't have to be overly rigid about her experience. If the caregiver in question has raised a few kids of her own and has volunteered with the local Girl Scouts troop for more years than she can remember, she probably has the necessary experience. Where you may run into trouble is if you hire a sweet young thing whose only exposure to the world of babies has been via televised episodes of *A Baby Story* — or if you hire an older woman who's still carrying around the same well-thumbed copy of *Dr. Spock's Baby and Child Care* that served her well when she was raising her own children during the 1950s and 1960s. After all, more than beehive hairdos have gone out of style over the past 50 years. Some of our child-rearing philosophies have too!

How long does she intend to run a family day-care business out of her home?

Don't be shy about asking the family day-care provider how long she intends to keep her family day-care operation up and running. Family day-care businesses tend to have a relatively short life cycle. Not only are they often tied to the life cycle of the family day-care provider herself (she may only be interested in caring for other people's children in her home while she's at home with her own children anyway), but there's also a high level of burnout among child-care providers in general and family day-care providers in particular.

Because caregiver consistency is important for young children (they're about as receptive to new child-care providers as they are to new vegetables!), you want to minimize the number of times you have to change child-care arrangements. So when you're evaluating family day-care arrangements, a key consideration is whether the family day-care provider is likely to be in business for as long as you're going to need her. Depending on the age of your child, that can be anywhere from a couple of months to four or five years. So you may want to pass on a particular family day-care arrangement if the provider intends to close up shop a year from now when her youngest child starts kindergarten or if she happens to mention that her husband's employer is going to transfer him out of state sometime next year.

Are any other businesses being run out of the same home as the family day care?

This is one of those questions that you may not think to ask a family day-care provider, but, trust me, it's one question you can't afford not to ask. Home-based businesses are very hot these days, so someone else in the same household may be running a home-based business that isn't exactly compatible with a family day-care operation.

Now before you assume that I'm talking about phone sex, drug dealing, and other unsavory occupations, think again. Something as seemingly innocuous as a home-based investment business can prove incompatible with a family day care. It may sound crazy, but I know of a case where the wife's day-care kids ended up being booted outside every time the husband's investment clients dropped by. (Hey, you can't have a client being distracted by the smell of baby poop or the screams of an angry toddler when he's trying to focus on his six-figure stock portfolio, now can you?)

Although you can argue that those kids didn't come to any actual harm (other than being treated like second-class citizens!), some home-based businesses can be downright dangerous. You'd have to think long and hard about letting your child spend his days at a family day care that's under the same roof as a small engine repair business, a woodworking shop, or some other type of business that involves the use of potentially hazardous equipment or materials. Or at least I would.

A less obvious hazard that you need to consider is the number of strangers who could potentially have contact with your child over the course of a day. Taking tremendous care to screen a child-care provider and then willfully turning a blind eye to the steady stream of strangers passing through her home day in and day out seems kind of ludicrous.

Which age group of children does she enjoy working with most?

Some family day-care providers have a real knack for working with babies and toddlers; others are much more comfortable working with preschoolers and school-aged children. So you want to find out which age group this family day-care provider works best with.

Unfortunately, if a family day-care provider has a space to fill in her family day-care setting, she may be so eager to fill it that she whitewashes the truth a little. Or a lot. So, naturally, you want to read between the lines by sizing up her reactions to and ability to interact with children of various ages. Obviously, if you're searching for a child-care arrangement for your extremely active 2-year-old twin boys, you want to zero in on someone who has a genuine love of toddlers, to say nothing of plenty of patience and stamina! (If she morphs into a Cruella DeVil look-alike the moment your boys start chasing one another around the room, you can pretty much scratch her off your list.)

Be sure to take note of how the family day-care provider handles any problems that occur during your visit to her family day care. You learn more about her child-care philosophies by watching how she handles a biting incident or a battle over a toy than by listening to her tell you how she would theoretically handle such an incident. If she seems unsure how to handle the incident or embarrassed that the children are behaving like this while you're visiting, she may not be as competent in dealing with young children as she would have you believe.

Is she comfortable dealing with this many children?

In some parts of the country, family day-care providers are allowed to care for as many as eight children under the age of 5 — more if the family day-care provider brings in a day-care assistant who is 16 years of age or over. But the fact that a particular family day-care provider is *allowed* to care for that many children doesn't necessarily mean that she *should* be doing it.

Not everyone has the patience required to hang out with a group of babies, toddlers, and preschoolers for 40 or more hours a week. In fact, few people have what it takes — something that helps explain the phenomenally high turnover rate in the family day-care profession. So one of the things to assess is whether she's generally able to maintain control or whether the day care is in a constant state of chaos. (Things are definitely not looking good if the toddlers start plotting a coup d'etat every time the family day-care provider leaves the room!)

Of course, there's a very fine line between allowing the inmates to run the asylum and running the day care like some sort of military school for tots. What you want to see is some sort of evidence that, despite the fact that the kids have her badly outnumbered, the family day-care provider is still in charge.

What are her child-care philosophies?

If your day-care fairy godmother is looking out for you, you may luck out and stumble across a family day-care provider who has gone to the trouble of putting her child-care philosophies in writing. The crème de la crème of family day-care providers will, indeed, go this extra mile. But, even if the family day-care provider that you're considering hasn't bothered jotting everything down on paper, asking her to state her child-care philosophies in a sentence or two is important. Obviously, you're looking for someone who understands that she's responsible for much more than merely keeping the children in her care safe: She should also be interested in designing an early childhood education program that promotes their healthy physical, emotional, intellectual, and social development.

Of course, simply listening to what she has to say isn't enough. You also need to watch how she interacts with the children in her care — the key reason for doing an onsite visit. The family day-care provider's body language will give you some pretty good clues as to her true feelings about the children she's with. If she pulls away slightly when a sticky-faced 1-year-old tries to give her a hug or becomes upset when a 2-year-old's enthusiastic crayon strokes extend off the page and onto the kitchen table, you can pretty much bet that she's not exactly in the running for Caregiver of the Year! Here are some points to consider when you're sizing up the family day-care provider's skills in dealing with young children:

- Does she sit with the children while they're playing?

- Does she make a point of singling out each child for some individual attention?

- Does she make a special effort to comfort and reassure a child who's feeling frightened or unhappy?

- Does she respond to misbehavior in a sensitive yet effective manner (for example, teaching rather than punishing children when they've misbehaved)? The next section has more on discipline.

- Does she know when she should and shouldn't intervene when a child is attempting to master a new skill?

- Is she enthusiastic about the children's achievements and accomplishments?

How well does she handle discipline problems?

Although you may like to believe that your child will be perfectly well behaved for her family day-care provider, the odds of her making it through her entire day-care career without so much as a single meltdown are pretty much slim to none. Whether it's being forced to suffer the indignity of sharing a much-prized bucket of blocks with her day-care arch enemy or being served a plate of broccoli on a day when she's simply not in the mood for green food that finally sends her over the edge, odds are the day will come when your angel-faced cherub does time in the time-out chair! That's why finding out upfront how the family day-care provider you're considering typically handles discipline issues is important. Ideally, you want to find a family day-care provider who understands that discipline needs to

✔ Be suited to a child's developmental stage and temperament

✔ Leave the child feeling good about herself

✔ Leave the caregiver feeling good about herself

✔ Be effective at teaching the child appropriate behavior

✔ Help to build upon the bond between the child and the caregiver

Having a frank discussion about what you consider to be acceptable methods of disciplining a child and what (for your family at least) is taboo is important. You may decide, for example, that spanking is never acceptable, but that time-outs are a great way of encouraging your 3-year-old to regain control.

How does she feel about toilet training the children in her care?

If one issue can practically have parents and family day-care providers coming to blows, it's toilet training. That's why finding out upfront if you and the family day-care provider belong to the same school of thought on potty training is a good idea.

If you're a firm believer in taking a relatively laid-back approach (for example, waiting for junior to give the adults in his life some sort of indication that he's willing to do something with that potty other than put it on his head), whereas the family day-care provider takes great pride in the fact that she's managed to train every child she's ever cared for on or before his second birthday, you could find yourself gearing up for the Mother of All Turf Wars!

What you're looking for is some evidence that she's willing to let your child and you take the lead — that when your child is showing signs of physical and emotional readiness and you've indicated that the timing is just right on the home-front (for example, you're *not* about to move to a new house or give birth to a new baby within the next 30 days!), she'll be ready to seize the moment. (But not a moment sooner!) The last thing your family needs is someone putting the heat on you and your child to hurry things up on the potty-training front so that she can get her last day-care kid out of diapers. (It's hard to say who'll be feeling the pressure more keenly: you or your child!)

That raises an important issue, by the way. While you're sizing up the caregiver, you want to get a sense of whether she's someone who's likely to accept that you're the one calling the shots when making parenting decisions. Although you may welcome or even solicit her advice on a particular issue — for example, how to convince your child to chomp down on her veggies rather than on the arm of the other 2-year-old at day care! — the caregiver shouldn't leave you feeling like she has all the answers and you don't. No working parent should have to put up with that kind of attitude on his way to and from work each day!

Does the family day-care provider insist that all the children take naps, whether they need one or not?

Something else to find out is where the family day-care provider stands on the whole nap issue — whether she believes that all children should take naps, whether they need one or not, or if she's willing to be a little more flexible.

If naps are set for a particular time (and it's not necessarily a bad thing to build some structure into the day-care day), ask the family day-care provider what accommodations are made for children who simply don't feel sleepy at the right time of day. Are they given the option of enjoying a quiet cuddle and a story, or are they expected to lie down quietly during naptime, whether they actually manage to make the full journey to dreamland?

And what about those children who feel the need for a nap an hour or two earlier than the rest of the group? Is there a quiet spot where they can lie down if they want to catch up on their sleep? According to the American Academy of Pediatrics, the American Public Health Association, and the National Resource Center for Health and Safety in Child Care, children should be given access to rest areas whenever they feel the need for sleep. In other words, family day-care providers should do their best to accommodate the pint-sized Rip Van Winkles in their care.

If the family day-care provider is really hung up on the whole nap issue — she's bound and determined that all the children in her care will take naps from 1 p.m. to 2 p.m. no matter what — you may want to consider that a bit of a red flag. I know one mom who pulled her child out of a family day-care arrangement after just one week after discovering that the entire day-care day was structured around the family day-care provider's burning need to see her afternoon soap opera. She somehow managed to train all the babies and toddlers in her care to fall asleep the moment the show began and to wake up just as the closing credits started to make their way down the screen. And what if a particular baby didn't happen to feel sleepy that day? Well, she just let her "fuss a little" until she got tired. Apparently, "fussing a little" meant being ignored until after that episode of *The Young and the Restless* was over.

What kinds of meals and snacks are served?

Although gourmet meals aren't required, you want to make sure that your child receives nutritious meals and snacks while he's at day care. You also want to make sure that the family day-care provider has a solid understanding of which foods are — and aren't — safe for young children. For example, which foods are most likely to result in choking, allergic reactions, or other emergency situations?

Ask the family day-care provider to show you some menu plans. Most family day-care providers are in the habit of coming up with menu plans for snacks and meals. Not only does planning ahead allow them to have the necessary grocery items on hand, but posting the upcoming week's menus in the cloakroom ahead of time also allows parents to work around the menus when planning the child's menus at home. (Pasta may be your child's favorite food, but that doesn't mean that he'll necessarily want to have it for lunch and dinner for three days running. But, then again, you never know!) Here are some points to ponder on the nutrition front:

✔ Are the meals varied, nutritious, and age-appropriate?

✔ Does the family day-care provider make an effort to keep mealtimes pleasant and unhurried?

✔ Does the family day-care provider ensure that an adult is always present when the children are eating? (To ensure adequate supervision, an adult should be within arm's reach of an infant who's learning to eat on his own and seated at the same table as a toddler.)

✔ Do the children determine how much — or how little — they want to eat (for example, this particular family day care doesn't have a clean-your-plate rule)?

✔ If you're intending to continue to breastfeed your baby after you return to work, how will the family day-care provider work with you to support that choice?

✔ Does the family day-care provider make a point of holding babies while they're drinking from a bottle? (Propping a bottle is dangerous, due to the risk of choking, and, what's more, it deprives an infant of much-needed human contact.)

✔ Are you expected to supply any of the food for your child (for example, breast milk, formula, infant cereal, and so on)?

✔ If you're expected to supply food, what type of refrigeration is available?

✔ Are you welcome to supply food if your child is a picky eater? Or does the family day-care provider stick to a firm "no food from home" rule when it comes to anyone older than babies?

✔ Are you responsible for supplying a high chair, feeding cups, or other types of feeding equipment?

✔ To what extent is the family day-care provider willing to accommodate children with food allergies, food intolerances, and special diets (for example, a vegetarian diet)?

Has she written down her various policies and procedures?

Unless the family day-care provider that you're considering worked as an HR consultant during her previous life, she's unlikely to greet you at the door with an entire binder jam-packed with policies and procedures. Just don't make the mistake of assuming that the absence of such a binder means that pretty much anything goes.

Most family day-care providers have some rules in place to prevent conflicts from arising between themselves and the parents of the children in their care. Because it's important to find out about the rules that have found their ways into the day-care playbook before you decide whether you want to play ball with a particular family day-care provider, you'll want to ask the family day-care provider if she has any written policies and procedures covering all the hot topics between parents and family day-care providers — late pickup fees, sick days, vacation days, and so on.

If she hasn't put these policies and procedures in writing, you need to quiz her about them just to make sure that the two of you are on the same page about all the important stuff. If you decide to use her services, you may want to put everything down in writing.

You don't have to get really formal about this by calling in a lawyer or even a professional writer. (Although, if you're in the market for a professional writer, I could definitely recommend a few good people!) All that matters is that you spell out the possible areas of contention in a friendly letter of agreement and you both sign, date, and retain a copy of the letter. It may seem like an unnecessary formality now, but, like a prenuptial agreement, it could save you a lot of grief down the road if the family day-care provider claims that she's sure she told you that her late fee is $10 a minute!

Does the family day-care provider charge a fee if parents are late picking up their children?

Although no working parent deliberately sets out to be late picking up her child from day-care, sometimes things don't exactly go according to plan. Whether it's an unexpected bridge closure that makes your drive home even more nightmarish than usual or a late-afternoon meeting with your boss that has you running behind schedule, the result is still the same: You show up at the family day-care provider's doorstep feeling like the biggest heel in the world.

Some family day-care providers are pretty understanding about the situation, provided it only happens once-in-a-blue-moon. Others throw the book at you right from the very beginning, charging you penalties that typically start at (gulp!) $1 per minute. To avoid conflicts with your family day-care provider and the need to take out a second mortgage to finance those late pick-up charges, you want to find out upfront where the family day-care provider stands on the whole late penalty fee. In other words, do you get one get-out-of-jail-free card or do the child-care penalties kick in the very first time you show up late?

What are the family day-care provider's policies regarding sick children?

Something else you want to find out right from the start is how the family day-care provider deals with sick kids. Does she refuse to accept any child who has as much as a sniffle (in which case you may as well just quit your job now and save yourself a lot of aggravation down the road!)? Or does she fall into the opposite camp, graciously allowing parents to send their kids to day care with typhoid fever, beriberi, or heaven knows what else because she doesn't want anyone to have to miss a day of work?

Assuming you luck out and find a family day-care provider who takes a reasonably sane approach to the issue of sick kids in day care (an issue that's discussed in greater detail in Chapter 12, by the way), your next question should be whether you're expected to pay for each day your child misses due to illness. Most family day-care providers expect you to pay for your child's space, whether it's used or not, although some will give you a break if your child comes down with a more serious illness that requires him to be away from day care for a couple of weeks while he's on the mend. This is definitely one of those issues that's easier to discuss in advance as opposed to in the heat of the moment, so don't be shy about asking about this right now.

Something else that's good to find out about in advance is under what circumstances you're likely to receive a call at work asking you to come and pick up a sick child. Will the family day-care provider call every time your child starts coughing (bad news if you've got a child who's prone to a nagging cough that can come and go for weeks at a time!), or will she hold off on picking up the phone until your child breaks out into a high fever or starts vomiting? Knowing this kind of information upfront is important because it can help you gauge how often you're likely to have to leave work to deal with a sick child if you choose to use the services of this particular family day-care provider.

What is the family day-care provider's policy about administering medication to the children in her care?

Look for evidence that the family day-care provider understands the importance of having some strict guidelines in place to deal with the administration of medications to other people's children. Most family day-care providers refuse to administer any sort of medication to a child unless they have the parent's prior written authorization. You'll be asked to fill out and sign a medication authorization form that includes the following types of information:

- ✔ Your child's name
- ✔ The name of the medication
- ✔ The date that medication should start and the date it should end
- ✔ The times when the medication is to be administered
- ✔ The frequency at which the medication is to be administered
- ✔ How you may be contacted in the event that your child exhibits any unusual symptoms or reactions to the medication.

Always provide the family day-care provider with any information you have about the side effects of any medications your child happens to be taking at the time — for example, give her a copy of the information slip that the pharmacist provided you with at the time you filled your child's prescription. That way, the family day-care provider is able to be on the lookout for any potentially dangerous side effects to the medication.

What would the family day-care provider do if your child required immediate medical attention and she couldn't get in touch with you right away?

Although it's generally a good idea to steer clear of a lot of what if's when you're interviewing the family day-care provider, some hypothetical questions are too important to leave unasked. This, obviously, is one of them.

What you're looking for here is some sort of concrete action plan — an understanding that, in the event of a bona fide emergency, the family day-care provider may have to seek medical attention directly rather than waiting for you to become available and deal with the situation firsthand.

To protect themselves from any legal fallout after the fact, many family day-care providers ask the parents to fill out a medical consent form authorizing them to take any emergency measures necessary to protect their child in the event that the parent is unreachable. For example, the family day-care provider can arrange for transportation to the hospital by ambulance or authorize any emergency treatments recommended by the attending physicians. A medical consent form typically contains the following types of information:

- ✔ The child's name
- ✔ The child's date of birth
- ✔ The child's Medicare number
- ✔ The name of the child's health insurance company

✔ The health insurance policy number

✔ The preferred hospital and clinic

✔ The name and phone number of the child's pediatrician

✔ Information about any drug allergies the child may have

✔ Information about any other medical conditions the emergency medical team would need to know about

✔ A statement indicating that you understand that you're responsible for picking up the tab for any costs incurred to the family day-care provider in obtaining medical treatment for your child.

Are parents welcome to drop by unannounced?

Find out if the family day-care provider that you're considering encourages parents to drop by unannounced, and be leery of any family day-care provider who won't agree to this sort of open-door policy. This shouldn't merely set off alarm bells in your head: It should have you grabbing your child and running for the nearest exit. Never, ever agree to leave your child in the care of someone who insists on such a policy. This is simply non-negotiable.

Does the family day-care provider take the children on field trips that require travel by car?

Trips by car to the fire department, police station, and the zoo can really liven up a family day-care program, but such excursions aren't without their risks. If you're not comfortable having your child traveling in someone else's car, you may want to seriously consider whether this family day-care program's going to meet your family's needs. After all, if you have to make alternative day-care arrangements every time there's a day-care field trip, you can find yourself stitching together an entire patchwork quilt of child-care arrangements.

Even if you do feel comfortable allowing someone else to drive your child around town, you want to make sure that the family day-care provider:

✔ Has a clean driving record (she can obtain a copy of her driving record from the state department of motor vehicles by paying a nominal fee, typically $5)

✔ Is able to produce proof of insurance

✔ Has enough child safety seats for all the children in her care or routinely arranges for parents to leave their children's car seats behind on days when a field trip is planned

✔ Ensures that the car seats are installed and used in accordance with the car seat manufacturer's instructions

---

Car seat safety

Don't take it for granted that your family day-care provider knows how to install your child's particular make and model of car seat. According to the National Highway Traffic Safety Administration, approximately 80 percent of child safety seats are improperly installed or used.

When used correctly, child safety seats play an important role in preventing needless tragedies: They're 71 percent effective in reducing the incidence of car accident fatalities in children under the age of 5.

How much notice do you have to provide if you have to withdraw your child from care?

Hopefully, you won't have to think about switching day-care arrangements for a very long time. But, as you've no doubt noticed by now, life has this way of throwing curveballs at you, and you can find that you no sooner settle your child into this particular family day-care arrangement when — whammo! — your employer transfers you out of state.

The last thing you need when you've had the rug yanked out from your life is finding yourself hit with another big surprise — like finding out after the fact that your family day-care provider wants four weeks' notice of your plan to withdraw your child from care. Although four weeks' notice is becoming the norm for center-based care, most family day-care providers are still willing to accept two weeks' notice. But don't just assume that's going to be the case. Find out now.

Consulting a Prospective Provider's References: Some Do's and Don'ts

If you've never had occasion to check someone's references before, the mere thought of cold-calling a complete stranger and asking her all kinds of questions about the family day-care provider you're considering may be enough to make you break out into a cold sweat. (Hey, maybe that's why they call it cold calling!)

Fortunately, reference checking doesn't have to be an exercise in torture. In fact, it really isn't all that different from interviewing a family day-care provider. The only difference is you're asking a third party the questions this time.

Here are the key do's and don'ts to keep in mind:

✔ **Do have a pen and paper handy.** That way, you can take detailed notes as you check each reference. (If you don't take notes, all the reference checks will start blurring together in your mind, and you'll have a hard time figuring out who to call if you have a follow-up question for one of the references.)

✔ **Do make a point of asking for concrete examples, whenever possible.** If one of the people providing a reference remarks that the family day-care provider was really patient with toddlers, ask her to explain how the family day-care provider would typically go about dealing with a toddler who was about to launch into a temper tantrum.

✔ **Don't be sure that the person providing the child-care reference is qualified to do so.** A reference from the family day-care provider's 18-year-old manicurist is pretty much useless for your purposes, unless, of course, the manicurist happens to be one of her day-care parents. You can also write off a reference from someone who hasn't spoken to the family day-care provider in the past five years — unless, of course, they're willing to spill the beans about the *reason* they haven't spoken to her for five years. (Who knows? It may be really juicy!)

✔ **Don't indulge your long-repressed desire to interrogate a witness à la *Law and Order*.** Instead, stick to questions like these that are straight-forward and specific:

- How long ago were your children cared for by this person?

- How long were they in her care?

- What were your children's ages at the time?

- Did the family day-care provider meet your expectations?

- Can you give me an example of a difficult situation that the family day-care provider handled particularly well?

- Can you give me an example of a time when you experienced a conflict or other difficulty with the family day-care provider? Was the situation ultimately resolved to your satisfaction?

- Do you think I should know anything else before making my decision about using the services of this family day-care provider?

✔ **Don't automatically assume that the person providing the reference is legit.** An easy way to double-check this is to make deliberate mistakes and see if she corrects you. Say "And she cared for your two boys?" knowing full well that the reference supposedly has two girls. If she forgets the true sex of her kids, she's either a fake or a pretty bad parent. You can pretty much rule her out as a reference on either count.

In addition to checking out the references that the family day-care provider offers, you also want to tap into the parent grapevine to see if anyone you know has heard anything good, bad, or indifferent about her. (Remember, she has a vested interest in only providing you with the names of references who are likely to describe her in the most glowing terms. You're more likely to get a less biased view if you can track down a reference on your own through your own circle of contacts. Obviously, this is much easier in a small community where everyone knows one another than in a large city, but it's always worth a try. You just never know when you're going to hit pay dirt on the reference-check front.

One final word on the subject of reference checks: Don't forget to ask the family day-care provider and any other adults who are involved in the family day-care business to consent to a criminal background check as well. Your local police department can tell you what's involved in setting one up and what you can expect to pay (around $20). It could very well be the best $20 you ever spend.

Chapter 8

Figuring Out Where Nursery Schools and Preschools Fit In

Think nursery schools and preschools are a relatively recent invention — the brainchild of the same generation of 1980s yuppie parents who managed to catapult educational toys into a multimillion dollar industry? Well, you may be surprised to discover that nursery schools and preschools have actually been around since the 1930s. In fact, they were originally designed to enable Depression-era preschoolers to benefit from what was then the latest research on early learning and socialization. Since that time, as the decades passed and mothers began re-entering the workforce in larger numbers, nursery schools and preschools began serving a second function by meeting the skyrocketing demand for childcare.

But enough with the history lesson. In this chapter, I talk about what nursery-school and preschool programs have to offer for today's generation of kids; what you need to know about various types of preschool programs (there's no such thing as a one-size-fits-all early childhood education experience); how to go about deciding whether your child would, in fact, benefit from such a program; and how to go about zeroing in on the program that's just right for your child.

Before I can get to all that, however, I want to take a moment to quickly pin down the preschool lingo.

Talkin' the Preschool Talk

Unsure where nursery schools and preschools fit into the child-care picture — or what these two terms even mean? You're not the only one who's confused.

Because the terms *nursery school* and *preschool* often are used interchangeably, and the line between child-care programs in general and early childhood education programs in particular (in other words, programs that emphasize learning) tends to be blurry at best, telling the difference between the two can become confusing — very confusing, in fact.

But I'm going to do my best to spell out key points you'll want to keep in mind to make sense out of the rest of the material in this chapter — kind of like a *For Dummies* book to this part of the *For Dummies* book!

The term *nursery school* typically is used to describe an early childhood educational program for 2- to 4-year-old children. Nursery schools almost always operate on a part-time basis (two to three hours per day, two to five days per week), and they tend to follow the school-year calendar (September to June). The term nursery school has gotten a bit watered down through the years, however, and is sometimes used to describe any part-time center-based child-care program, regardless of whether it has a strong early childhood educational component.

The term *preschool* typically is used to describe an early childhood educational program for 3- and 4-year-old children. Preschools traditionally operate on a part-time basis (two to three hours per day, two to five days per week), and they tend to follow the traditional school-year calendar (September to June). In recent years, however, the lines between preschool and center-based child-care have blurred, so much so that enrolling your child in a full-time center-based child-care program that is, for all intents and purposes, a full-time preschool program is now possible.

And if that isn't confusing enough, regional variations exist when it comes to using the terms *nursery school* and *preschool.* Programs that are described as preschool programs in some parts of the country are described as nursery schools in others, and vice versa.

No consumer watchdog agency governs the use of the terms *nursery school* and *preschool.* Some programs claiming to be nursery-school or preschool programs deliver little more than basic "keep 'em safe" custodial-quality care. The terms *can* be used to describe everything from a grass-roots program operating on a shoestring out of a rundown church basement to an Ivy League preschool that charges as much as $20,000 per year in tuition to a cultural enrichment program that is designed to give preschoolers early exposure to the arts.

Would your child benefit from a preschool program?

Unsure whether or not your child would benefit from a preschool program? This quick, five-question quiz can help you decide. The more "yes" answers you get, the more confident you can feel that a preschool program is the right choice for your child.

1. **Does your child enjoy socializing with other children?** No rule says that a child *must* be a social butterfly to thrive in a preschool setting. If there were, preschool directors would have an awfully difficult time filling all those preschool spaces. However, adjusting to the preschool environment is easier for a child when he's more inclined to greet a new group of friends with great gusto instead of clinging to your coattails (literally!) and hoping those other kids just go away. Bottom line? If your child can't wait to go to monthly playgroup and always badgers you to have a friend or two or ten over to play, then that's a pretty solid indication that he'll probably have a great time at preschool. (Of course, you don't have to rule out preschool entirely for a slow-to-warm-up child. He may simply need a bit more time to ease into his new environment — something a caring and sensitive preschool teacher should be able to help him with.)

2. **Does your child tend to do well in group situations?** It's one thing to enjoy having a friend over to play in the backyard; it's quite another to spend every morning playing with a room full of kids your own age. When you know from past experience that your child is comfortable in large groups, you won't spend too much time worrying about whether preschool is the right environment.

On the other hand, if your child seems totally stressed while playing with two or more children, preschool may not necessarily be up her alley.

3. **Would your child benefit from some added stimulation?** If your 3-year-old seems to grow bored with the family day-care situation that served so well when he was a baby and a toddler, it may be that your child's craving a bit of added stimulation. Rather than removing your child from the family day-care environment entirely, you may simply want to top that arrangement off with a part-time preschool program.

4. **Is your child reasonably self-sufficient?** Although the preschool teacher isn't going to expect your child to show up on the first day of school knowing how to tie shoelaces, zip up a jacket, and do everything completely on her own (or if the teacher is, she's dreaming in Technicolor!), a certain degree of self-sufficiency is, if not expected, at least highly welcome. The reason is obvious: If the teacher has to help ten kids wriggle into their outerwear whenever outdoor playtime rolls around, it'll be time to come back inside long before the last child's jacket is even zipped up! (Of course, kids who aren't terribly self-sufficient when they first arrive at preschool soon learn to be. You'll no doubt be amazed by all the new skills your child picks up during her first few weeks and months: carrying her plate over to the counter after she's finished having her bedtime snack and putting her storybook back on the shelf after you're finished reading to her. You may swear there's an entirely different child living in your home!)

(continued)

(continued)

> **5. Does your child communicate well with other adults?** A child who finds it relatively easy to express wants and needs finds settling into the day-care environment much easier than a child who is painfully shy. So your child's temperament is an important point to keep in mind when you're trying to determine whether preschool will work well. (For more about how your child's temperament affects your various child-care choices, see Chapter 3.) That's not to say that you should rule out preschool entirely for an exceptionally shy child: You should simply be aware that he may require some additional support in settling into his new surroundings.

Because the distinction between what constitutes a nursery school and what constitutes a preschool is such a fine one, and having to say "nursery schools and preschools" repeatedly with every reference throughout the remainder of this chapter gets kind of wordy, I'm going to stick to using the term *preschool* to describe both preschools and nursery schools from this point forward. (I just wanted to let you know upfront so that you wouldn't think my discussion of nursery schools had fizzled out for no good reason. I have a method to my madness.)

Getting the Lowdown on Different Types of Preschool Programs

So you've decided that your child will benefit from a preschool program. Now all you need to do is figure out *which* preschool program — a question that's a whole lot easier to ask than it is to answer, of course!

Although you may be tempted to assume that any program that's listed in the preschool section of your local Yellow Pages is bound to be serving up pretty much the same thing, you'd be speaking in rather broad generalities. It's kind of like grouping wine and grape juice together under the "grape-based beverages" category — something that's technically accurate, for sure, but not likely to score you many points with the group of friends who thought you were bringing out the *vino* when you offered them "a splash of grape."

The five basic types of preschool programs are

- ✔ Programs that emphasize academics
- ✔ Programs that emphasize learning through play
- ✔ Programs that are rooted in a specific school of thought

✔ Religious preschools

✔ Cooperative preschools

The next few sections take a look at each type in more detail. However, noting that some preschools manage to fall into more than one category is important. In fact, it's quite possible, for example, for a cooperative preschool to be operated by a religious organization and to emphasize learning through play. And if that same preschool happens to subscribe to a particular school of thought, it may even fall into a third category. Who knew the world of preschool education could be so complicated!

Programs that emphasize academics

A preschool program that places its emphasis on teaching academics to young children is called an *academic learning program.* Academic learning programs are much less popular than they were back in the flashcard-powered 1980s when yuppie parents eagerly forked over the big bucks for any preschool program that promised to give Junior the academic edge.

In recent years, a backlash against this style of learning has occurred, not just because Yuppies themselves have gone out of vogue, but rather a solid body of research shows that plunking a typical 3-year-old in a classroom and trying to use the same sort of teaching methods you'd use on a much older child is counterproductive. Remember, 3-year-olds are not merely short 10-year-olds; they're developmentally different in all kinds of ways.

Does that mean that academic learning programs have gone the way of the dodo bird entirely? Well, not exactly. Despite the fact that this style of teaching young children is highly dated and flies in the face of today's more progressive teaching methods, some parents continue to seek out these types of programs in the mistaken belief that doing so will give their child a much-needed leg up in an increasingly competitive world. And as long as parents are eager to fork over the necessary cash, preschool operators will be happy to give them the academic learning programs they think their children need. After all, supply-and-demand economics plays out even in the world of preschools.

Programs that emphasize learning through play

At the opposite end of the early childhood educational spectrum are programs that emphasize learning through play — in other words, programs that promote a child-centered, teacher-supported approach to learning.

This school of thought is the most current on the preschool education front and is in keeping with educational philosophies of the National Association for the Education of Young Children and other leading authorities in the field of childhood education. If you hear early childhood education experts talking about such-and-such a policy being in keeping with "developmentally appropriate practice" (DAP), what they're talking about are programs that put the child in the driver's seat when it comes to early learning.

Of course, putting the child in the driver's seat does not imply that the teacher is left standing at the side of the highway. The teacher's job is to create a stimulating environment that sets the stage for playing and learning and then to support the child's resulting journey of exploration.

Programs rooted in a specific school of thought

Next, I'm going to quickly run through three popular types of preschool programs that are rooted in a specific school of thought, namely Montessori schools, Waldorf schools, and schools that use High/Scope curricula in their programs.

Of course, before you get your heart totally set on sending your child to a preschool that adheres to any particular educational philosophy, you want to do a quick check of what's available in your community. The majority of preschools tend to follow more of a Heinz-57 model as opposed to strictly adhering to the tenets of a particular educational philosophy.

Montessori schools

Montessori schools are based on the teachings of Maria Montessori, an Italian physician who pioneered the so-called *Montessori Method* back in 1907 after spending a great deal of time watching how children learn. She concluded that children learn best when they're given the opportunity to make their own choices and to learn by doing. In other words, it adheres to the principle that children are born with the ability to absorb information from the world around them, and that there is therefore no need to rely on traditional methods of teaching to instill knowledge in children.

As you may suspect, given what I've just told you about Maria Montessori's educational philosophies, Montessori schools emphasize a child-centered approach to learning. Rather than being forced to fit into a curriculum that has been designed to meet the needs of every other child the same age, children in Montessori schools are encouraged to progress at their own pace by making use of special learning materials that are designed to provide the child with feedback about whether she has mastered a particular skill: there's only one "right" answer.

Children typically work individually or in small groups. Teachers (or guides) play much less active roles in a Montessori classroom than they do in a standard preschool environment because Montessori followers believe

- That children learn by doing
- That when additional assistance is required to accomplish a particular task, the best teacher for that child in need of assistance is another child who has just recently mastered the same skill

Because children in the same classroom may vary in age by up to three years (children in the early childhood classroom at a Montessori school range in age from three to six, for example), this type of informal child-to-child mentoring tends to happen quite naturally.

Of course that doesn't mean the teacher plays a totally hands-off role. On the contrary, the teacher is responsible for modifying the classroom environment on an ongoing basis to ensure that it continues to meet the needs of the children in that classroom. Because the Montessori method of classroom instruction differs considerably from traditional methods of classroom instruction, early childhood educators who choose to teach in Montessori schools must receive specialized training. In the U.S., teachers can obtain such training through the Association Montessori Internationale (www.montessori-ami.org; phone 585-461-5920 for the U.S. branch office in New York City) and the American Montessori Association (www.amshq.org; phone 212-358-1250).

The Montessori method continues to be quite popular nearly a century after it was first pioneered. Approximately 7,000 Montessori schools operate around the world, including about 4,000 within the U.S.

Waldorf schools

Waldorf schools are based on the philosophies of Rudolf Steiner — the founder of the first Waldorf school, which was housed at the Waldorf Astoria cigarette factory in Stuttgart, Germany at the end of World War I. Steiner believed that each person is made up of three important elements — the spirit, the soul, and the body — and that young children develop these three elements by being immersed in nurturing surroundings. Consequently, Waldorf schools provide a homelike environment that is designed to encourage creative play.

More than 800 Waldorf schools operate around the world, including 180 in the U.S. You can find out more about Waldorf Schools by visiting the Association of Waldorf Schools of North America Web site at www.awsna.org or by calling the association at 916-961-0927.

High/Scope program

In the High/Scope program, responsibility for learning is shared between child and teacher. The teacher is responsible for providing the child with opportunities for learning and the child is responsible for making choices about the materials that are used and activities that are carried out throughout the day.

The High/Scope curricula identify 58 key experiences preschoolers need to have and group those experiences into the following ten categories:

- Creative representation (activities that involve imitation, recognition, and role-playing)
- Language and literacy (storytelling, dictating stories, and other means of communication)
- Initiative and social relations (making choices, problem-solving, and relationship-building skills)
- Movement (activities that encourage movement)
- Music (singing, playing instruments)
- Classification (describing shapes, sorting, and matching)
- Seriation (putting things in order)
- Numbers (comparing, arranging, and counting objects)
- Space (activities that encourage children to explore spatial relationship)
- Time (starting, stopping, sequencing)

You can find out more about the High/Scope program by visiting the High Scope Web site at www.highscope.org or by calling 734-485-2000.

Religious preschools

Some — but not all — preschools operated by churches make learning about religion part of the preschool curriculum.

When you're considering a religious preschool, you want to inquire about its other educational philosophies — whether it supports a child-centered or teacher-driven method of learning and whether it tends to be more academically oriented or more oriented toward a philosophy of learning through play.

Cooperative preschools

Cooperative preschools (sometimes referred to as parent participating preschools) are schools that are operated by parent-run cooperatives. The first cooperative preschool in the U.S. was started in 1916 by a group of 12 faculty wives at the University of Chicago, and they've been a popular child-care option ever since.

Figuring out why cooperative preschools continue to attract a sizeable following of parents nearly a century after they were first invented isn't difficult. Consider the following:

✔ **You can save yourself a bundle of cash.** You can expect to slash your preschool fees in half by choosing a cooperative preschool as opposed to a regular preschool. The reason is simple: You're paying partially in cash and partially in labor. You see, in addition to writing a check once a month to the cooperative that runs the nursery school, you may also have to donate a fair chunk of your own time (or line up a friend or family member to put in this time on your behalf, when your job doesn't allow you to take any time off during the day). You typically serve a *duty day* (or preschool shift) in the school every other week, an evening a month for the co-op board meeting, and a couple of Saturdays a year for the school maintenance crew, fundraising activities, and so on. (Be sure to find out whether your duty day involves helping a licensed preschool teacher or serving as the preschool teacher yourself. There's a world of difference in how that experience can play out for all concerned.)

Some schools accept nonparticipating parents, who pay a slightly higher fee because they aren't contributing the same amount of time to the co-op as the other co-op parents, so don't rule out a cooperative preschool that comes highly recommended simply because you don't think you have the time to devote to the co-op yourself. There may be a way around the problem.

✔ **You can ease the transition between home and school for you and your child.** I know, I know: it's the *child* who's supposed to get the separation anxiety. Well, from what I've seen, sometimes parents have a tougher time separating than kids. When you're feeling rather torn about the idea of sending your child off to preschool, you may want to consider going the co-op route to ease the transition a little. Not only will you be totally up to speed about what's happening behind the scenes at the school, which is one of the advantages to being privy to all those board of directors discussions, you'll also actually be in school a couple of days a month when it's time to do your duty days. This time at school gives you the chance to get to know your child's preschool friends and familiarize your-self with his preschool routines — something that can help your child to feel much more at home.

Co-op preschools also provide some less tangible benefits. Having been this route three times myself (my older three children all attended the same cooperative preschool), I can tell you from firsthand experience that belonging to a cooperative preschool can be a wonderfully enriching experience for you and your child. In fact, I still keep in touch with my now 15-year-old daughter's preschool teacher and many of the parents I met during her time at the school.

They don't necessarily work for every family, however. Some parents find that there can be some downsides to serving those duty days alongside your kid — particularly a kid who has a hard time separating from Mom and Dad. Your child may cling to you rather than focus on the activities and the learning, and she may have a rough time sharing you with the other kids. ("What do you mean you're pouring juice for her first? But you're *my* Mom!")

If you'd like to find out more about what cooperative preschools have to offer, you may want to get in touch with Parent Cooperative Preschools International (www.preschools.coop; phone 800-636-6222) or check out the Cooperative Schools Web site at www.coopschools.com.

Outlining the Must-Ask Questions for the Preschool Director

After you've decided that you'd like to enroll your child in a preschool and you've come up with a list of preschools you'd like to check out, you want to get the preschool director on the phone so you can ask some preliminary questions. Then, assuming your phone call goes well, set up a time to check out the preschool in person. The sections that follow discuss what to ask during each phase of *Operation Preschool Investigation*.

Telephone prescreening

Telephone prescreening can be a huge timesaver for a busy parent. You can quickly cut to the chase and obtain answers to all your need-to-know questions. It may even eliminate the need to conduct an onsite visit when it's painfully obvious right from the start that a particular preschool program isn't going to meet your family's needs.

Parents behaving badly

The competition to get into certain Ivy League preschools can be so fierce that desperate parents are doing whatever they can to give their kids the edge at application time. In fact, according to a recent article in *The New York* *Times,* some parents actually are paying private consultants up to $300 an hour for assistance in filling out preschool application forms, with the hope of increasing the odds that little Madison or Jordan will score an acceptance.

To make sure you gather as much information as quickly and efficiently as you can, write out your questions ahead of time and time your call during one of the less busy times of day when the preschool director is more likely to have time to talk. That means avoiding the morning drop-off, afternoon pickup, and lunch hour periods.

Here's what to ask once you get the preschool director on the phone:

Do you have any spaces available?

Most preschool programs register students for the fall session in early spring. If you don't start shopping around for a space for your child until early summer, you may have a hard time finding an opening at all. Some of the better preschools (or I should say the more *in-demand* preschools) manage to fill their programs years in advance, so you may discover to your dismay that you missed out on your chance to enroll your child in the local Ivy League preschool because you failed to get your child's name on the waiting list the day he was born! (What *were* you thinking?)

How long is the waiting list?

When the preschool is full but has an excellent reputation, find out just how long the waiting list is. If it isn't too long, you may decide to check out the facility, fill out the necessary paperwork, and add your child's name to the waiting list in the hope that you eventually manage to win this round of preschool roulette. And you may. Some families with children enrolled in the program may move out of town or otherwise rethink their preschool decision, which can open up a spot for your child.

Sometimes the only way to secure a space at more in-demand preschools is by playing the waiting-list game. So don't let the waiting-list issue put you off. On the other hand, don't have blind faith that the preschool fairy is going to magically come through for you and your child: Keep on pounding the pavement and checking out other options until your child is guaranteed a space somewhere. After all, having too many options is better than having too few.

What are the hours of operation?

Preschool scheduling issues tend to be make-it-or-break-it propositions for parents who hold down full-time jobs in the paid labor force. When the preschool doesn't open until an hour after you're due at work, and the program runs for only three hours, you have to figure out what your child is going to do when preschool isn't in session and you're still at work.

If your child already is being cared for by an in-home child-care provider, such as a nanny, it may simply be a matter of arranging for your caregiver to transport your child to and from preschool at the appropriate times of day.

But if your child is being cared for by a family day-care provider, you may have to arrange for your child's transportation. For example, you may either have to arrange your work schedule so that you can take your daily breaks at the times of day when your child needs to be shuttled between preschool and family day care or ask your children's grandparents whether they're willing to do this bit of chauffeuring on your behalf. A family day-care provider may, after all, be reluctant to take on this job because it would mean having to make twice-daily trips to and from preschool with all the other children in her care in tow. This kind of extra trip may not only wreak havoc with some of the children's naptimes, the family day-care provider may find that other parents are unwilling to have their children lugged about in a stroller in all kinds of weather or driven around town in the family day-care provider's car, just so your child can make it to preschool. This situation can be a very sticky one for all concerned.

The preschool's hours of operation are less likely to be of concern to you, on the other hand, when you're at home full-time with your other children — unless, of course, you have to fit the twice-daily preschool run around your need to be home on time to meet your other children's school bus. I know from firsthand experience that every stay-at-home mom is in desperate need of an executive assistant or, at the very least, a clone! In this case, carpooling with other parents whose children attend the same preschool can save you hours and hours in the car, so be sure to make a point of finding out who is driving in from what parts of the city. Who knows? Maybe one of your child's preschool buddies happens to live on the next street.

Does the preschool shut down at certain times of the year? If so, when?

Most preschools follow the local school calendar, shutting down during summer months, Christmas holidays, and spring break. You want to find out exactly when the preschool that you're considering closes its doors, just in case the dates in question don't mesh particularly well with the rest of your life. Trying to juggle conflicting schedules is never fun, so you want to know upfront exactly what you're dealing with.

What are the ages of the children in the preschool?

You need to know the answer to this question for two reasons:

- Finding out whether your own child is eligible to enroll in the preschool. A preschool for 3- and 4-year-olds won't meet your immediate child-care needs, after all, when your child just turned 2.

- Getting a feel for the flavor of the program. A preschool program that groups 3- and 4-year-olds together (a so-called mixed-age group) has a very different flavor than a preschool program that groups children on the basis of age (a so-called single age group).

Although mixed-age groups have many advantages — your child won't have to adjust to a new teacher *and* a new group of friends upon graduating from the 3-year-old room to the 4-year-old room — it's nevertheless possible for the youngest children to be nearly two years younger than the oldest children, something that can affect the types of field trips that a preschool teacher is willing to take the children on. After all, taking a group of relatively tame almost-5-year-olds on a behind-the-scenes tour of the local donut shop is one thing, but trying to repeat that same field trip with a group of children who only recently celebrated their third birthdays is a completely different story.

Do children have to be fully toilet-trained to enroll in the program?

Diapers are a no-no at many preschools, so if your child is still in diapers, you need to find out upfront whether children have to be fully toilet-trained to attend a particular preschool.

If the preschool requires children to be fully trained and you're looking for some additional insights on the potty-training issue, you may want to pick up a copy of *Potty Training For Dummies* (Wiley) by Diane Stafford and Jennifer Shoquist, M.D. — the ultimate bathroom read!

What are the fees?

Something else you want to find out over the phone is what you can expect to pay in terms of fees. Preschool fees vary tremendously. You can pay as little as $50 a month for a two-day-a-week, half-day space at a cooperative preschool or as much as $2,000 a month for a full-time space in one of the so-called Ivy League preschools. (If there's marble in the foyer, you're probably not going to get away with bargain basement fees!) If the fees seem hefty, find out whether the school offers scholarships or discounts to families with limited incomes or families with more than one child enrolled in the preschool. Sometimes price breaks are available for the taking.

Are the preschool's philosophies relatively in sync with your own educational philosophies?

Most preschool programs have mission statements or other written materials that are designed to convey to parents exactly where that program is coming from, philosophically speaking. As I discussed in the earlier section on "Getting the Lowdown on Different Types of Preschool Programs," you can expect to encounter some radically different approaches to learning in the preschool setting. As a result, you want to make sure that you're completely up to speed — and totally in agreement with — the educational philosophies that govern the preschool setting that you're considering.

Is the center licensed and accredited?

The ideal is finding a preschool that is both

- **Licensed.** A licensed preschool is one that meets basic state regulations governing the operation of child-care facilities.

- **Accredited.** An accredited preschool is one that has gone through some sort of accreditation process to obtain the child-care world's equivalent of a Good Housekeeping Seal of Approval. See Chapter 5 for more on accreditation.

What caregiver-child ratio does the preschool maintain? What is its group size?

A study conducted by the National Research Council found that when the teacher-child ratio is kept suitably low (the National Association for the Education of Young Children recommends maximum caregiver-child ratios of 1:10 for 3- and 4-year-olds):

- A more extensive interaction occurs between child and teacher.

- The teacher is better able to modify the preschool program to meet the individual needs of that child.

- The teacher is less likely to be restrictive and controlling.

Group size is also important. The National Research Council study found that smaller groups (the National Association for the Education of Young Children recommends a maximum group size of 20 for 3- and 4-year-olds):

- Encourage children to initiate play more often

- Provide teachers with more opportunities to engage in extended conversations with the children in their care

- Enable teachers to mediate interactions between children and encourage problem solving and exploration

What kind of training does the teacher have?

Find out what kind of training the preschool teacher has received — whether at an accredited college or university, or whether she's merely a graduate of Matchbook U or some other educational institution of rather questionable quality.

Training is one area where you really can't afford to compromise. A recent study conducted by the National Research Council identified a clear link between the caliber of the teacher and the quality of the program. The study went on to recommend that anyone teaching in a preschool environment have at least a bachelor's degree in a field related to early childhood (for example, developmental psychology, early childhood education, or early childhood special education).

While you're discussing the caliber of teachers, be sure to find out what the school does when it needs substitute teachers — more specifically, how the substitute teachers are recruited and screened. You want to see some evidence that appropriate hiring procedures are in use and reference and background checking methods are in place. (See Chapter 5 for more on these types of checks.)

Conducting your onsite visit

Assuming that you're impressed with what you find out on the phone, you want to schedule an onsite visit so you can check out the preschool in person. The following sections explain what you'll want to figure out during your onsite visit.

Is the preschool environment designed to meet the needs of young children?

According to the National Association for the Education of Young Children, the ideal early childhood environment is one that is "dynamic and changing but predictable and comprehensible from a child's point of view." In other words, it serves up a perfect balance of stimulation and routine.

Because children benefit more from being the ones in charge of their own learning (as opposed to having the preschool teacher telling them what they should be learning and when), the best preschool classrooms are made up of clearly defined activity centers that enable children to initiate play on their own. When you're checking out a preschool classroom, ideally you'd like to see most, if not all, of the following types of learning centers represented:

✔ **Arts and crafts center:** Arts and crafts activities provide young children with opportunities to work on their fine-motor skills and their hand-eye coordination skills; to experiment with various types of materials; to learn about color, shape, form, and texture; to learn how to use tools like scissors and paintbrushes; to express their feelings through their artwork; and to develop pride in their own creative abilities. When you're sizing up the quality of the art program at a particular preschool, be on the lookout for

- **Art supplies that feature nontoxic ingredients:** Although perhaps past the crayon-biting or yummy-glass-of-paint-water stages, your child's still likely to get art supplies on or in his hands and mouth, so make sure that nothing is in those art supplies that can be harmful.

- **Preschooler-friendly art supplies and tools:** When the program serves 3- and 4-year-olds, look for slightly chunkier markers, paintbrushes, and pencils (which are easier to manipulate), as well as thinner versions of these products that are designed for use by older children.

- **A variety of "found" art materials:** The best preschool programs encourage children to incorporate everyday items into their works of art. You'll find bins of cotton balls, dried pasta, cloth scraps, coffee filters, old greeting cards, fabric and paper lace, muffin papers, paper towel rolls, pine cones, Popsicle sticks, rocks, sea shells, and other treasures just waiting to be used in some truly fabulous way by a budding Picasso.

- **Child-driven art projects:** Look for evidence that children are encouraged to come up with their own art ideas rather than simply carry out the director's instructions and assemble the same craft as every other child in the classroom in robot-like fashion.

✔ **Dramatic play center:** As the name suggests, dramatic play involves acting out scenes from real life through role-playing, dress-up, playing with hand and finger puppets, and so on. Dramatic play gives children the opportunity to boost their vocabularies, develop their fine- and large-muscle skills, work on their hand-eye coordination, experiment with people and things, face problems and come up with creative solutions on their own, express emotions they may not feel comfortable expressing on their own, and start making sense of the world around them. Dramatic play can actually help make kids smarter because it requires more abstract thinking: that empty cardboard box isn't a cardboard box anymore — it's a rocket ship ready to zoom the budding astronauts off to the moon!

✔ **Building blocks center:** Although a bucket full of wooden blocks may seem almost quaintly old-fashioned in this era of high-tech educational toys, most play experts agree that actually more play value can be found in a typical bucket of blocks than the latest educational toy. Playing with blocks gives children the chance to think creatively and to experiment with spatial relationships. They also get the chance to acquire some basic math skills as they begin learning about size, quantity, length, and shape. And because blocks can be worked into pretend play as well, a child can use her set of blocks to make a stable for her ponies or a ramp for her race cars — blocks are a toy that can grow with a child.

✔ **Sensory play center:** When we were growing up, they called it sand play or water play, but nowadays, you're more likely to hear these activities being grouped into the broader *sensory play* category. Whatever you call it, there's no question that kids love sensory play, and it's great for their brains. Sensory play isn't limited to sand and water play; it basically refers to any activity that stimulates your child's senses. That can be finger painting, squishing modeling clay through their fingers, or listening to the beat of a drum. Sensory play provides your child with a fun and stimulating way to learn about the world along with the chance to master such basic mathematical concepts as volume and measurement, gravity, and displacement. (Who knew science could be this much fun?)

✔ **Music center:** Music helps your child develop listening skills, promotes the development of auditory memory, stimulates imagination, and even encourages relaxation and unwinding. That's one reason why some preschool teachers actually encourage a child who's clearly feeling frazzled to retreat to the music center for a bit of preemptive R&R. Most preschool programs have some basic musical instruments on hand for children to play with (either commercially manufactured or handmade) as well as a tape recorder or CD player that can be used for listening to music. And, of course, singalong time is a key feature of group time in most preschool programs.

✔ **Math center:** It may be sometime yet before your child starts dazzling you with knowledge of the Pythagorean theorem, but that doesn't mean it's premature to start thinking about a mathematical education. Preschool activities that are designed to encourage children to group, sort, measure, and count help develop the basic math skills that will serve your child well when starting school.

✔ **Science center:** The entire world is a laboratory to a growing child, so you want a preschool environment that takes advantage of your child's innate curiosity by providing plenty of opportunities to discover gravity and other scientific principles. The science corner in a preschool may consist of magnifying glasses and some objects from nature, and books about the wonders of the natural world.

✔ **Active play center:** Sometimes referred to as the gross-motor-skills center, the active play center in a preschool is the area where more active play can take place. It may consist of an indoor climber, some ride-on toys, an indoor obstacle course, or something as simple as some gym mats on the floor for the children to tumble around on. Most preschools provide children with opportunities for indoor and outdoor active play, so be sure to check out the playground area, too.

✔ **Preprinting center:** Preprinting activities help children develop the fine-motor skills required for writing (understanding how to hold a pencil, how to move the pencil across the page from left to right, and so on) and an appreciation for the role that the printed word plays in our lives. A preprinting center may include paper and pencil work (mazes that encourage a child to guide a pencil around the page).

✔ **Puzzle center:** Puzzles are highly appealing to young children and give them the opportunity to practice fine-motor and problem-solving skills. Puzzles often are placed on shelves along with age-appropriate games (cooperative games rather than competitive games are best for children in these age groups) and other toys and activities that are easiest to play with on a tabletop (certain types of construction sets, pegboards, large beads, and lacing cards).

✔ **Book center:** Early exposure to books can help children develop an array of skills, including those that involve listening, auditory memory, visual memory, and critical thinking. It also can improve your child's attention span. Children can discover how books work — for example, the same words jumping off the page no matter who is reading the book and, in our culture, at least, reading the text from left to right and the book from front to back. When you're checking out the book center at the preschool, be sure to note whether the preschool teacher tries to bring books to life by making suitable props available (for instance, having a couple of firefighters' costumes on hand for the children to dress up in while reading a book about firefighters), encouraging miniature play (giving the children some miniature figurines to use as actors acting out key scenes from the story — or maybe even giving the story an entirely different ending), and doing some related activities (making blueberry pancakes after reading *Blueberries for Sal*).

Does the program allow for individual and group activities?

Look for a physical setting that provides cozy spots for playing alone and large, open areas that are ideal for group activities like circle time (a time when all the children and the teacher come together for a shared group activity — perhaps singing or reading a book together). You also want to look for a mix of small group activities, such as a small group of children playing together at the water table, and large group activities, like an end-of-morning singalong.

Does the program allow plenty of opportunities for free play?

Although some structure is desirable, you don't want your child's day to be overprogrammed, so ask to see a copy of the daily itinerary. If every moment of the day is scripted, the environment may be overly rigid. You want to see evidence that the schedule allows some time for *free play,* or play that is initiated by the child and that zeroes in on activities of interest to the child.

Do the children seem to be happy and settled?

If the children in the classroom seem restless or distracted, or if they generally seem to run around or wander around aimlessly, it may be that the activities that are available to them simply aren't interesting enough or that the children need greater support from the teacher in focusing on and engaging in the activity at hand.

Of course, you'll also want to take note whether the teacher insists that the children sit still for prolonged periods of time. That kind of regimented approach to learning is not appropriate either.

What you're looking for is evidence that the children in the program seem happy and that they aren't having any trouble at all keeping themselves busy — the true hallmark of a kid-friendly preschool program.

Does the preschool teacher relate well with the children?

Not everyone has a knack for working with preschoolers because they require so much time, patience, and energy. The preschool teacher's body language tells you much about how comfortable she is in dealing with preschool children and managing any behavioral problems that happen to arise. Does the teacher seem tense and frustrated or calm and confident?

You also want to find a teacher who understands that her role is to help the children in her classroom acquire new skills and expand their horizons — something that inevitably means letting kids puzzle things out for themselves rather than always rushing in to do everything for them at the first possible sign of frustration. (Sometimes what's easier for the teacher isn't necessarily in the best interests of the child.) You can pick up some additional pointers about assessing caregiver's skills in Chapter 6.

What are the preschool's basic operating policies and procedures?

Be sure to inquire about the preschool's policies and procedures so that you know how the school handles sick children, discipline problems, mid-year withdrawals, overdue fees, and so on.

Does the preschool measure up in terms of health and safety?

Don't get so caught up in sizing up the quality of the program that you take basic health and safety for granted. You can pick up some pointers on what to look for in a large group setting by checking out the health and safety material in Chapter 6.

Is the center director willing to provide you with the names of other parents who are willing to act as references?

The best way to get a solid sense of the quality of a particular preschool is by talking to other parents whose children currently are enrolled in the program and parents whose children were enrolled in the program in the past. Hearing from a mix of present and past parents to call upon for reference checks is best because each contributes a slightly different perspective. A parent whose child is currently enrolled in the preschool can bring you up to speed on current practices, while a parent whose child graduated from the preschool a year or two ago has less of a vested interest in keeping the center director happy, and thus may be more willing to speak frankly about the preschool and its director. See Chapter 6 for more about the art of doing reference checks. (Trust me, it truly is an art!)

Part III

In-Home Childcare: Deciding Whether Nanny or Uncle Danny Can Do the Job

The 5th Wave   By Rich Tennant

"I don't know Ms. Peep, but I just have a good feeling about you as a nanny to watch over our kids. They're out in the yard right now. Why don't you go out and say Hello?"

In this part . . .

If you're hoping to find your very own Mary Poppins (or at least a reasonable facsimile), then you've found your way to the right part of the book. The next few chapters are all about nannies and other in-home child-care providers, including the sometimes-sticky option of hiring a relative to care for your child. I discuss the key issues you need to keep in mind if you're thinking of hiring an in-home child-care provider, and I arm you with a list of must-ask questions for everyone from Granny to Mary Poppins. (You weren't going to just let Mary waltz in without an interview, were you?)

Chapter 9

Searching for an In-Home Caregiver: Mary Poppins, Where Are You?

You've checked out your various child-care options and set your sights on hiring a nanny. In fact, friends and family members may even be starting to drop some not-so-subtle hints that you're becoming a bit obsessed with this whole nanny thing. (Perhaps it's *The Sound of Music* pillowcases that grace the pillows on your bed or the fact that the *Mary Poppins* DVD lives in your home entertainment system these days!)

Hey, being passionate about your child-care choices helps if you're about to embark on a nanny search. Hiring a nanny is a much more complicated process than searching for a vacancy in the nearest family day care (see Chapter 7) or day-care center (see Chapter 6). (If you haven't checked out your other options, you may want to flip back to Chapter 2 before committing to this route.)

This chapter tells you the plain, unvarnished truth about what it takes to emerge victorious in the most challenging event at the Child-Care Olympics: the Nanny Recruitment Marathon! I talk about the various types of in-home caregivers (so that you can be sure it's actually a *nanny* you want), give you the lowdown on what's involved in recruiting domestically as well as hiring overseas, and offer some tips on interviewing prospective nanny candidates and writing a nanny contract that won't come back to haunt you. (Not all nannies fall into the Mary Poppins or Maria von Trapp category, after all!)

Nanny talk

The meaning of the word *nanny* used to be quite clear, but the term has been watered down considerably over the years. Not everyone who calls herself a nanny necessarily has a nanny school diploma hanging on her wall.

Some parents refer to any in-house child-care provider as a nanny, even if the child-care provider hasn't taken a single course in child development in her entire life. (Of course, some parents totally hate the term *nanny*, feeling that it positively oozes pretension when it's used to describe anyone other than a nanny school

graduate. These people gravitate toward either the less-than-politically correct term *sitter,* which is best used to describe the teenager who provides occasional care so you get escape for a kid-free meal at a restaurant, or the horribly politically correct *caregiver.*)

Some geographical variations definitely exist when it comes to the use of the word *nanny.* The very same child-care provider who may be called a *sitter* in some parts of the country is magically repackaged as a nanny the moment she sets foot in other locales.

A Nanny by Any Other Name

Before you get serious about your nanny search, you want to make sure you have the nanny lingo down. A nanny by any other name may not necessarily be a true nanny! (Heck, even a nanny by the *same name* may not necessarily be a true nanny these days, as you're about to discover.) And if you don't know exactly what kind of "nanny" it is you're hiring, it's pretty tough to be clear about that person's training, experience, and overall suitability for the job of caring for your child. Here's what you need to know about each of the categories of in-home child-care providers that you're likely to encounter when you launch your nanny search.

- ✔ **Nanny:** Technically speaking, a nanny is someone who's graduated from a bona fide nanny school (a school that specializes in the training of nannies).

  Although anyone who graduates from a nanny school is definitely a nanny, you can't be sure that everyone who calls herself a nanny is necessarily a nanny school grad. To try to unmuddy the waters at least a little, some nanny school graduates are now starting to refer to themselves as *professional nannies.* So if you're looking for a true nanny (a nanny school graduate), that's something to keep in mind.

- ✔ **Au pair:** Although people sometimes use the term au pair to describe any young person who provides childcare on a *live-in basis,* the term was originally used to describe a cultural exchange program founded by the U.S. State Department that allows a young person from a foreign country to exchange child-care services for the chance to live and study in the United States. You can find out more about the pros and cons of hiring an au pair in Chapter 2.

✔ **Baby nurse:** A baby nurse is someone you hire to help out during the early weeks after the birth of a new baby. She helps you learn all the baby-care ropes and serves as an extra pair of hands so that you can catch up on some much-needed sleep. In many ways, a modern-day baby nurse fills the role played by previous generations of grandmothers who made themselves available for a couple of weeks to help the new parents adjust to life in their post-baby universe.

✔ **Housekeeper:** Fortunately, the term housekeeper is a lot less political than some of the other terms you encounter in the world of nannies. A housekeeper is generally just that — someone who helps clean your house, cook your meals, and so on. (Think Alice from *The Brady Bunch*!) Most bona fide nannies and many other in-home child-care providers object to being asked to serve as both child-care providers and housekeepers. So make sure you're clear about whether you're looking for a housekeeper or a nanny. You may have a hard time finding someone who's willing to do both jobs — or to do both jobs well.

Finding a Professional Nanny

If you decide to recruit a professional nanny (someone who's graduated from a bona fide nanny school), allow at least a couple of months if you're recruiting an American nanny (professional nannies are in chronically short supply) and six months to a year if you're hiring a nanny from overseas — cutting through all the Bureau of Citizenship and Immigration Services' (BCIS) red tape takes time.

If you're planning to hire a domestic or foreign nanny, you want to do the following:

✔ Check out nanny schools.

✔ Tap into the nanny network.

✔ Conduct a domestic search if you plan to hire someone from the U.S. You can either work with a nanny agency or conduct the search on your own.

✔ Conduct a foreign search if you plan to hire overseas. Because of the massive red tape involved, plan to work with either a nanny agency that specializes in foreign recruitment or use the services of an immigration attorney.

Checking out nanny schools

If you're willing to consider a brand-new nanny (as opposed to a more seasoned nanny), go right to the source at recruitment time: Call a nanny school. Ask if they can provide you with a bit of information on their program and if they offer any sort of recruitment service to help match up their graduates with would-be employers. The American Council of Nanny Schools (517-686-9417) can provide you with a list of accredited nanny schools, so it's definitely worth your while to put a call into that particular organization.

Tapping into the nanny network

Don't overlook the power of the nanny network. Birds of a feather flock together, and nannies are no exception. One of the best ways to find a new nanny is to ask other nannies whether they know of another nanny who's looking for work.

Resist the temptation to try to lure away the nanny next door by promising her an extra $50 a week. It'll cost you a lot more than that to scrape the tomatoes off your house when your neighbor gets wind of what you've done! Besides, stealing someone else's nanny isn't a nice thing to do. So repeat after me: Thou shalt not covet thy neighbor's nanny.

Doing some quick research

You may find scanning the classified ads in your local paper or doing a little online searching helpful when you begin your search. These methods are sure to get you some leads. Just be sure to proceed with caution. The leads you generate this way are leads on complete strangers.

Although doing online searches and scanning the want ads can no doubt provide you with a lot of willing applicants, don't let your enthusiasm about finding a pool of willing nannies cause you to overlook the need to be extra vigilant at reference-checking time. These folks are all total strangers after all. You don't even have a friend of a friend who can vouch for them.

Using an agency to recruit domestically

If you're in a hurry because your previous nanny left you in the lurch or you simply don't want to deal with all the headaches associated with the recruitment process, working with a nanny agency (an employment agency that specializes in matching up nannies with would-be employers) may be your best bet.

Finding your nanny through a nanny search offers a number of benefits, such as the following:

- ✔ **Saves you time:** Instead of having to advertise the position yourself, wait for the applications to trickle in, and then wade through mountains of applications from often shockingly under-qualified applicants, the nanny agency cuts to the chase and provides you with a short list of pre-qualified candidates to choose from. Reputable agencies also conduct thorough background and reference checks. Because reference checking can be time-consuming and can potentially land you in legal hot water if you don't know what you're doing, some families choose to use the services of nanny agencies for this reason alone.

  How these agencies pre-qualify candidates varies. Before you decide to do business with a particular agency, find out how that agency screens candidates.

- ✔ **Frees you from having to handle salary negotiations:** The agency can handle the salary negotiations on your behalf. This service is particularly valuable when the supply of nannies is tight and the truly crème de la crème nannies can pretty much dictate their own employment terms. You can also expect the agency to provide salary and benefits consulting (in other words, to give you a rough idea of what other families in your area are offering so that your nanny doesn't get lured away by a better offer), to conduct thorough background and reference checks, and to either consult on nanny bookkeeping and tax matters or to refer you to a company that specializes in these issues.

- ✔ **Offers a guarantee:** Some nanny agencies are willing to mediate if any disputes arise between you and your nanny, but this service tends to expire around the same time as the 90-day warranty that most nanny agencies provide with their nannies. (Agencies that offer this type of warranty are willing to find you a replacement nanny at no extra cost if the first nanny doesn't work out or decides to exit stage left the first time she has to change a dirty diaper.)

You can expect to pay a registration fee of $100 to $200 plus a fee equivalent to one month of the nanny's wages if the agency is able to help you find the nanny of your dreams. (Make sure you're the only one paying the nanny agency, by the way: You want to steer clear of agencies that double dip by collecting fees from both nannies and families.)

If you choose to go the nanny agency route, make sure you're getting what you're paying for — or at least what you *think* you're paying for. Expect a reputable nanny agency to interview you in order to get a sense of your family's wants and needs and then to conduct pre-interviews with a series of qualified nanny candidates in the hope of finding a good match for your family. Also expect the nanny agency to do some initial pre-screening on your behalf — conducting background checks, reference checks, and so on.

Obviously, you want to be sure that the agreement you have with the agency comes in writing. With a written agreement, you can see in black and white what your fee does and doesn't cover. You're handing over a fair chunk of change, so you want to be sure you're getting your money's worth.

Not all nanny agencies practice due diligence when screening nanny candidates. And some online nanny "agencies" are little more than online databases that allow you to search for a prospective nanny. (If you read the fine print at some of these Web sites, you see that the "agencies" aren't guaranteeing the quality of these applicants at all: They're simply slapping up an online database and charging both parties money to be listed in it.) That's not to say that all online nanny agencies are less than above board, of course. Some highly respected real-world nanny agencies offer their services via the Internet, too. But the burden is on you, the prospective consumer, to figure out who's offering full nanny agency services and who's merely offering a watered-down imitation of such services.

Being prepared for overseas recruitment

Some families decide that they want their children to be exposed to a British nanny or are eager to find a nanny who can provide their children with intensive exposure to another language, so they decide to recruit and hire a nanny from overseas.

If you're thinking of hiring a nanny or other domestic worker from overseas, you're going to need a chain saw to cut through all the government red tape. The process of recruiting from abroad can be painfully slow, and you have to be prepared to guarantee that the person you're *sponsoring* (in many cases a total stranger!) won't become a burden to society by embarking on a life of crime or ending up on the welfare rolls. To hire a nanny from a foreign country, you have to act as her sponsor. Sponsoring her is the only way that she can obtain the green card she needs to live and work in the U.S. Because the paperwork is so complex and the penalties for any inadvertent foul ups so severe, most families who decide to recruit nannies from overseas either work with a nanny agency that specializes in overseas recruitment or hire an immigration attorney who understands the ins and outs of immigration law.

But even these safeguards don't guarantee clear sailing ahead. Getting a green card today is harder than it was even a few years ago because of the increased emphasis on homeland security. Another difficulty is that before you can hire a foreign worker, you have to prove that no equally qualified American is available to do the job (no small feat given that nannies are technically classified as unskilled workers in the eyes of the government bureaucrats).

So you have to decide whether you have the nerves of steel and the financial resources required to get involved in overseas recruitment. Those immigration attorney bills can quickly add up. Ditto for the commission for the nanny agency you're working with.

You need to be clear right from the start exactly what you're paying for and what — if any — guarantees the agency or attorney offers. No across-the-board rules exist when it comes to international recruitment, so you need to go in with your eyes wide open.

Turning to Other In-Home Caregivers

If you're open to the idea of hiring someone other than a professional nanny, you may decide to play more of a hands-on role in the recruitment campaign. Your two key strategies will, of course, be to beat the bushes for referrals and (if that doesn't produce a suitable pool of applicants) to run an advertisement in your local newspaper or on an online job board.

By the way, I continue to use the term *nanny* throughout this section, even though I'm no longer talking about professional nannies per se. I use the term in a generic sense to cover any type of in-home caregiver.

Referrals

Word-of-mouth is always your best bet when finding out information about hiring a nanny. Not only are you more likely to get the scoop about a great nanny who's new to the area and looking for work, but you also benefit from the reassurance that comes from knowing that she comes highly recommended by your best friend's sister. You can find out more about generating these types of referrals in Chapter 1.

Advertising

If your word-of-mouth campaign doesn't pan out (or you simply want to hedge your bets by conducting a two-tiered approach to Operation: Find a Nanny), you may consider rolling out a small advertising campaign as well. In addition to running your nanny recruitment ad in the local newspaper, you may want to post it on local bulletin boards and online job boards.

Make sure you word your job ad carefully so that you limit the pool of applicants. After all, you don't want every under-qualified Tom, Dick, or Harriet in town to apply. Of course, even if you go to the trouble of clearly spelling out any specific requirements for the position (for example, the nanny must have a driver's license), you can still expect to hear from a fair number of driving-school dropouts who are hoping to dazzle you with their other qualifications. Here's a quick snapshot of what you should include in your ad:

✔ **The job title:** Remember to specify if you're in the market for a part-time or full-time nanny and whether the position is live-in or live-out.

✔ **A brief description of the job duties:** If you're paying by the word, keep it short and to the point: for example, "To care for our three preschoolers in our home.")

If you want to provide additional information about the position, you may want to refer job applicants to a Web page you've created for this purpose. If you have your own family Web site, you can use that, or you can create a Web site by going to `www.geocities.com`, `www.tripod.com`, or `www.homestead.com`, or one of the other free Web page services.

✔ **The kinds of qualifications you're seeking:** Spell out what you're looking for in black and white: for example, "An experienced nanny with early childhood development and first-aid training."

✔ **Any other specific job requirements:** Make sure you specify whether the nanny needs to have a valid driver's license, whether you're willing to consider only non-smokers, whether you'll only consider applicants who have experience in caring for children who have special needs, and so on.

✔ **Your geographical location:** Would-be applicants will want to know where the job is located, so make sure you include your city and state in your ad.

✔ **How soon you require the nanny's services:** Indicate the approximate starting date in the ad: for example, "Position to start immediately" or "Nanny required after September 1."

✔ **The salary range:** Some parents prefer to negotiate the salary with individual applicants rather than committing themselves to a specific salary range upfront. Others prefer to run the salary range in the ad in order to limit the pool of applicants to candidates who are willing to consider a salary in that range. How you choose to handle this perennial hot potato is up to you.

✔ **How applicants should apply:** Indicate how the applicants should apply: by phone, fax, e-mail, or mail.

If you're not comfortable having your home mailing address run in the ad (after all, you're basically announcing to the world that you have children and they live at such-and-such address), ask that applications be routed to a post office box that you've set up for this purpose. You can set up such a mailbox at companies like Mail Boxes Etc. for as little as $10-$20 per month.

Smoke gets in your eyes

Second-hand smoke poses a serious health hazard to young children, so you have every right to insist that nanny candidates be non-smokers or, at the very least, that they refrain from smoking in your child's presence. If you want to brush up on the facts about kids and second-hand smoke, check out the numerous fact sheets on this topic at the Tobacco-Free Kids Web site: www.tobaccofreekids.org.

Playing Nanny Roulette: Interviewing Candidates

When you begin receiving applications, weed through them and eliminate the less than top-tier candidates. After you have your list of potential nannies, start contacting them to set up interviews. Unless you're planning to turn your face-to-face interviews into a week-long endurance test for yourself, you want to weed out as many potential applicants as possible by phone. Then, with any luck, you're left with a short list of four to six candidates to interview in person.

Although you may be tempted to whittle the list down to just one or two, bear in mind that the number of no-shows for nanny interviews can be rather alarming. So hedge your bets by lining up six interviews, if you can swing it. With any luck, you'll end up with at least two or three candidates to choose from.

Acing the phone interview

You're all set to pick up the phone and dial — or are you? Don't even think about making those calls until you're clear about what you can and can't ask during an employment interview. As a general rule, plan to steer clear of questions that ask about the job applicant's race, religion, national origin, sex, marital status, parental status, family or child-care plans, family background, sexual orientation, or any other issue that may force the person applying for the job to reveal information that's protected by law. The only possible exception is if the information in question is directly relevant to the job, but even then you want to tread carefully. Very, very carefully.

Now that you have an idea of what you *shouldn't* be asking, you probably want to know what you *should* be asking, as well as what you should tell the candidate about yourself and your situation. In this section, I list and discuss the types of questions you may want to ask when screening potential applicants by phone. I also discuss how to wrap up the phone interview.

Are you looking for full-time work?

You need to know upfront whether the nanny's schedule is reasonably flexible or whether she's only available to work the contracted hours and not a minute more. She may, for example, be taking university courses two nights a week or juggling a weekend job — something that can pose a problem for you if your job requires a lot of out-of-town travel and you're counting on her to pinch-hit for you on an as-needed basis.

You also want to find out how keen she is about accompanying your family on your summer vacation if you're hoping to have her tag along to provide some built-in childcare while you're traveling. (Hey, bringing your own nanny beats using the dial-a-stranger service that doubles as childcare in some hotels!) Some nannies see these paid holidays as a perk (hey, what's not to like about a free vacation?), while others view them as an unwelcome intrusion into their private lives (would you want to holiday with *your* boss?) So make sure you know upfront whether the nanny is keen on accompanying your family on vacation or whether she'd rather pass on the round-the-clock employer-employee bonding experience!

What made you choose a career as a nanny?

In addition to looking for some bona fide evidence that she actually genuinely enjoys working with young children (hint: a little enthusiasm is definitely in order), you want to try to figure out why the candidate has chosen to work as an in-home child-care provider instead of operating her own family day-care business or working in a day-care center. Maybe she's a highly motivated self-starter who prefers to work as a solo act as opposed to being part of a team of child-care professionals. Or she may be a total social misfit who has difficulty getting along with other human beings — child or adult. (Needless to say, you want to know which label fits.)

How long have you been working with young children?

Ideally, you want to find a nanny who has a bit of experience under her belt. Otherwise, your kids will end up serving as unwitting guinea pigs while she acquires real-world experience. Of course, you have to let common sense be the deciding factor here. If you come across a nanny school graduate or other similarly qualified applicant who's super-keen and seems to have a lot on the ball, you may decide to give her a chance even though she hasn't actually clocked a lot of time in the nanny trenches. There's no hard-and-fast rule that a veteran nanny is always better than a brand-new nanny. In fact, a nanny who has been at it for too many years and who's no longer getting much enjoyment out of her profession is definitely not a better choice than someone who's embarking on her career with tremendous enthusiasm. So you go with your gut instincts on this one.

When you're tallying up the nanny's years of experience, make a distinction between the number of years she's spent working in child-care centers and other group settings and the number of years she's spent working as a nanny. Some child-care professionals who positively thrive in child-care centers find nanny work to be extremely isolating, even lonely, so if this is the nanny's first job in a non-group setting, you're running the risk that she may decide that the life of the nanny isn't for her after all, in which case you'll be back to pounding the pavement.

What ages of children have you cared for in your previous positions?

This question will, of course, only apply to those nannies who have actually had some on-the-job experience, but assuming she's had at least one job as a nanny, knowing whether she's only worked with babies or whether she's an old pro at dealing with toddlers and preschoolers — or vice versa — is helpful. The skills required to take care of a baby are, after all, very different from those required to care for an older child, so you want to make sure that the nanny you're considering is up for the challenge. (See Chapter 3 for more about important age issues you should keep in mind when choosing childcare.)

What were your duties at your most recent job?

You want to ask this question for two reasons:

- ✔ To get a sense of how skilled the nanny is at caring for young children
- ✔ To try to find out whether she's fudged a little on her résumé

If she was seldom left alone with the children (for example, one of the children's parents was generally on the premises while she was working), she may be stretching things a little to be calling herself a nanny. (She may have been more of a *mother's helper* — a child-care provider who acts as more of an assistant than a stand-in for the child's parents — than a nanny.) If, on the other hand, she was regularly entrusted with three children under the age of five for a week at a time while her employer attended out-of-state business conferences, you can be pretty sure that her previous employer felt reasonably confident about the nanny's caregiving skills. (That trust is kind of an unspoken vote of confidence.)

What was your reason for leaving?

You can discover a lot about a nanny by considering her reasons for leaving her previous position. If, for example, she chose to move on because she had a personality conflict with her previous employer, you may want to ask yourself if her personality could cause similar difficulties in your relationship with her. In other words, is history likely to repeat itself?

What kind of training have you received?

Although no official standards govern the education and training of in-home child-care providers, you probably want to look for a nanny whose skills are at least comparable to those of a child-care provider working in an out-of-home child-care setting. She should have some basic training in early childhood development, infant– and child–first aid, and so on. (See Chapters 6 and 7 for more about what specific types of training are recommended for day-care center staff and home day-care providers.)

Can you give an example of when one of the children in your care was completely out of control? How did you deal with the child?

Recruitment experts say that judging an applicant on the basis of proven past behavior is better than judging the candidate on hypothetical predictions of future behavior. You can paint wonderful pictures of how you'd *like* to think you'd handle future situations (after all, all that's needed is an active imagination and an ability to anticipate the kinds of answers that the interviewer is looking for). What really matters is how we actually handle ourselves in real-world situations, and the only way to get a sense of that is to ask the nanny to describe her past behavior.

Of course, the possibility always exists that she's lying about her past behavior, making up amazing stories about how she handled every single child-rearing challenge she ever faced in her previous jobs with a degree of patience and creativity that puts even the Mary Poppins and Maria von Trapps of the world to shame. But at least you have a fighting chance of hearing a story that's at least partially routed in real life instead of a complete and utter work of fiction!

Are you willing to do a bit of light housework?

If you're looking for someone who's willing to make dinner and do a bit of laundry, state your expectation upfront. Springing your game plan on the nanny after the fact isn't fair at all and can lead to tremendously hard feelings all around.

And if light housework does happen to find its way into the job description, make it totally clear that you understand and agree that her first priority must be the children. You don't want her shoving your baby in the baby swing for hours at a time so that she can have a gourmet dinner waiting for you at the end of the day. Nor do you want her ignoring your toddler's pleas for potty assistance because she was in the middle of switching laundry loads. Anything she accomplishes on the housekeeping front should be considered a bonus, after all; her real job is caring for the kids.

And don't be surprised, by the way, if your request that a prospective nanny scrub the toilets, wash the windows, and clean out the eaves in her spare time is greeted with a click at the other end. Remember, you're trying to recruit a child-care professional, not a serf!

Are you legally permitted to work in the U.S.?

Although you may feel a little awkward asking this question, Uncle Sam leaves you little choice. If she's in the country illegally and you end up hiring her, you can find yourself in major hot water with the Bureau of Citizenship and Immigration Services (BCIS).

If she claims she's eligible to work in the U.S., insist that she bring the appropriate documentation to the interview. (See Chapter 11 for some specific guidelines on what documents are acceptable in the eyes of the BCIS.) If you don't follow the fed's rules to the letter, you can find yourself subject to fines or even imprisonment.

If we were to hire you, when are you available to start work?

This question may seem like a total no-brainer, but add it to your list anyway so that it doesn't get overlooked. You need to know whether the nanny is available to start work immediately or whether she's shopping around for a position that starts a few weeks or months down the road.

If she's currently working for someone else, she is morally or contractually bound to provide her current employer with a couple of weeks of notice. Even if you're absolutely desperate for someone to step in and make your child-care nightmares go away right now, don't pressure the nanny to leave her current employer in the lurch. Not only does this behavior increase the likelihood that she'll leave you in the lurch someday (perish the thought!), but it also isn't fair to ask her to burn — or dynamite — her bridges with her current boss. She may need a reference from that family someday, and they're not likely to speak kindly of her if she left them scrambling for a replacement because *you* insisted that she be on the job first thing Monday morning or lose her crack at the position.

Taking the opposite approach and ruling her out just because you have to wait a couple of weeks for her to become a free agent is equally foolish. If she's a top-notch candidate, she's worth waiting for, so simply come up with some sort of temporary backup child-care plan and bide your time. Good things are worth waiting for, right? (See Chapter 12 for some tips on coming up with alternative child-care arrangements that may meet your short-term child-care needs.)

Are you willing to undergo a background check at our expense?

If the nanny candidate becomes angry or upset when you tell her that you require a background check as a condition of employment, that can be a solid indication that she has something in her background that she'd rather you not discover. It may be something fairly innocuous, like some unpaid parking tickets, or it may be something more serious, like a conviction for child abuse or welfare fraud.

Don't be thrown by her reaction. Remember you're well within your rights to make this request. Corporations routinely go this route at hiring time, so why would you be any less thorough in checking out the person who will ultimately be entrusted with caring for your child? See Chapter 5 for more on background checks.

Are you willing to undergo a pre-employment medical exam?

Some families require that nannies undergo a medical examination prior to being hired in order to find out if the nanny has a serious drug problem or other health problem that could interfere with her being able to carry out her job responsibilities in a safe and responsible manner. If you decide to ask this of the prospective nanny, offering to pick up the tab is only fair. Your health-care provider can provide you with a fee schedule for this type of service. See Chapter 5 for more about pre-employment medical exams.

Moving things along

Assuming the phone call has gone well thus far, you probably want to wrap up the call by telling the nanny a bit more about your family and the job requirements (for example, the number and ages of your children, where you live, the specific employment duties, the hours of employment, whether the position is live-in or live-out, and so on.) This wrap-up gives the nanny a chance to ask you questions about the position, too. (Remember, she's going to be interviewing you at the same time!) If you both decide that she and your family sound like a good fit, you can then move to the next step — setting up a time for a face-to-face interview.

Making the in-person interview count

After you come up with a list of candidates who've passed the phone interview process, you're ready to schedule interviews with the remaining nanny finalists. (I know, I know: This operation has the makings of a new reality TV show — *Nanny Interview Survivor!*)

When scheduling your appointments with the nanny candidates, be sure to allow at least an hour for the face-to-face interview so that you have a chance to ask all your questions and still have time to introduce the nanny to your children. (You may want to arrange for a friend or family member to take care of your kids in another part of the house so that they aren't underfoot during the interview. After all, staying focused on the interview is pretty hard if your toddler is constantly interrupting you to whine for a drink!)

In this section, I list and discuss some of the key questions you want to ask during face-to-face interviews.

Damned lies and statistics department

Are you tempted to pass on the whole background-check process because it sounds like a complicated and expensive proposition? Here's a statistic that may help change your mind.

Approximately 15 percent of background checks turn up some sort of criminal history that was not mentioned on a job application form or during a job interview.

If you are offered this position, are you prepared to make at least a one-year commitment to our family?

Looking for a nanny isn't a process you're likely to want to repeat anytime soon, so make sure that the nanny you're interviewing is willing to make at least a one-year commitment to your family. Besides, having a revolving door of child-care providers isn't good for young children, so you want to find a stable child-care arrangement for your child's sake as well as your own.

Of course, you're unlikely to be able to enforce this kind of verbal agreement in court, but the nanny will know right from the start that she's not likely to get much of a reference from your family if she bails on you halfway through the year.

What are your salary expectations?

If you didn't tackle the salary issue in your job advertisement, you want to raise it during the employment interview so that the nanny has some idea of what you're prepared to pay, and you have some sense of what she's willing to accept.

Determining the nanny's salary is all about negotiation and compromise, so try not to drop your cup of coffee if the figure she pulls out of the sky when you ask her about her salary expectations is way above your budget. Simply let her know that you hadn't anticipated paying quite that much and ask if there's any room for negotiation. Or, alternatively, let her know that you need to spend a little quality time with a calculator and a pad of paper and that you'll let her know later on if you can at least come close to meeting her salary expectations.

Don't assume that you have to meet her salary demands to the penny. When nannies decide whether to accept a particular position, the salary being offered is just one of the factors they consider. If she likes your family and is keen to work in your particular community, she may be willing to settle for a slightly lower salary. Of course, you can sweeten the deal by throwing in a few perks like a health insurance package, a gym membership, and a promise of a bonus at contract renewal time if she's still working for your family. (I swear, corporate merger and acquisitions specialists could learn a few tricks about the art of closing the deal from parents in the nanny trenches!)

May I see the documents that prove you're eligible to work in the U.S.?

Don't allow yourself to be so charmed by the nanny candidate that you forget to get this important bit of hiring business out of the way. You don't want to extend an employment offer and then remember after the fact that you forgot to verify that she's allowed to work in the U.S. So ask her to put her money where her mouth is — at least for employment eligibility — and show you her passport, her certificate of U.S. citizenship, her certificate of naturalization, or whatever other documents she brought along to establish her identity and employment eligibility. See Chapter 11 for guidelines on what documents the Bureau of Citizenship and Immigration Services accepts as proof of eligibility to work in the U.S.

May I have a list of references?

Don't forget to ask the nanny for a list of references and for permission to conduct a detailed background check. You probably want her to sign a form granting you permission to do a bit of digging; not only will it provide you with a bit of protection if she decides to slap you with a lawsuit if you happen to dig up something particularly untoward that affects your hiring decision, but it also increases the likelihood that the people you approach for reference checks feel free to speak openly and honestly about her abilities.

Would you like to meet the children?

Obviously, the only correct answer to this question is a hearty yes! (A "No, not really" should cause you to feed her application into the paper shredder immediately!) Allowing the nanny to meet the children allows you to assess the chemistry between the two of them and to determine how confident and competent the nanny appears to be in dealing with young children.

When the nanny meets your child, her actions speak louder than words. If she gets down to your child's level and gently engages your child in conversation and play without being so overbearing as to send your child running for cover, you can assume you're dealing with a veteran of the nanny scene. If, on the other hand, she rushes in to give your completely shell-shocked toddler a sloppy kiss in a misguided attempt to score points with you, you know for certain that you're dealing with a rank amateur!

Here are the key things to watch for when observing the way the nanny interacts with your child:

✔ **Genuine warmth and caring:** The nanny's body language and voice tone should give you some distinct clues about how in tune she is with your child's needs. (Of course, you also want to consider whether she clicks with you. After all, you're going to work with her on a daily basis!)

✔ **Professionalism:** Look for someone who seems clear about her professional boundaries. You don't want someone who's going to try playing the role of your best buddy. You want someone who's prepared to play the role that she's been hired to play — namely the role of your employee.

✔ **A solid understanding of what children can and can't do at various stages of development:** If the nanny hands your 6-month-old a book with paper pages and then seems surprised when your child rips the book, she's clearly clueless about infant development — something that should have you thinking twice about entrusting your precious baby to this person's care.

Although you want to give the nanny and the kids 20 minutes or so to get to know one another, all good things — including good job interviews — must come to an end. When it's time to wrap things up, thank the nanny for her time and let her know when you'll be getting back to her with your decision. (You'll want to do that relatively quickly, by the way, both out of courtesy to her and to reduce the risk that she'll get snapped up by another family in the meantime.)

Checking references

Just make sure you're completely clear about what you can and can't ask before going into detective mode. Trying to obtain information about an applicant's age, sex, or membership in another protected class (for example, religious group) for the purpose of unlawfully discriminating against that applicant is against the law.

If you're feeling a bit squeamish about conducting these types of reference checks yourself, don't be afraid to outsource this job to someone else. Most reference-checking firms tell you everything you could ever want to know about a prospective nanny for $200 or less. And if the nanny you hire proves to be completely incompetent — she ends up being a reckless driver who hits one of the neighborhood kids while he's riding his bicycle — you may have a measure of protection if his parents decide to come after you with some sort of a negligent hiring lawsuit (for example, they try to make the case that you didn't scrutinize the nanny's past carefully enough before extending an offer of employment). You may be able to prove that you did your homework to the best of your ability: It was the reference-checking company that messed up.

If you decide to hire someone from a reference-checking firm to do your dirty work, make sure you're clear about how he goes about searching police department, court, motor vehicle, credit bureau, Social Security Administration, and Bureau of Citizenship and Immigration Services records. Electronic database searches aren't adequate substitutes for in-person record checks because some electronic databases are badly out-of-date, and, what's more, you can miss important data simply because an incorrect or imprecise search term was used. (Gotta love computers!) See Chapter 5 for more on the art of reference checks.

Hitting the Jackpot: Hiring Your Very Own Mary Poppins

Lady Luck has been smiling down on you and you've managed to find the nanny of your dreams. Now you just need to wrap up the necessary loose ends and close the deal. In this section, I tell you how to do just that, specifically:

- ✔ How to make the job offer
- ✔ What your nanny contract should contain

Just one quick word of caution before I get down to business: Don't be in a big hurry to put in calls to the nannies who didn't make the final cut until your first choice nanny has actually signed the employment contract. You want to have at least one other good candidate in mind as a backup in case your first-choice nanny ends up turning down your job offer.

Making the job offer

When you're certain that you have, in fact, reached child-care nirvana and stumbled across the nanny of your dreams, the next logical step is to make her a job offer.

Although you can make an employment offer verbally or in writing, the key advantage to making the offer in writing is that you reduce the chances of having any misunderstandings down the road. What some parents like to do is to call ahead to see if the nanny is still interested in the job and then let her know that they'll be hand-delivering a written offer to her home later that day for her to review and hopefully sign.

If you decide to make a written offer of employment to your nanny, make sure that it touches on all the key points, namely the salary and benefits, details about the probationary period, the hours of employment, and so on. You may also want to indicate in your offer of employment that the nanny will be required to sign an employment contract as a condition of employment, and enclose a copy of that contract.

Putting it in writing: The nanny contract

Wondering what a nanny contract is all about? Well, keep reading.

Sometimes referred to as a *work agreement,* the nanny contract is a written agreement between you and your nanny that spells out the terms of her employment. The contract functions like a prenuptial agreement in that it's designed to anticipate situations that can lead to difficulties in your "marriage," and it spells out the terms of your "divorce" should you and your nanny choose to part ways.

Knowing what to put in the contract

Whether you decide to write the nanny contract yourself or have it prepared by a lawyer, you want to ensure that it contains each of the following types of information:

- ✔ **Basic contact information for each party:** Nanny contracts typically start out by listing your name and address and the nanny's name and address. Contact information is standard fare for any legal document, after all.

- ✔ **The nanny's Social Security number:** The contract should specify the nanny's Social Security number. (Naturally, you want to see her actual Social Security card to verify that the number is legit — not just some nifty number she made up on her way to the job interview! Hey, you can't be too careful about these things. See Chapter 11 for more on what else you need to do to verify that she's eligible to work in the U.S.)

- ✔ **The date the nanny will start working for your family:** Put this date in writing so that you and the nanny are perfectly clear about when she's coming on board and so that you both have a permanent record of her official starting date — something that can prove valuable down the road when you start discussing wage increases and contract reviews.

- ✔ **The nanny's hours of work:** The contract should spell out what the nanny's hours will be on a day-to-day basis and whether she's willing to put in any overtime on evenings and weekends if you're out of town on business. Obviously, you need to ensure that any agreement that you and your nanny come to regarding her hours of work is in full compliance with state and federal labor laws. (If you're not quite sure about the rules, flip to Chapter 11 to find out what you need to know in order to stay on the good side of Uncle Sam and his buddies in the Department of Labor. Trust me, you don't want 'em for enemies.)

✔ **Standard wages:** The contract should clearly state the nanny's gross wages on a per pay period basis (for example, $1,500 every two weeks). You may also want to indicate the net amount she'll receive on each paycheck after all the appropriate state and federal taxes have been deducted from her wages. (Although the nanny doesn't have any say about whether employment taxes and Social Security taxes are deducted from her paychecks, she decides whether she'd like you to remit her income taxes on her behalf or whether she'd like to handle her taxes herself. You're required by law to offer to remit these taxes on her behalf, so don't forget to have this conversation with her. See Chapter 11 for more on staying out of hot water with the IRS.)

✔ **Overtime wages:** The contract should also state what rate of pay will be paid for any overtime hours your nanny works. Obviously, you need to ensure that you're in full compliance with all applicable labor laws. See Chapter 11 for more information.

✔ **Baby bonus:** Offering your nanny an increase in pay if you ask her to care for an additional child is pretty standard, so you may want to spell out in her contract that she'll receive a 15 percent raise (or whatever the two of you agree is fair) when she starts caring for the new baby, too.

✔ **Benefits:** The way to a nanny's heart is through her benefits package; so don't forget to spell out in the contract all the benefits you intend to offer her. (You do intend to offer at least a few benefits, don't you?) Although the most sought-after benefit by far is a decent health and dental plan (which the employer fully or partially pays for), other perks like paid sick days, paid personal days, and a free gym membership score major points with your nanny. Some families find that knocking a couple of thousand dollars off the salary they're offering and investing those dollars in benefits is better because a decent benefits package generally helps attract a higher caliber of nanny.

✔ **Probationary period:** If your nanny needs to complete a probationary period before she becomes a permanent employee, make sure that the contract makes the terms of the probationary period clear. And if you're planning to give her a small raise at the end of her probationary period, you want to spell out the conditions of the raise in black and white, too.

✔ **Room and board:** If you're hiring a live-in nanny, the contract should mention the fact that you're providing room and board and specify which types of household expenses she's expected to pay for out of her own wages, like long-distance phone charges.

✔ **General house rules:** Whether she's living under your roof or not, your nanny needs to be clear about your house rules, like whether she's welcome to use the family computer while the children are napping, whether she's allowed to entertain her friends in your house, whether she can smoke in front of your children — issues that can lead to major problems down the road if they're not dealt with upfront.

✔ **Job responsibilities:** The contract should spell out the key job responsibilities (for example, feeding and dressing the children, taking them to the park when the weather is suitable, putting them down for naps, disciplining them, and so on). If you prefer to write up a more detailed job description, you can attach it as a separate appendix.

✔ **Transportation:** Make sure the contract specifies whether the nanny is expected to transport your kids around town by public transit, whether she has your permission to drive your child around in her vehicle, or — if she doesn't own a car — whether she has your permission to drive your car. (Obviously, you need to ensure that she has a valid driver's license and arrange for the appropriate car insurance if she's going to drive your car. And you need to talk about who pays for gas under what circumstances: For example, if she's allowed to use your car for personal errands on occasion, is she expected to pay for her own gas?)

✔ **Out-of-pocket expenses:** The contract should make it clear that the nanny will be reimbursed for any reasonable out-of-pocket expenses under a certain dollar amount (say $20) that she incurs while on the job, but that she needs to get your prior approval before purchasing any big-ticket items.

✔ **Discipline policy:** You may want to spell out your family's discipline policies: For example, which methods of discipline you support and which ones you don't. That way, if a disagreement about discipline arises down the road, you can point out that you made your expectations clear right from the start.

✔ **Emergency contact information:** The nanny needs to know exactly what she should do and whom she should call in the event of an emergency if she's unable to get in touch with you. You may also want to attach signed releases authorizing your nanny to administer medication or make emergency medical decisions on your behalf. Remember, time can be precious when a child's seriously injured or ill.

✔ **Confidentiality clause:** You don't want your family's dirty laundry to be aired at the park and the playground or (even worse) on a daytime talk show, so make sure your contract includes a confidentiality clause. At a minimum, the clause should specify that the nanny is forbidden from discussing, publishing, or otherwise disclosing any confidential information related to your family's personal or business affairs.

✔ **The time period that the contract covers:** The contract should clearly spell out the time period that it covers. Nanny contracts are typically renewable on an annual basis. Some parents find that offering an annual signing bonus at contract renewal time works well. That way, the nanny has an incentive to renew her contract with you. And don't make the mistake of assuming that you'll be able to force the nanny to work for your family for an entire year if she decides to accept a better offer after only a few months. Nanny contracts simply don't work that way.

✔ **An exit clause:** Talking about ending your relationship with your nanny before the two of you have even started working together may seem odd, but coming to an agreement about how the two of you will part ways before things start getting messy is always best. At a minimum, your contract should spell out how much notice you will require from your nanny if she decides to quit and how much notice you will give her if you decide you no longer need her services. You also want the contract to state that, upon termination, the nanny is required to hand over the keys to the house and the family car as well as any property belonging to you and your children. (Hopefully, the contract's provisions will save you from having to go to court to regain custody of your 3-year-old's much-loved stuffed bunny.)

Preparing to sign on the dotted line

Sometimes it's stickier for the employer to terminate the contract than for the employee, so make sure you're fully up to speed on your rights and responsibilities as an employer before you decide you want to go the nanny route. If you're already having nightmares about the possibility of being hit with a wrongful dismissal suit or being saddled for life with the nanny from you-know-where, then the life of the nanny employer isn't necessarily for you. See Chapter 11 for more on the ins and outs of being an employer before you get in over your head.

You may sleep better if you decide to have your homegrown contract reviewed by an employment lawyer. He can ensure that you haven't inadvertently violated any state or federal employment laws — a mistake that can cause you major grief down the road. You may spend a couple of hundred dollars upfront for this kind of contract advice, but it may very well protect you later on if a disgruntled nanny with an axe to grind launches a lawsuit against you.

When you and the nanny are both in agreement about the contract terms, it's time to sign on the dotted line — literally. You need two copies of the contract — one for you and one for the nanny. You both need to sign and date every copy so that you both end up with a fully executed copy for your files. Remember, an unsigned contract isn't worth the paper it's written on.

Chapter 10

All in the Family: Hiring a Relative to Do the Job

*H*iring a relative to care for your child is a popular option — so popular, in fact, that child-care professionals have even given this form of care its own name: *relative care.* Relative care can be the best possible form of care — provided that the arrangement works for you, your child, *and* the relative providing the care. If it doesn't, it can put a huge strain on your relationship — very bad news indeed, given that you're likely to bump into this person at family reunions and other family functions for many years to come. (So much for "firing" the child-care provider if things don't work out.)

Overlooking the potential pitfalls is easy when you're dealing with people you know and love. So, in this chapter, I make a point of zeroing in on potential trouble spots so that you can go into any relative-care arrangement with your eyes wide open. I cover everything from intergenerational safety concerns to parent-caregiver turf wars to disagreements about child-rearing issues.

It's all relative

Wondering which relatives are most likely to be involved in providing childcare? According to the U.S. Census Bureau, grandparents are responsible for providing childcare to 21 percent of children under age 5 and to 15 percent of children between the ages of 5 and 14. Siblings and other relatives are responsible for providing childcare to 12.8 percent of children under the age of 5 and to 17.3 percent of children between the ages of 5 and 14.

Identifying the Pros and Cons of Hiring a Relative

Thinking about hiring a relative to care for your child? Make sure that you're perfectly clear about the pros and cons of going this route before you start arm-twisting Grandma or Uncle Danny into playing Mary Poppins.

Considering the pros

Having a relative rather than someone outside the family care for your child has lots of advantages. Here are the key points to consider:

✔ **The relative is likely to be someone you've known for a very long time.** Leaving your baby in the care of someone that you know well is a lot less scary than entrusting her to the care of a complete stranger who happened to respond to your classified ad in the paper. Even after you do all the requisite background checks on the stranger, you may still wonder whether you have a handle on what she's really like.

✔ **Hiring a relative allows you to nurture and build on existing family relationships.** If your mother-in-law is going to care for your baby when you return to work, the transition may be a little less rocky than if you were trying to help your baby get used to a complete stranger. After all, she already has a relationship with Grandma. And, even more important, your child will have a chance to forge a very special bond with Grandma during the months and years ahead — a truly priceless gift for all concerned.

✔ **Your relative may be more willing to accommodate your schedule than a complete stranger would be.** Because your relative likely has a long-standing personal relationship with you, she may be more willing to work around your schedule (for example, providing evening or weekend care if your job requires that you work off-beat hours) than a total stranger may be. Your mother or mother-in-law, for example, may be eager to do whatever she can to help you be successful on the job because she wants you to be able to provide a good standard of living for her grandchildren. (For other tips on finding childcare that works if you work nonstandard hours, see Chapter 13.)

✔ **Your relative may be willing to give you a bit of a break on the price.** If your father agrees to take care of his grandchildren while you're at work, he's likely doing it more for love than for money, so he probably won't demand an exorbitant rate of pay. (Of course, you won't want to take advantage of Dad's goodwill by underpaying him or, worse, not offering to pay him at all. Unless he absolutely insists that you allow him to work for free, you should expect to pay fair market value for his services.)

Weighing the cons

Of course, hiring a relative to care for your child has several disadvantages. Before making your final decision, you'll definitely want to consider whether some of these points apply to your situation:

✔ **You may be bringing too much emotional baggage along for the ride.** If your relationship with your mother has always been somewhat rocky, you may not want to complicate it further by adding an employee-employer dimension. (Remember that old novelty song "I'm My Own Grandpa!" Well, you could do a modern-day version of that song about being your mother's boss — except this version of the song wouldn't necessarily be a fun party song. It would probably come out sounding like more of a heart-wrenching country western ballad!)

✔ **The relative may be doing this out of a sense of obligation to you rather than a genuine desire to meet your child-care needs.** Perhaps you held down two jobs when you first graduated from college so that you could help put your kid sister through school, too. Now that she's home raising her 6-month-old quintuplets, she can't very well turn around and refuse to provide childcare for your newborn twins, too, now can she? Never mind the fact that she's likely to be massively overloaded and exhausted if she tries to take care of this brood of babies on her own (to say nothing of breaking every recommended caregiver-child ratio in the book!): She may force herself to rise to the occasion out of some long-standing sense of obligation to you.

Child-care arrangements that are born out of a sense of obligation rarely work out well for either party — an important nugget of information to tuck away in your head in case you have an entire laundry list of relatives who happen to be indebted to you!

✔ **Some hidden strings may be attached.** This is more likely to be an issue if your parents or in-laws are providing child-care services for free so that you and your partner can save up your money to make a down payment on a house or otherwise get ahead financially. If this is the case and you and your partner announce that you're taking the kids to Disneyland for a midwinter vacation, you may find yourself on the receiving end of a huge lecture from your parents about how they're making all these sacrifices so that you can pay off your house, and now you're acting like a spendthrift.

✔ **Your relative may not take her job responsibilities seriously enough.** Odds are, your sister-in-law wouldn't ask if she could take a stranger's child with her while she hit the bank, the gym, the post office, and the grocery store. If she has your child in tow, however, she may expect to be able to run these types of errands. After all, she's doing you a favor by providing childcare for your family, now isn't she? Relatives like this often fail to grasp that, if you're paying her for her services, you have every right to expect that your child will spend her days as any other day-care kid would: playing with toys and doing arts and crafts — not playing Junior Errand Girl! And if you're not paying for your relative's services, you may want to give serious thought to the hidden costs of the "free" childcare you're receiving. After all, your child isn't likely to get much out of the child-care experience if she's spending her days standing in line at the grocery store or the bank.

✔ **Not every relative has what it takes to be a great child-care provider.** Pause and think about the motley assortment of characters who are in a typical family tree — Cousin Jimmy, who got fired from his job at the Acme Widget factory because he couldn't figure out which end of the widget was up (yikes — what if he has the same problem with toddlers?); Mean Aunt Martha, who is notorious for smacking any child who comes within swatting distance of her at family reunions; and Great-Grandpa Fred, who is a proud graduate of the Children Should Be Seen and Not Heard School of Thought. You can see that some relatives shouldn't be entrusted with a goldfish, let alone a small child. Don't let the fact that you or your partner may share some of the same DNA with these people blind you to their faults. Scrutinize them as carefully as you would any other child-care provider. If they don't pass muster, go back to the drawing board and start exploring other child-care options.

✔ **Conflicts with the relative who is providing childcare can affect the entire family.** If you run into difficulties with the relative in question over the quality of the care she's providing to your child, you may get the evil eye from more than just her: That entire side of the family may decide to turn on you. And if the child-care provider who's causing you grief happens to be your mother-in-law, your marriage could suffer some serious collateral damage as a result. Are you willing to risk it?

- ✔ **You may get more unsolicited advice from a relative than you would if you were dealing with a complete stranger.** Although unwelcome advice giving can be a potential trouble spot in any parent-caregiver relationship, it tends to be more of a problem when relatives are involved, particularly if the relative providing the care is a member of the older generation. I talk more about this issue in the following section, "The Generation Gap Revisited."

- ✔ **Your child is more likely to be abused by a relative than by any other adult in his life.** This is one of those statistics that can't help but send a chill down your spine: According to the nonprofit think-tank Public Agenda, a child is 50 times as likely to be physically or sexually abused by a relative than by a stranger. Although most parents tend to worry more about the stranger who works in the day-care center, their child is at far greater risk while in a relative's care. So if you're considering relative care because you think it's a safe option, think again: The numbers don't bear this particular theory out.

- ✔ **Parting ways with a relative can get very, very messy.** If the child-care arrangement doesn't work out and you decide to look for an alternate child-care arrangement — or, alternatively, your sister-in-law leaves you in the lurch after just a week or two of providing care to your child — hard feelings are likely on both sides. This is one key disadvantage of having a relative care for your child: You have to find a way to make your relationship with this person work long after the two of you have officially parted ways. If things don't work out and you end up parting ways on less-than-friendly terms, you're still likely to have to make small talk over the dinner table at Thanksgiving.

As you can see, you must consider a lot of "cons," but that idea shouldn't scare you away from relative care. A lot of these potential problems can be side-stepped if you're willing to take a business-like approach right from the start. If you can manage to put aside the fact that the child-care provider in question is Dear Old Dad and treat him like you would any other child-care provider, you'll be well on your way to reaping the rewards of relative care.

Revisiting the Generation Gap

Each working day, more than 5 million grandparents in the United States provide childcare to their grandchildren. Although most of these child-care arrangements work out well for all concerned, not every grandparent-grandchild child-care arrangement is necessarily made in heaven. Here's what you need to know to tilt the roulette wheel in your favor.

Too blue to care

A recent study found that 20 percent of grandparents who are responsible for caring for young children 30 or more hours a week meet the criteria for clinical depression. You should at least consider the possibility that your family member may be becoming depressed if you notice one or more of the following symptoms of depression:

- Persistent sad, anxious, or "flat" mood

- Feelings of hopelessness or pessimism

- Feelings of guilt, worthlessness, and helplessness

- Loss of interest or pleasure in hobbies and activities that were once enjoyed, including spending time with the grandchildren

- Decreased energy or fatigue

- Difficulty concentrating, remembering, or making decisions

- Insomnia, early-morning awakening, or oversleeping

- Appetite and/or weight loss or overeating and weight gain

- Thoughts of death or suicide

- Suicide attempts

- Restlessness and irritability

- Persistent physical symptoms that do not respond to treatment, such as headaches, digestive disorders, and chronic pain

Obviously, if your relative is depressed, you will need to make alternate child-care arrangements.

Why grandparents can make terrible — or terrific — child-care providers

Grandparents can make either terrible or terrific child-care providers, depending on the circumstances. If they're in good health and genuinely interested in providing childcare to their grandchildren, the results can be truly magical. If, however, they're in poor health but feel forced to provide childcare to their grandchildren because their children seem to have few other options, the results can be nothing short of disastrous.

You can easily trick yourself into believing that your parents are as young and vital as they were during your own growing-up years. However, you need to look at your parents realistically and be honest with yourself — and them — in deciding whether they're up to the challenge. You won't be doing anyone a favor — not yourself, not them, and certainly not your child — you allow them to take on a responsibility that's simply too much for them to cope with at this point in their lives.

That was then, this is now: Intergenerational safety concerns

Although many grandparents do an admirable job of bringing themselves up to speed on current safety practices, some seem to get stuck in a bit of a time warp, stubbornly sticking with whatever practices were in vogue when they were raising their own kids a generation earlier.

Obviously, this attitude can pose a major problem if you're planning to leave your child in your parents' care while you go to work. You won't have much luck focusing on your work if you're constantly worrying about whether your father-in-law is using your baby's car seat properly (or even at all!).

Here are some tips on getting older relatives on board about safety:

✔ **Give your parents and/or your in-laws a crash course on the art and science of modern-day parenting.** In some communities, you can sign up for workshops designed to teach grandparents everything they need to know about the current thinking on child development, child health, and child safety.

If you can't find any such courses in your community, you may want to swing by the Consumer Product Safety Commission's Web site to print out a copy of *A Grandparents' Guide for Family Nurturing & Safety*. The booklet, written by pediatrician and author T. Berry Brazelton and Consumer Product Safety Commission Chairman Ann Brown, contains tips on child-proofing your house for your grandchildren and using safe sleep practices when putting babies in bed to sleep. You can print out a copy of the booklet at `www.cpsc.gov/cpscpub/pubs/grand/704.html`, or if you prefer, you can obtain a hard copy by requesting Item 606E from the Consumer Information Center, Pueblo, CO 81009.

✔ **Make sure that your parents and in-laws follow your instructions about child safety.** A study conducted by Nissan North America, Inc., found that 12 percent of grandparents admit that they don't use child safety seats for children age 6 and under who are traveling in their cars.

And, speaking of car seats, make sure that your parents and in-laws know how to use and install your child's car seat: A study conducted by the National Highway Traffic Safety Administration found that up to 80 percent of child safety seats are either improperly installed or incorrectly used. Your parents and in-laws should carefully review the installation instructions in the manual that came with the car seat as well as the owner's manual for their vehicle.

You also may want to direct your child's grandparents to the following two resources:

- "Car Safety Seats: A Guide for Families," which can be found on the American Academy of Pediatrics Web site at `www.aap.org/family/carseatguide.htm`

- The Safety Seat Guide page at the National Safe Kids Campaign Web site at `www.safekids.org`

✔ **Don't be afraid to take a hard line when it comes to your child's safety.** This is a situation where there simply isn't any room to compromise. If your in-laws won't childproof their home to your standards, you may have to insist that they take care of your child in your home rather than their own.

On a related note, watch out for grandma's purse or grandpa's bag. A study conducted by the U.S. Consumer Product Safety Commission and the Poison Information Center at the Children's Hospital in Birmingham, Alabama, revealed that 36 percent of childhood poisonings with prescription drugs involved a grandparent's medication. The researchers found that grandparents often store medications in containers that are not child-resistant and that these containers are often left on tables, on kitchen counters, or in purses — all within easy reach of a young child.

Turf Wars: Deciding Who's the Boss

A few years ago, someone came out with a T-shirt that said, "If Mom Says No, Ask Grandma!" It's not hard to see why these T-shirts sold like hotcakes: Those words are so true. Grandma and Mom don't always see eye to eye on child rearing. Although wrangling with these sorts of issues is no big deal if you see Grandma only once a month, it's a whole different ballgame if she takes care of your child full time while you go to work. In such a situation, you want to make it clear right from the start that you're the one calling the shots. (If you're the parent, you get to make the decisions. End of story.)

That's not to say that you won't welcome Grandma's or Grandpa's input on important issues. After all, if they're caring for your child on a regular basis, they're going to come up with some very helpful strategies for managing everything from your child's temper tantrums to her potty training resistance. But it's important that you are the one who makes the calls when it comes to discipline methods and other key child-rearing issues (after taking Grandma and Grandpa's two cents into account).

If your mother or mother-in-law can't accept that simple fact (or she mistakenly assumes that, because she's spending eight hours a day with your baby while you're at work, she knows your baby better than you do), then you'll probably want to rethink your choice of a child-care provider. Otherwise, you may find yourself embroiled in a multigenerational tug of war that could get very ugly indeed.

Of course, turf wars can be a problem in any relative care arrangement, which is why you should make it clear from the start that you're the one making the key parenting decisions involving your child.

There's nothing wrong with asking your relative for input. In fact, it's a good idea to do so on a regular basis. For example, if your brother-in-law has already toilet trained his own four kids, he may have tons of great tips to share with you on toilet training your child.

If you run into turf wars with the relative who is caring for your child, chances are it will be over discipline issues or child-rearing issues. People tend to have strong opinions about these matters, so it's only natural that you may become embroiled in the odd tug of war. This section offers some tips on dealing with these perennial hot potatoes.

Resolving conflicts over discipline issues

Discipline issues can be a source of major grief. You may feel that your relative is being too strict or too lenient with your child, something that can quickly lead to hard feelings all around. She, in turn, may feel that you're spoiling your child terribly and that she's being forced to do all the discipline dirty work for you.

Before you both start pointing fingers and second-guessing one another's discipline decisions, make sure that you have an accurate picture of what's really going on — no easy feat if you're relying on your child's take on the situation.

If your 4-year-old keeps complaining that "Cousin Janie is mean," find out exactly what she's talking about (is Cousin Janie actually being mean, or is she simply refusing to allow your child to color on the walls and swing from the chandelier?) and then sit down with your cousin to discuss the specifics in a nonconfrontational way.

You may find out that your cousin *is* being a little hard on your child — perhaps she expects your high-energy preschooler to behave as well as her much more docile school-aged child. If so, you may want to express your concerns that her expectations may not be age-appropriate or that she's not considering your child's temperament when setting behavior expectations for your child.

With any luck, she'll respond in a professional manner and be open to this sort of feedback. If, on the other hand, she becomes angry and defensive, you may want to think about searching for another child-care provider.

Dealing with disagreements over child-rearing issues

Disagreements over basic child-rearing issues are also quite common. More often than not, these types of conflicts tend to be triggered by one or more of the following issues:

- Sleeping
- Feeding
- Toilet training
- Spoiling a baby
- Using the TV as a baby sitter

Sleep squabbles

To nap or not to nap? That is the question.

If your toddler has clearly outgrown her need for a nap but your sister-in-law insists on plunking her in a crib for a two-hour siesta regardless, you're likely to end up with a very unhappy toddler on your hands.

As much as your sister-in-law may want a midafternoon break herself, forcing your child to take a nap is unfair if she no longer needs one. Besides, you'll probably have an even bigger problem at the end of the day: a toddler who's still making like the Energizer Bunny at 11 p.m.!

The best way to handle this particular issue is to let your sister-in-law know about the late-night fallout you're experiencing as a result of her forced-naps policy and to suggest some possible compromises. Perhaps a half-hour of quiet time when the lights are dimmed and everyone listens to soft music might serve as a suitable substitute for a full-blown nap.

Of course, some people run into the opposite type of sleep problem when they're dealing with relatives: a relative who refuses to put their child down for a nap. Whether it's a soft-hearted Granny who can be easily convinced to let a reluctant toddler forgo naptime or a busy sister-in-law who ends up running errands when your baby should be getting her much-needed nap, the result is the same: You end up with an overtired and mega-crabby tot on your hands.

Once again, your best bet is to simply shoot from the hip and let Granny or your sister-in-law know how her lax stance on the naptime issue affects your child during her non-day-care hours. That may be all it takes to convince your relative of the importance of that afternoon nap.

Food fights

You can head off a lot of battles over feeding issues by being totally clear about your expectations right from the start. Explain at the outset what types of foods you want your child to eat and when you want her to eat her meals and snacks.

If you're dealing with an older relative, make sure that he's fully up to speed on the latest infant feeding practices. Otherwise, you could walk in one day and discover to your horror that your father-in-law is feeding your 6-week-old baby a bottle of the same evaporated milk and corn syrup "formula" that his own kids drank a generation earlier — or that he's told your toddler that she has to eat everything on her plate before she's allowed to get down from the table.

One easy way around the first problem is to simply let your father-in-law know that you'll supply all your baby's meals and snacks until your child is ready for table food. That way, you have far greater control over what does — and doesn't — end up in your child's mouth.

The second one's a little trickier. You may have to sit down with your father-in-law and let him know that pediatricians are now advising parents not to force their kids to eat beyond the point of hunger. If you want to cite an outside authority to help you make your case, you may want to present your father-in-law with a copy of the American Dietetic Association's mealtime tips sheet: `www.wellpoint.com/healthy_parenting/mealtimetips.html`. It summarizes all the current thinking about giving kids healthy messages about food.

Toilet training

Toilet training is more likely to become an issue between you and the relative caring for your child if the relative in question is a member of the older generation. Attitudes toward toilet training have changed dramatically over the course of a generation. Although 90 percent of children were trained by their second birthday back in 1961, just 22 percent of 2-year-olds today can make the same claim.

If your mother or mother-in-law took great pride in the fact that she had all her kids out of diapers before they turned 2, she may be eager to see history repeat itself with her grandchildren. If you don't share her eagerness to sign your toddler up for toilet training boot camp, you'll need to have a frank discussion with her about your approach to toilet training. If she's not willing to follow your lead on this issue, you may want to rethink your plans to have her care for your child.

Spoiling a baby

The current generation of child-rearing experts makes it pretty clear that you can't really spoil a young baby by meeting that baby's needs. (In fact, there's a solid body of research to show that babies whose needs are responded to in a timely and sensitive manner actually cry less and are better able to soothe themselves as they grow.) Previous generations of child-rearing experts, however, didn't necessarily subscribe to the same school of thought, however. Consequently, if you've arranged for an older relative to care for your baby, you may find yourself disagreeing with this relative about this all-important issue.

If your mother or mother-in-law is worried about spoiling your baby, she may be reluctant to respond to your baby's needs as quickly or as often as you'd like — something that's likely to seriously compromise the quality of care that your baby receives. Bottom line? You're likely to find yourself going back to the child-care drawing board.

TV time

Most parents have pretty strong feelings about the TV-viewing issue. They're eager to limit the number of hours that their kids spend plunked in front of the tube. (By the way, the American Academy of Pediatrics is all for limiting TV viewing time for young children, too. These physicians don't recommend any TV time at all for children under the age of 2.)

This opinion is all well and good if you're lucky enough to have a relative who sees eye-to-eye with you on the TV-viewing issue. If, however, the relative caring for your child has a tendency to use the TV as a baby sitter so that she can make a few midmorning phone calls or get a head start making dinner late in the afternoon, she may not be overly thrilled by your no-TV stance.

In this case, you have to decide whether you're willing to compromise on the issue or whether you'd prefer to start pounding the pavement in search of another child-care provider.

Approaching your relative about a problem

While you won't want to micromanage the relative caring for your child, you can't turn a blind eye to obvious problems. For example, if you think that your mother is pressuring your 2-year-old to start the toilet-training process before your toddler is fully ready, you'll definitely want to speak up.

Your mother is likely to be more receptive to your feedback if you express your concerns from your child's perspective. Instead of saying, "I think you're rushing the toilet-training issue," say, "I don't think Jenna is ready for toilet training yet. She doesn't seem to be showing a lot of the signs of physical and emotional readiness that her pediatrician went over with me during her last checkup." (By the way, cite your child's pediatrician's opinion wherever possible. Most relatives will back off on a particular child-rearing issue if they think you have your child's pediatrician in your court.)

Of course, you also want to give some thought to the timing of your discussion. If you can tell from your mother's body language that she's frustrated and exhausted after a particularly grueling day of caring for your toddler, you'll probably want to postpone the discussion until she's in a more receptive frame of mind. Inviting her out for breakfast or lunch on the weekend may work well. Not only is the pace likely to be a little more relaxed because it will just be the two of you, but you also won't have to compete with your toddler for your mother's attention.

Have a potentially controversial discussion on neutral turf: No one needs to feel at a psychological disadvantage because of where the discussion is being held.

If your mother consistently gets on the defensive whenever you express concern about her handling of a particular child-rearing issue, you may want to think twice about using her child-care services. Your child's caregiver, blood relative or not, should respect your wishes when it comes to your children's care.

The Write Stuff: Avoiding Trouble Spots with a Written Agreement

You may not feel comfortable asking your cousin or your mother-in-law to sign a formal child-care contract (see Chapters 7 and 9 for information on what family day-care and nanny contracts typically include). Having *something* in writing is generally a good idea, however, even if it's only a friendly letter of agreement summarizing the key points of your child-care arrangement. (Remember that you want to keep this aspect of your relationship with your relative on a solid business footing in the hope of saving yourself endless grief down the road.)

At a minimum, the letter of agreement that you draft should touch upon the following points:

- ✔ The pay rate and pay schedule
- ✔ The hours of care
- ✔ Whether the childcare will be provided in your home or in your relative's home
- ✔ How many vacation days you're willing to provide each year and whether these will be paid vacation days

✔ How sick days will be handled

✔ How you want the child-care provider to handle any discipline problems that arise

✔ What the child-care provider needs to know about your child's regular daily routine

✔ How the child-care provider should contact you in an emergency.

Here are the key points to keep in mind when you're drafting each section of your letter.

The pay rate and pay schedule

You wouldn't think of asking a complete stranger to agree to work for you without first having a frank discussion about pay rates and pay schedules, so you shouldn't expect your relative to show up for her first day of work without knowing when — or even whether — she's going to get paid. This is a discussion that definitely needs to happen sooner rather than later.

And speaking of pay rates, don't make the mistake of assuming that your mother or mother-in-law owes it to you to provide free child-care services because the child in question happens to be her grandchild. Expect to pay the going rate for childcare. If her budget allows it, she may decide to give you a bit of a break on the price (or even do it for free, either because she wants to help you get on your feet financially or because she's simply tickled pink at the thought of spending time with her grandchild), but you shouldn't assume that you're entitled to free childcare. Your mother or mother-in-law has already done her time in the parenting trenches, after all.

The same thing applies to pay schedules, of course. Assuming that you can simply write Mom a check for childcare whenever you happen to think of it isn't fair or reasonable. Make a point of handling the business part of your relationship in as business-like a manner as possible. If you would ordinarily provide any other child-care provider with a series of postdated checks at the start of the month as payment for her services, extend the same courtesy to the relative caring for your child.

The hours of care

Something else you want to sort out ahead of time is the hours of care. If you're operating under the understanding that your mother-in-law is providing full-time care, and she's operating under the understanding that she's providing full-time care *except* when she has a doctor's appointment, hospital fundraiser, or senior citizens club bus trip, you could be headed for trouble.

This is more likely to be a problem, by the way, if your *father*-in-law is providing *free* childcare. Because he's doing you a favor by not charging you for his services, he may feel that you should be grateful for whatever time he's willing to give you and not get your shorts in a knot about the days when he decides to do his own thing. What he's losing sight of, however, is the fact that you're unlikely to have an unlimited number of vacation days to cover all of his absences. And when you've burned through all your vacation days to cover your father-in-law's various senior citizens club excursions, you may decide that the free childcare that he has been providing really isn't such a great bargain after all.

Whether the care will be provided in your home or the caregiver's

Will that be your place or mine? It may sound like a tacky pick-up line, but it's actually an important question to ask your relative when you're sorting out your child-care arrangement. Here are some points to consider when you're trying to decide which scenario will work best for all concerned:

- ✔ **How big a factor is convenience for you?** If you have to be on the road by 5 a.m. each morning and your kids are still in dreamland then, you may feel quite strongly that you want your relative to provide care in your home. If, on the other hand, your mornings aren't quite this crazy, dropping your kids off at your mother-in-law's on your way to work may not be a big deal.

- ✔ **How comfortable do you feel about leaving this particular relative alone in your house while you're at work?** I know, I know: Technically speaking, your relative isn't actually going to be home alone. Your 6-month-old will be supervising her! But that may not be enough to set your mind at rest if Cousin Rachel is notorious for being a snoop and you have visions of her flipping through your bank statements, reading your e-mail, and checking out your lingerie drawer the moment you pull out of the driveway. As a rule, the Cousin Rachels of the world are best confined to their own home turf, so you may want to give serious thought to having her care for your child at her place, not yours.

- ✔ **Is this person currently providing childcare to other children?** If your sister-in-law already has a thriving home day-care business or is at home with a couple of her own children, she may not necessarily be willing to uproot herself and spend her days at your place. Of course, if you can offer her a few added perks — access to a fully fenced backyard complete with state-of-the-art playground equipment, for example — she may at least consider the possibility if she's got only her own kids to think about. (The parents of any kids in her day care probably wouldn't be overly keen about having their kids uprooted in this way, but you never know. It's something you could talk about anyway.)

✔ **Which environment has the most to offer?** Something else you want to consider is the child-care environment in each home and whether your child would benefit more from spending her days in her own home or in your relative's home. Don't forget to take into account community resources that are available at each location. For example, if your father-in-law lives across the street from a public library that offers all kinds of terrific drop-in programs for young children and next door to a community center famous for its learn-to-swim program, you may want your child cared for in his home so that your child can take advantage of these great programs. (Of course, if your mother-in-law insists on keeping her crystal collection on display throughout the house and your father-in-law's power tool collection is within easy reach of anyone who saunters into the basement, you need to decide whether the advantage of nearby fun activities outweighs the potential household dangers.)

✔ **Are you ready to deal with all the governmental red tape that goes along with hiring a domestic worker?** If your relative will be caring for your child in your home, odds are that she meets the federal government's definition of a domestic worker, so you need to ensure that you're in full compliance with all the appropriate labor laws. See Chapter 11 for a full picture of what's involved.

When you've figured out what will work best for you, see whether your relative has any strong feelings about the issue. Find out whether either arrangement is okay with her or whether she has a preference.

Vacation days

Although you may not think to broach the subject of vacation days with a relative, odds are that she'll want some time off at some point during the year. You may as well find out sooner rather than later how much time she wants to take off and when.

And while you're talking vacations, you also want to talk about how many days of paid vacation you're prepared to offer. A general rule that works for many families is to offer the child-care provider — whether a relative or a nonrelative — the same number of weeks of paid vacation that they themselves receive. In other words, if your employment contract entitles you to three weeks of paid vacation, you may want to offer that same amount of paid vacation to the relative caring for your child. Of course, you're not legally required to do so by law. It's simply a nice thing to do and something that will earn you a lot of brownie points with your relative.

Sick days

You also want to spell out your sick leave policies in the letter of agreement — specifically, whether you can offer your child-care provider a certain number of paid sick days per year. (Once again, you may want to turn to your own employment contract for inspiration.)

Discipline policies

Disagreements over discipline tend to be a perennial trouble spot when family members provide child-care services for one another. That's why it's a good idea to spell out your discipline policies in your letter of agreement For example, you may want to clarify whether you use verbal reprimands, time-outs, the removal of privileges, or some other techniques when you're disciplining your child at home, and which methods you want your relative to use when she's disciplining your child.

You may also want to attach a list of your major family rules so that the child-care provider can try to ensure some degree of consistency. (For example, if hitting your little brother is taboo at home, it should be taboo at day care, too.)

A description of your child's daily routine

If the relative who will care for your child has spent a lot of time with your child, you may be able to skip this particular section of the letter of agreement. But if the visits between the two of them have been sporadic at best, you want to describe your child's daily routine in detail: when she goes down for her morning and afternoon naps, what kinds of foods she eats at lunchtime and snacktime, and so on. This information helps to ease your child's transition too. (See Chapter 15 for more tips on easing your child into day care.)

Emergency contact information

Even if you feel totally confident that your relative knows exactly how to reach you in an emergency, make sure that your letter contains this all-important information, too. That way, you won't have to worry about your sister-in-law panicking and forgetting your office and cell phone numbers in the heat of the moment.

After you've finished jotting down all the key points, e-mail a draft of your letter to the relative who will be caring for your child and ask him to add his two cents, too. He may raise some additional issues that hadn't even occurred to you. And the more of these issues you can discuss and resolve upfront, the less likely you are to run into trouble down the road.

Keeping Your Relationship on Track

An ounce of prevention is worth a pound of cure when it comes to relationships, and family relationships in particular. Here are some tips on keeping your relationship with the relative who is providing childcare on track:

✔ **Lay the groundwork for regular communication.** Communication can easily fall by the wayside when you're dealing with a family member. You may be hesitant to initiate a discussion about any problems that arise, or you may be so rushed at the start and end of each day that you simply don't do as good a job of communicating as you should.

To get around this problem, you may want to consider these suggestions:

- Put a notebook in your child's knapsack or diaper bag so that you and your relative can easily swap notes back and forth about your child's care.

- Touch base by phone at least once a week so that you can identify any little issues before they snowball into bigger issues.

- Arrange to go out for coffee at least once a month so that you can have a more in-depth discussion about how things are going.

✔ **Be sure to express your appreciation for the service your relative provides.** Don't fall into the all-too-common trap of taking your relative for granted. Whether he's related to you or not, he provides a valuable service to your family for which he deserves both praise and recognition.

✔ **Deal with any problems head-on.** If you're not happy about the way your sister-in-law handled a particular situation involving your child, have a frank discussion about the problem so that the two of you can agree about how to handle similar situations in the future. Don't expect these kinds of problems to solve themselves on their own — because they rarely do.

✔ **Encourage your relative to network with other child-care providers.** Find out whether your community has a child-care providers' association and, if so, encourage your relative to join it so that she can get to know other child-care providers. These contacts can be not only a great source of information on community resources but also a terrific source of moral support on the less-than-great days in the child-care trenches.

✔ **Be prepared to invest in your relative's ongoing professional development.** Offer to pick up the tab for any professional development courses your relative may want to take to improve his skills. For example, maybe he wants to take the courses required to obtain accreditation through the National Association for Family Child Care's family child-care accreditation system or the National Association for the Education for Young Children's accreditation program; see Chapter 5 for more about these two highly respected accreditation programs.

Chapter 11

Me? An Employer?: Hiring Domestic Employees

You may not necessarily see yourself as "the boss," but that's exactly what you become the moment you decide to hire a nanny or another in-home child-care provider. (Who knew that getting bumped up to the executive suite was this easy?) Of course, along with the jazzy new job title comes an entire truckload of employer-related responsibilities — responsibilities that you may not even be aware of until after you've had your wrist slapped by Uncle Sam. That's the reason I wrote this chapter: I wanted to give you a bird's-eye view of what you're getting yourself into, for better and for worse, the moment that you and the nanny say your "I do's."

Employee or Independent Contractor? Say What?

Of course, the first thing you need to figure out is whether you're entering into an employer-employee relationship with the child-care provider in question — or whether she is actually working as an *independent contractor* (a self-employed business person).

This question is critical because if the child-care provider is operating as an independent contractor (for example, she's operating a family day-care business as opposed to caring for your child in your home), you don't have to worry about all the employer-employee red tape that's described at length in this chapter.

In most cases, however, nannies and other in-home child-care providers meet the IRS's criteria for employees, not independent contractors. In case you aren't in the habit of downloading tax law interpretation bulletins from the IRS Web site just for kicks, allow me to quickly summarize the key criteria that the IRS uses in determining whether a particular worker falls into the employee or independent contractor category.

- ✔ **Who's responsible for determining where and when the work occurs?** If you're the one responsible for dictating the hours of employment and deciding where your child is cared for (in your home, for example), chances are the child-care provider is your employee rather than an independent contractor.

- ✔ **Is the child-care provider working for you, or is she working for other families, too?** A family day-care provider who runs her own home-based business is considered to be an independent contractor rather than your employee. If you're sharing a nanny with another family, but she's providing this care to your two families exclusively and this care is being provided in one of your homes, she's likely considered an employee in the eyes of the IRS.

- ✔ **Are you offering your nanny any employee-type benefits, such as a pension plan, vacation pay, or sick pay?** If you offer your nanny these types of benefits, you'll have a hard time trying to make the case to Uncle Sam that she's an independent contractor.

- ✔ **Is your working relationship likely to be long-term?** If the nanny will be working for you for a short period of time rather than on an ongoing basis (for example, she's simply filling in for a week or two while your regular family day-care provider is home recovering from emergency surgery), she may, in fact, meet the definition of an independent contractor.

- ✔ **Is she being paid through an outside agency?** If you contract the nanny's services through a nanny agency and you pay the agency rather than the nanny directly, she's technically the agency's employee rather than your own. (Don't make the mistake of assuming that you'll save a lot of money by hiring your in-home child-care provider through a nanny agency. They still have to pay the nanny taxes, so they'll have to pass this expense on to you, plus the usual overhead and markup.)

Make sure that you're totally clear about whether your nanny is an employee or an independent contractor. If you incorrectly assume that she's an independent contractor when, in fact, she's technically your employee, you may find yourself liable for back taxes, penalties, and interest even years after the fact. (Uncle Sam is particularly unforgiving in these types of situations.)

You can find out more about the criteria that the IRS uses in deciding who does and doesn't meet the definition of an employee by requesting a copy of *Publication 15-A: Employer's Supplemental Tax Guide* from your local IRS tax office or by downloading a copy from the IRS Web site: www.irs.gov.

If you're still befuddled after reading the guide — or perhaps even more befuddled after making your way through this hefty document! — you can save yourself further headaches by asking the IRS to make a definitive ruling on whether your nanny is an employee or an independent contractor. All you need to do is to fill out a *Form SS-8: Determination of Worker Status for Purposes of Federal Employment Taxes and Income Tax Withholding* and then file this form with the IRS. The IRS will then let you know whether you should be treating your nanny as an employee or as an independent contractor. Voilà! Problem solved.

Considering Whether You Have What It Takes to Be Someone's Employer

Up to this point in the chapter, I've focused on the government's definition of what it means to be someone's employer. I haven't even touched on the bigger issue: whether you actually want to take on this responsibility.

Are you prepared to invest the required time and energy?

Until you've sat on the other side of the desk, you may underestimate just how much time and energy goes into being someone's boss. The following are some questions to ask yourself. (These questions have no right or wrong answers. They're simply designed to give you a snapshot of some of the behind-the-scenes HR responsibilities that you can expect to shoulder if you go the nanny route.)

- Are you willing to devote the necessary time and energy training your nanny and researching your own responsibilities as an employer?
- Do you have solid interpersonal skills? Do you tend to get along well with others?
- Do you have strong leadership qualities? Are you able to motivate, inspire, and generally bring out the best in others?
- Are you willing to be "the heavy" if the nanny's job performance isn't up to snuff?

Your answers to these questions should help you to decide whether you have what it takes to be someone's employer. Not everybody does.

Are you an administrative whiz?

The paperwork associated with hiring and keeping a nanny can be quite a burden. For whatever reason, the various government departments seem to repeatedly lose sight of the fact that a family that hires a nanny doesn't necessarily have an entire payroll and human resources department at its disposal to help it cut through all the governmental red tape.

If you're getting bogged down by all the administrative work associated with employing a nanny, or you're worried that you may end up overlooking something you were supposed to be doing and end up in major hot water with Uncle Sam, you have an alternative. But that alternative doesn't come cheap.

You can hire a nanny payroll firm to handle all the assorted paperwork and remittances on your behalf. On average, you can expect to pay about $1,000 per year to have the firm calculate your nanny's paychecks, prepare your tax returns, and do all the related bookkeeping on your behalf. Some families figure that this is a small price to pay to transfer all the administrative burden to someone else, so you may want to consider this option if your budget can swing it.

Of course, if you're an administrative whiz who gets a great deal of personal satisfaction from balancing your checkbook to the penny and who looks forward to tax season because filling out all the tax forms is so much fun, you don't need to call in any outside help. This nanny thing is going to be an absolute cakewalk for you.

Knowing Your Responsibilities

Ignorance of the law is no excuse, especially when you're the one in charge. If you're thinking seriously about hiring a nanny, you need to make sure that you're fully up to speed about all the responsibilities that go along with being someone's employer, namely

- ✔ Verifying that the nanny is, in fact, eligible to work in the United States
- ✔ Deducting the appropriate Social Security and Medicare taxes and paying unemployment taxes on your nanny's wages

Employment eligibility verification

The Bureau of Citizen and Immigration Services requires you fill out a *Form I-9* whenever you hire a new employee. The purpose of this form is to demonstrate that the person you've hired is eligible to work in the United States.

Filling out this form requires a bit of a tag team effort. One section needs to be completed by the employee, and another section needs to be completed by the employer. The form requests the following pieces of information:

✔ The nanny's first and last name and middle initial and, if applicable, the nanny's maiden name

✔ The nanny's address

✔ The nanny's date of birth

✔ The nanny's Social Security number

✔ The nanny's employment status, namely whether she's

- A citizen or national of the United States

- A *Lawful Permanent Resident* (in which case you need to provide her alien number)

- An alien who's authorized to work until a particular date (in which case you need to provide her alien number or admission number)

✔ A statement about whether the nanny received any help with the preparation of her section of the form (for example, assistance from an immigration agent or translator)

✔ Details about the document or documents you've reviewed in order to verify the nanny's employment eligibility, including

- Type of document

- Issuing authority

- Document number

- Expiration date

✔ Your name and title

✔ The business name (if applicable)

The document verification section of the form is critical: Your nanny is required to produce one or more documents to verify that she's legally entitled to work in the United States. Hiring someone who's unable to produce these documents is against the law, so you're responsible for making sure that she produces them and that the documents are legit.

What follows are answers to some of the most frequently asked questions about checking your nanny's documents.

What types of documents am I allowed to accept as proof of identity and employment eligibility?

As you may expect, the U.S. Bureau of Citizenship and Immigration Services has very strict rules about what types of documentation you're allowed to accept as proof of identity and employment eligibility. In fact, it breaks this list of types of documents into three categories:

- ✔ List A (documents that establish both identity and employment eligibility)
- ✔ List B (documents that establish identity)
- ✔ List C (documents that establish employment eligibility)

If the nanny is able to produce a valid document from List A, that's the only document you need to see. If, however, she isn't able to produce a document from that list, you need to see a document from List B *and* a document from List C. (See Table 11-1 for complete details.)

Don't request any document that isn't specifically listed in Table 11-1. Doing so could leave you open to a charge of discrimination.

Table 11-1   Lists of Acceptable Documents to Demonstrate Identity and Employment Eligibility

Workers are required to produce one document from List A, or a document each from List B and List C. Illustrations of many of these documents appear in Part 8 of the Handbook for Employers (M-274).

List A: Documents that Establish Both Identity and Employment Eligibility	List B: Documents that Establish Identity	List C: Documents that Establish Employment Eligibility
U.S. Passport (valid or expired)	Driver's license or ID card issued by a state or outlying possession of the United States, provided it contains a photograph or information such as name, date of birth, gender, height, eye color, and address	U.S. Social Security card issued by the Social Security Administration (other than a card stating it's not valid for employment)

List A: Documents that Establish Both Identity and Employment Eligibility	List B: Documents that Establish Identity	List C: Documents that Establish Employment Eligibility
Certificate of U.S. Citizenship (INS Form N-560 or N-561)	ID card issued by federal, state, or local government agencies or entities, provided it contains a photograph or information such as name, date of birth, gender, height, eye color, and address	Certification of Birth Abroad issued by the Department of State (Form FS-545 or Form DS-1350)
Certificate of Naturalization (INS Form N-550 or N-570)	School ID card with photograph	Original or certified copy of a birth certificate issued by a state, county, municipal authority, or outlying possession of the United States bearing an official seal
Valid Foreign Passport with I-551 stamp or attached INS Form I-94 indicating unexpired employment authorization	Voter's registration card	Native American tribal document
Permanent Resident Card or Alien Registration Receipt Card with photograph (INS Form I-151 or I-551)	U.S. Military card or draft record	U.S. Citizen ID Card (INS Form I-197)
Unexpired Temporary Resident Card (INS Form I-688)	Military dependent's ID card	ID Card for use of Resident Citizen in the United States (INS Form I-179)
Unexpired Employment Authorization Card (INS Form I-688A)	U.S. Coast Guard Merchant Mariner Card	Unexpired employment authorization document issued by the INS (other than those in List A)
Unexpired Reentry Permit (INS Form I-327)	Native American tribal document	

(continued)

Table 11-1 *(continued)*

Workers are required to produce one document from List A, or a document each from List B and List C. Illustrations of many of these documents appear in Part 8 of the Handbook for Employers (M-274).

List A: Documents that Establish Both Identity and Employment Eligibility	List B: Documents that Establish Identity	List C: Documents that Establish Employment Eligibility
Unexpired Refugee Travel Document (INS Form I-571)	Driver's license issued by a Canadian government authority	
Unexpired Employment Authorization Document issued by the INS that contains a photograph (INS Form I-688B)	Clinic, doctor, or hospital record (for persons under age 18 who are unable to present a document listed previously)	
	School record or report card (for persons under age 18 who are unable to present a document listed previously)	
	Day care or nursery school record (for persons under age 18 who are unable to present a document listed previously)	

How can I tell whether the documents are valid or are something the nanny whipped up on her home computer?

Any modern-day nanny who's serious about trying to pull one over on Uncle Sam is going to produce some fairly sophisticated fraudulent documents, so you're unlikely to encounter smudgy ink or documents with glaring errors (misspellings of "United States of America," for instance) unless you're dealing with a rank amateur. You're more likely to run into highly impressive-looking documents that don't actually carry any official standing in the United States or any other country. So how is someone other than an immigration lawyer supposed to tell the difference? By relying on good old-fashioned common sense, that's how.

All that Uncle Sam asks of you is that you examine the documents and try to determine whether they're genuine. If you're not sure what the various types of documents listed in Table 11-1 are actually supposed to look like (just in case you're not in the habit of reading immigration manuals for fun), you may want to download a copy of the *Handbook for Employers*

(M-274) from the Bureau of Citizenship and Immigration Services Web site: www.immigration.gov/graphics/lawsregs/handbook/hnmanual.htm. The manual includes photographs of sample documents, so you have a rough idea what to look for when you're verifying the nanny's documents.

Just one word of caution on the document verification front: You can get yourself in major hot water if you refuse to accept authentic-looking documents from a foreign country. This refusal could be considered employment discrimination, leaving you open to a nasty and costly lawsuit.

If you feel like you're in a bit of a Catch-22 here — you're worried about getting in trouble with the feds if you accept fraudulent documents, but you're scared about getting sued by the nanny if you question the authenticity of her passport from a country you've never even heard of before — you may want to contact your local Bureau of Citizenship and Immigration Services office for assistance. You can either check your local phone book or use the online directory at the Bureau of Citizenship and Immigration Services Web site: www.immigration.gov/graphics/fieldoffices/service_centers/.

Am I allowed to accept a photocopy of a document?

The only documents you're allowed to accept are the originals. The reason is obvious: The potential for document fraud increases astronomically the moment you hit the print button on a photocopier. Uncle Sam only provides for one small exception to this across-the-board rule: You're allowed to accept a certified copy of a birth certificate instead of the original.

And just so you don't get on the wrong side of the federal immigration authorities, here's something else you need to know: You may not accept a laminated Social Security card as evidence of employment eligibility if a note on the reverse side of the card states "not valid if laminated." Metal and plastic reproductions of Social Security Cards aren't acceptable, either, by the way. Once again, too much potential for fraud.

What should I do if the nanny keeps "forgetting" to bring her documents with her to work?

Don't let the nanny get away with playing the "I forgot my documents" game. Federal laws require that you verify your nanny's eligibility for employment within three days of the start of her employment. (Some government documents actually stipulate that this task should be completed no later than the close of business on the employee's first day of work.)

If you let things slide for more than a day or two, you could end up with a very sticky situation on your hands. While Uncle Sam allows you to terminate the employment of any employee who fails to produce the required documentation within three business days of the date upon which employment began, it gets a bit trickier (and from a legal standpoint, a bit more perilous)

to try to get rid of an employee after this point solely on the grounds that she hasn't ponied up the necessary documents. If you find yourself in such a situation, you will likely want to get some legal advice on what you need to do to get rid of the nanny without getting slapped with a wrongful dismissal lawsuit.

You also need to ensure that you're applying the same standards of document verification to all your domestic workers. (Assuming, of course, that you have other employees. Not all of us have a butler, maid, chauffeur, and chef on staff!) If you're seen as playing favorites, you could end up getting your hand slapped by Uncle Sam, your disgruntled nanny, or both.

Can we fill out the Form I-9 prior to the nanny's first day of work?

Absolutely. In fact, filling it out ahead of time is a pretty good idea. Instead of having to verify the nanny's passport while you're trying to attend to all the other things you have to worry about during your nanny's first day on the job (not the least of which is your child's reaction to this new person), you'll be able to scratch at least one item off your list of things to do.

The nanny lost her passport recently. All she had to show me was a receipt proving that she's applied for a new one. Can I accept this?

Yes, you can accept this receipt as temporary proof that the nanny is eligible to work in the United States. But you have to remember to follow up and ask to see her new passport after she receives it. (If an employee has applied for a replacement document and is able to produce a receipt for the replacement document, the employee must produce the actual document within 90 days of the date when employment begins.)

What happens if there's some sort of problem with the nanny's documents after all?

If you checked the nanny's documents and submitted a properly completed Form I-9 to the government, you can't be charged with an employment verification violation. (That's good news, by the way, because the penalties associated with such a violation are pretty hefty, ranging from fines of up to $10,000 for each incident in which you hired an "unauthorized alien" — government lingo for an illegal worker — to imprisonment. And if you think that you have child-care problems now, just try to arrange around-the-clock childcare for the next five years while you do your time in prison!)

Just so you're perfectly clear, you'll be able to stay in the good graces of the federal immigration authorities if you have

✔ Ensured that your nanny completed Section 1 of Form I-9 completely at the time of hiring

✔ Reviewed the documents that the nanny presented to you and determined that they appear to be genuine and that they appear to belong to the person presenting them

✔ Fully completed Section 2 of the Form I-9 yourself and signed and dated the employer certification

✔ Retained Form I-9 for the appropriate period of time (see the section "How long do I have to keep the Form I-9 on file?" later in the chapter)

✔ Made Form I-9 available to the immigration authorities upon request

If you follow all those steps, you won't find yourself in the hot seat if it turns out that the nanny you hired is working in the country illegally.

What do I do with the Form I-9 after it's filled out?

After the Form I-9 has been fully filled out, you file it away. (It's not like a tax return that you have to file with the government. You simply store it with your other employment-related records.)

How long do I have to keep the Form I-9 on file?

The federal government requires you to keep Form I-9 on file for three years after the date that your nanny began work or for one year after the termination of her employment, whichever is later, but some state employment departments recommend that you keep all employment records for up to seven years to protect yourself against any employment-related claims down the road. Just make sure that you file the form in a safe place: You must be able to produce a copy if an immigration inspector asks to see it.

Some employers choose to keep a photocopy of the nanny's documents in order to prove that they did, in fact, verify them. If you decide to go this route, don't make this mistake of assuming that photocopying the documents gets you off the hook from fully completing the Form I-9. Photocopy or no photocopy, you could find yourself in major hot water if the immigration authorities were to show up on your doorstep and find that the form was incomplete.

My nanny only has a temporary work authorization. Do I need to go through this process again when her work authorization expires?

Yes, unfortunately, you do. You have to re-verify your nanny's employment eligibility when her work authorization expires. (You could inadvertently end up with an illegal worker on your payroll if you didn't re-verify — something that would land you in major trouble with federal immigration authorities.) You can either fill out Section 3 (Updating and Reverification) of the original Form I-9, or you can start a new Form I-9.

Make sure that your nanny knows that she needs to apply for new work authorization at least 90 days before the expiration date of her current work authorization. Otherwise, her original work authorization may expire before her request for a new work authorization is heard by the *immigration adjudicators* (the people responsible for making immigration decisions). If her new application isn't adjudicated within 90 days, the immigration authorities will grant the nanny an extension of up to 240 days to allow time for her new work authorization to make its way through the adjudication system.

Our nanny quit two years ago to go back to school. Now, we're about to hire her again. Do we have to get her to fill out another Form I-9?

If you still have her original Form I-9 on hand (you're supposed to keep it for a year after the two of you parted ways or three years after the date of original hire, whichever is longer), you can have her update the original form by completing Section 3 (Updating and Reverification).

If you no longer have her original Form I-9 on file, you'll have to start from scratch and fill out a new Form I-9.

Can I hire an outside agency to verify the nanny's employment eligibility for me?

You can ask an employment agency to do some of the legwork for you, but you're still ultimately the one who's responsible for verifying that the nanny is who she says she is and that she's eligible to work in the United States. Like it or not, the buck stops with you.

Am I required to report new hires to the state employment office?

Yes, this requirement is another bit of governmental red tape that ends up getting dropped in your lap when you hire a nanny. To find out exactly what's involved in reporting new hires in your state, contact your state employment office. (Check under "Employment" in the state government listings in your phone book.)

Employment taxes, Social Security, Medicare, and more

You've no doubt heard all the buzz about the various "nanny taxes" that employers are required to remit to the government if they happen to employ a nanny or other in-home employee. Although you may be tempted to try to avoid paying these nanny taxes in the hope of trimming your payroll costs — tax experts estimate that playing by the nanny tax rules boosts payroll expenditures by approximately 11.1 percent — you may want to think twice before making this gamble.

You see, trying to dodge the nanny tax can be very risky business indeed. If you get caught, you may find yourself on the hook for your share of the back taxes, the nanny's share, plus the usual penalties and interest. You even leave yourself open to criminal prosecution if you knowingly lied on your tax return about the fact that you owed nanny taxes. (Remember that when you sign on the bottom line of your tax return, you're swearing that your return is true, correct, and complete. If you lie, you're committing *perjury,* which is a major federal offense.)

Although some folks argue that the risks of getting caught are virtually nil, they're being overly optimistic. If your former employee were to apply for unemployment benefits, worker's compensation benefits, or Social Security benefits even many years after the fact, the IRS could come after you to try to collect any unpaid nanny taxes. (The nanny tax has no three-year statute of limitations on errors or omissions. You're on the hook, period.)

So the best advice I can give you on this particular subject is to simply accept the fact that nanny taxes are part of the cost of hiring a nanny and fork over the necessary cash to the IRS. If nothing else, you'll sleep better at night knowing that you're playing by Uncle Sam's rules.

And now that I have that bit of business out of the way, allow me to give you the lowdown on the various types of taxes you should know about to stay on Uncle Sam's good side, namely

- ✔ Federal income tax
- ✔ Social Security and Medicare
- ✔ Federal Unemployment Tax (FUTA)
- ✔ State taxes

Obtaining an Employer Identification Number (EIN)

Collecting employment taxes is one of the least fun aspects of being an employer. These taxes are a pain to calculate, a pain to collect, and a pain to remit. Unfortunately, Uncle Sam doesn't give you a lot of choice in the matter. If you meet certain criteria (see Table 11-2), you're required to play tax collector, whether you like it or not.

Table 11-2	Do You Need to Pay Employment Taxes?

Social Security and Medicare Taxes

If you . . .	Then you need to . . .
Pay cash wages of $1,400 in 2003 or more to any one household employee **Note:** You're not required to count wages paid to your spouse, any child age 20 or younger, your parent (see note immediately following), or any employee age 17 or younger at any time in 2003 (unless working for you is this person's primary occupation) **Note:** You're only required to pay Social Security and Medicare on wages paid to your parent if both the following conditions apply: (a) Your parent cares for your child who is either (i) age 17 or younger or (ii) has a physical or mental condition that requires the personal care of an adult for least four consecutive weeks in a calendar quarter; and (b) your marital status is one of the following: (i) you're divorced and have not remarried; (ii) you're a widow or widower; or (iii) you're living with a spouse whose physical or mental condition prevents him or her from caring for your child for at least four continuous weeks in a calendar quarter.	Withhold and pay Social Security and Medicare taxes

Federal Unemployment Tax

If you . . .	Then you need to . . .
Pay total cash wages of $1,000 or more in any calendar quarter in 2003 to household employees **Note:** Don't count wages you pay to your spouse, your child age 20 or younger, or your parent.	Pay federal unemployment tax

The information in this table reflects the rules that were in place for the 2003 tax year. For updates on tax changes for subsequent years, download an up-to-date copy of Publication 926: Household Employer's Tax Guide from the IRS Web site: www.irs.gov.

Of course, before you can report employment taxes or start issuing tax statements to employees, you need to apply for an *Employer Identification Number* (EIN), which is a nine-digit number that the IRS uses to identify the tax accounts of employers. You can apply for an EIN by mail by completing Form SS-4, or you can apply by phone. (Call your local IRS office or visit the IRS Web site for details: www.irs.gov.)

If you haven't received your EIN by the time your first tax payment is due, you'll have to make your deposit directly to the IRS. (You won't be able to make your payment via a financial institution until you receive your EIN.)

Whatever you do, don't hold off on making your payment until you receive your EIN. The penalties for making late payments are fairly hefty, ranging from 2 percent for deposits that are made one to five days late to 15 percent for accounts that are still unpaid after the IRS has sent you an official notice that your account is past due. (Ouch!)

Federal income tax

Although you aren't required to withhold income taxes from your nanny's paychecks, she may want you to anyway to avoid getting hit with a hefty tax bill in the spring. If she asks you to withhold income tax and to remit it to the government on her behalf, you'll need her to complete and sign a *Form W-4: Employee Withholding Allowance Certificate.* This form, which summarizes her filing status and how many exemptions she qualifies for, will assist you in calculating how much tax you should withhold from each paycheck.

By the way, you may find yourself having to advance tax money to the nanny if she happens to qualify for the Earned Income Credit (a federal tax credit for low-income workers). If she provides you with a properly completed *Form W-5: Earned Income Credit Advance Payment Certificate,* you'll be required to advance her some of this credit on each paycheck.

For more on tax issues, see *Publication 926: Household Employer's Tax Guide,* available from any IRS office or from the IRS Web site: www.irs.gov.

Social Security and Medicare

Social Security taxes fund old-age, survivor, and disability benefits for workers and their families, and the Medicare tax pays for hospital insurance. After the wages you pay your nanny reach a certain threshold determined by the IRS (in 2003, that threshold was $1,400 per year), you're required to pay both these taxes on your nanny's wages.

Technically speaking, you and the nanny are responsible for each paying half of the Social Security and Medicare taxes, but many employers choose to cover both the employer and employee portions of these taxes. Because the two taxes amount to 15.3 percent of the total wages, and her share is half this amount, picking up the tab for her half would cost you 7.65 percent of her wages.

Whether you decide to pay the total cost or just your share, you're the one who's responsible for ensuring that these taxes get remitted to the IRS.

Federal unemployment tax

The Federal Unemployment Tax Act (FUTA), in conjunction with state unemployment systems, provides compensation to workers who've lost their jobs.

The FUTA tax typically amounts to 6.2 percent of your employee's FUTA wages. However, you are able to take a credit of up to 5.4 percent against the FUTA tax, which brings the net tax down to just 0.8 percent, provided that you paid all your previous year's state unemployment taxes on time.

Depending on where you live, you may be required to pay both the federal unemployment tax (the FUTA tax) and the state unemployment tax. Or you may only be required to pay one or the other. To find out about the rules in your state, contact your state unemployment tax agency. (Check the government pages of your local phone book.)

State taxes

Even if you don't actually have to fork over any cash for any federal taxes, you may still be required to pay taxes for unemployment and workers' compensation insurance. In most states, you become liable for state employment taxes as soon as your total payroll (for all employees, not just a single employee) exceeds $1,000 per calendar quarter. Of course, this threshold is much lower in some states. It's just half this amount ($500) in New York and the District of Columbia.

Conforming to Health and Safety Regulations

Your home isn't just your home anymore. It's also somebody's workplace. So you need to be extra conscious of safety and liability issues that this situation can present to you, the employer.

Three points that warrant special consideration are

- **Occupational safety and health:** You have a number of specific responsibilities under the terms of the Occupational Safety and Health Act of 1970. Specifically, you're required to provide your employee with a place of employment that's free from recognized hazards that are causing, or are likely to cause, death or serious harm.

  You can find out more about your responsibilities in this area by getting in touch with the U.S. Department of Labor Occupational Safety and Health Administration. Either call your local office (you can find the phone number in the government pages of your phone book) or visit the OSHA Web site at www.osha.gov.

✔ **Worker's compensation:** If your state has a worker's compensation program and domestic workers are required by law to participate in this program, you may have the option of either participating in the state-run program or purchasing a private policy.

You can get the lowdown on the rules in your state by visiting the U.S. Department of Labor Employment Standards Administration Office of Workers' Compensation Programs Web site: `www.dol.gov/esa/owcp_org.htm`.

✔ **Insurance:** You want to be sure that your homeowner's insurance policy and your car insurance policy provide adequate coverage, especially with regard to liability. Obviously, the best time to ensure that you have adequate insurance coverage is before something bad happens, not after the fact, so this detail is one that you definitely want to attend to before your nanny's first day on the job.

Keeping Nanny Happy

After you find the nanny of your dreams (or at least a reasonable facsimile!), you want to do whatever you can to keep her. (You don't want to have to repeat the hiring process anytime soon, do you?) This final section of the chapter talks about what you can do to help your nanny settle into her new job and how you can make the annual performance review process work for — not against — you.

Operation orientation

Although you may *think* that the hiring process is finished the moment the ink dries on the hiring agreement, you still have one important detail to attend to — your nanny's orientation. The following are the key points to cover when your nanny shows up for her first day of work:

✔ **A tour of the premises:** Don't make the mistake of thinking that you only have to give the nanny the grand tour if you happen to live in especially grand surroundings. She needs a tour of the premises even if your estate consists of a tiny one-bedroom apartment. You want to ensure that she knows how to operate the microwave, the dishwasher, and any other appliances that she's likely to need to use during her work day; that she's able to find your child's clothes and toys; and that she knows exactly where you keep the first-aid kit and other emergency supplies.

✔ **A review of daily routines:** Make sure that you take time to go over your child's daily routines: when he likes to get up in the morning, what he likes to eat for breakfast, what types of games he enjoys, and so on. *Hint:* You can make life a lot easier for your caregiver and your child if you jot down the key points for her. That way, she can refer to your notes if she draws a blank and can't remember how your baby's favorite stuffed animal, Mr. Bunny, gets laundered in the event of a diaper explosion!

✔ **A discussion of safety procedures in the home:** Make a point of discussing fire evacuation procedures, reviewing the guidelines for bathtub and swimming pool safety, and passing along other important safety information. *Note:* If you have an infant, also remind her of the importance of following the American Academy of Pediatrics' recommendations concerning safe sleep practices for infants in order to reduce the risk of Sudden Infant Death Syndrome (SIDS).

✔ **Emergency contact information:** Don't worry about coming across as paranoid or overprotective if you point out to the caregiver that you've taped an entire laundry list of emergency contact numbers next to the phone, including your personal cell phone number, your work cell phone number, your office phone numbers, and so on. The nanny will appreciate the fact that you want to make it easy for her to get in touch with you if some sort of a crisis happens. And be sure to update this information on a regular basis — daily even, if your work location changes from day to day. You're not being overprotective — you're being a caring parent and a considerate employer.

✔ **A tour of the neighborhood:** Give the nanny a quick tour of the neighborhood so that she's able to find her way to the local park, the playground, the corner store, and, of course, the hospital. Making sure that she feels at home in her new surroundings, including the community, is important. So make a point of taking the time to help her settle in. It will be time well spent. *Note:* If the nanny will be responsible for driving your child around town, you may want to let her do the driving while you're giving her the grand tour: It'll give you a chance to size up her driving skills and to ensure that she knows how to use your child's car seat properly.

Giving performance reviews

Wondering how often you should review your nanny's job performance?

Many parents who employ nannies find that conducting an initial performance review at the end of the three-month probationary period and then again on the contract renewal date works well. If you haven't signed a formal employment contract with your nanny (see Chapter 9 for more on that subject, by the way), you may want to conduct your nanny's performance review on the anniversary of her hiring date.

And while you're reviewing your nanny's job performance, take a moment to double-check that you're still in full compliance with state and federal employment laws, particularly laws regarding minimum wages and overtime rates. You don't want to find yourself in hot water with the labor department because the wages that you pay your nanny don't meet the legal minimums. *Note:* If the minimum wage rate in your state is higher than the federal minimum wage, you're required to pay the state minimum wage.

Depending on the results of your nanny's annual performance review and what you discover about federal and state minimum wage rates, you may decide to offer your nanny an increase in salary and/or an increase in benefits. Some families find that building bonuses into subsequent contracts works well: for example, having escalating bonuses that kick in as the nanny accumulates each subsequent year of service with the family. Such bonuses not only give her an added incentive to live up to the terms of the contract, but they also reduce the likelihood that the next-door neighbors will be able to lure her away with the promise of an extra $50 per week. (Hey, it happens.)

So, you want to hire a nanny?

The following checklists can help remind you of the various employment-related duties that are associated with employing a nanny.

When you first hire a nanny, you need to . . .

✔ Verify that she can legally work in the United States

✔ Report the fact that you have hired her ("new hire" reporting) to your state employment office

✔ Find out whether she would like you to withhold income tax from her paychecks and, if so, have her fill out a Form W-4 so that you can calculate the appropriate amount

✔ Determine whether you need to deduct Social Security and Medicare taxes from your nanny's paychecks (see Table 11-2, earlier in this chapter)

✔ Determine whether you need to pay the Federal Unemployment Tax (FUTA; see Table 11-2)

✔ Find out whether you need to pay state taxes (call your state tax office for information and assistance)

Each time you pay your nanny, you need to . . .

✔ Withhold Social Security and Medicare taxes (if applicable)

✔ Withhold federal income taxes

✔ Make advance payments of the earned income credit (if she qualifies for this credit)

✔ Keep detailed records of all payroll transactions. According to the IRS, you should record the dates and amounts of each of the following items: your employee's cash and noncash wages; any employee Social Security tax you withhold or agree to pay for your employee; any employee Medicare tax you withhold or agree to pay for your employee; any federal income tax you withhold; any advance Earned Income Credit (EIC) payments you make; any state employment taxes you withhold

By February 1 of the following year, you need to . . .

✔ Obtain an Employer Identification Number (EIN), assuming that you haven't already

✔ Provide your employees with copies B, C, and 2 of *Form W-2: Wage and Tax Statement*

By March 1 of the following year, you need to . . .

✔ Send Copy A of *Form W-2: Wage and Tax Statement* to the Social Security Administration.

By April 15 of the following year, you need to . . .

✔ File *Schedule H (Form 1040): Household Employment Taxes* with your previous year's federal income tax return (Form 1040). Do not use Schedule H if you choose to pay the employment taxes for your household employee with your business employment taxes. Instead, include the Social Security, Medicare, and federal income taxes for the employee on the *Form 941: Employer's Quarterly Federal Tax Return* that you file for your business.

Part IV
Wanted: Part-Time and Occasional Childcare

The 5th Wave   By Rich Tennant

I'd ask you to babysit, but I already have a relative with a bullhorn and experience in crowd control.

In this part . . .

You may want to think of this part of the book as the Child-Care Solutions Department — the place to turn to when you have an odd child-care problem that's causing you major grief. Here you find chapters on lining up backup childcare, finding childcare when you work non-standard hours, and hiring a teenage baby sitter — three perennial hot potatoes in the world of childcare.

Chapter 12

When Plan A Fails: Having a Backup in Place

In This Chapter

▶ Gauging the significance of a child-care Plan B

▶ Determining whether your child is too sick to go to day care

▶ Devising a backup arrangement for when your nanny is ill

▶ Finding solutions for the short- and long-term

Working parents have a Murphy's Law, and it goes something like this: The more critical it is for you to work on any given day, the greater the likelihood that your child will come down with the flu or your nanny or family day-care provider will be called out of town to deal with a family emergency.

These last-minute curveballs can be nerve-racking and frustrating — unless, of course, you have a child-care backup plan in place. For example, if you've already arranged for your mother-in-law to pinch-hit on those days when you find yourself left holding the child-care ball, then what may otherwise be a catastrophic start to your day suddenly becomes a thoroughly manageable hiccup. You simply call upon your child-care fairy godmother (your mother-in-law), call the office to say you'll be a few minutes late, pour an extra cup of coffee while you wait for your mother-in-law to arrive, and then merrily go on with your day. (Or at least that's how it would play out in a perfect world. Things don't always go quite that smoothly.)

This chapter is all about child-care backup plans — why you need one and how you can go about coming up with a virtually foolproof one. (I say virtually foolproof because even if you were to ask an entire team of risk analyst experts to dream up every possible worst-case scenario on the child-care front, they'd be bound to overlook something that could mess up your child-care plans. I'm talking real life after all — and real life *involving small children*, to boot! — not some carefully scripted TV show.)

Realizing Why Every Working Parent Needs a Plan B

Having a child-care backup plan can reap tremendous dividends at home and at work. It minimizes the number of times you have to go AWOL from your job to deal with a child-care crisis, which reduces your stress level at home, too. And, face it: Regardless of what type of childcare you choose to use — in-home childcare, family day care, or center-based childcare — you're going to need to resort to backup eventually.

Kids are sometimes too sick to go to day care

Dealing with sick kids is a fact of life for most working parents. According to the National Association for Sick Child Daycare, more than 350,000 children under the age of 14 are absent from school or childcare each day due to illness.

Your present childcare and the nature of your child's illness determine whether or not it's business as usual on the child-care front or whether you need to move on to Plan B.

Your child-care arrangement

Your child's illness may be no big deal — or it may be a huge catastrophe for you, depending on your child-care arrangement. Consider how a simple outbreak of the chickenpox, for example, can affect your child-care situation when your child is either too sick or too contagious to head to day care.

- ✔ **In-home childcare:** If you have an in-house nanny who is fully immune to chickenpox, you may not experience a lot of childcare-related road bumps as a result of your child's chickenpox outbreak. In fact, you may not notice too much out of the ordinary, except, of course, for the presence of an itchy-speckled person who is about ten thousand times grumpier than usual! Assuming your child doesn't have anything seriously wrong (a few kids end up reacting quite severely to the chickenpox and can become seriously ill, but these cases are quite rare), you may not need to take any time off work. So other than making regular pit stops in the children's department of the library to load up on storybooks and videos to keep your child entertained while she's on the mend, things are likely to be pretty much business as usual for you.

- ✔ **Family day care:** If your child usually attends family day care, you'll no doubt find that she becomes persona non grata the moment she erupts in spots. Even though the chickenpox virus likely has already been shared all around the day care, some family day-care providers prefer that parents keep their kids home when they are clearly ill. If you absolutely have to work that week, arrange for a friend, family member, or healthcare worker to come into your home to care for your child while you go to work or try to find her a space in a sick child day-care center that accepts children with chickenpox. (Not all sick child day-care centers are willing to take kids with chickenpox, so start giving some thought to Plan C, too.)

✔ **Center-based childcare:** If your child's child-care center operates a sick child day-care program as well, and the sick child day-care program is willing to accept children with chickenpox, you don't have a lot of worries on the child-care front. But if, like the majority of parents, you have your child enrolled in a child-care center that isn't able to accommodate children with the chickenpox, you'll need to come up with an alternative child-care arrangement in a hurry — either in-home childcare provided by a friend, family member, or healthcare worker, or center-based childcare in a facility that specializes in caring for sick children and that accepts children with the chickenpox. (I talk more about day-care centers for sick children in the section, "Short-term care options: Pinch-hitting for a day or two" later in this chapter.)

How sick is too sick?

How sick does a child have to be to stay home? That's truly the $10,000 question for every working parent.

You don't want to complicate your life unnecessarily by keeping your child home from day care every time he comes down with a case of the sniffles — nor do you want to earn the ire of the child-care center director (to say nothing of every other parent whose child attends that particular day care) by sending your child to day care while he's a walking-and-talking germ machine.

The following are the key points to consider when you're trying to decide whether sending your child to a group day-care arrangement is okay or whether you'd be better off keeping him home.

✔ **Is your child well enough to participate in the child-care program?** If your child is too tired to participate in the child-care program, think seriously about keeping him home unless the center or family day care is especially equipped to care for mildly ill children. Sending him to day care if all he's really up for is taking catnaps on the sofa at home isn't fair to your child, the child-care provider, or even the other children.

✔ **Is your child's illness contagious?** You won't score too many points with the family day-care provider or the other day-care parents if you spread your child's chickenpox around the day care, so keep your child home (or, failing that, send him to a sick child day-care center instead) if he's come down with some sort of contagious illness. (*Note:* If you're not sure what types of illnesses are contagious and at what points a child is infectious, see Table 12-1.)

Table 12-1   Sick Kids and Day Care: When to Send Them to Day Care and When to Keep Them Home

Type of Illness	Symptoms	How It's Transmitted	Is It Okay to Send Your Child to Day Care?
Respiratory and related conditions			
Bronchiolitis	Starts out like the common cold, but after a few days, coughing, wheezing, and breathing difficulties may occur; irritability and difficulty eating are also common	Bronchiolitis is caused by a virus that results in the swelling of the small bronchial tubes, and it can be transmitted through exposure to someone with an upper respiratory tract illness.	Bronchiolitis is spread easily through saliva and mucus, so keep your child home until she is feeling better.
Common cold	Fever, runny nose, and a small amount of coughing	The common cold is caused by a respiratory virus that is spread from person to person via airborne droplets containing the virus or via contaminated hands and/or objects.	The common cold is most infectious from one day before until seven days after the onset of symptoms, so chances are the germs have already been shared around the day care by now. You can send your child to day care as long as she's feeling well enough to participate in the program.
Croup (Laryngotracheitis)	A fever and/or a cough that resembles a seal-like bark	Croup can be spread from person to person via airborne droplets containing the virus or via contaminated hands and/or objects.	Children with croup are most contagious during the early days of illness. Keep your child home while her symptoms are most severe and only send her back to day care when she feels well enough to fully participate in the program.
Ear Infections	Earache, irritability, fever and cold symptoms	Ear infections aren't infectious.	Your child can go to day care as long as she's feeling well enough to participate in the program.
Influenza	Fever, chills, and shakes; extreme tiredness or fatigue; muscle aches and pains; and a dry, hacking cough	Influenza (or the flu) is caused by a respiratory virus that is spread from person to person via airborne droplets containing the virus or via contaminated hands and/or objects.	Your child is unlikely to feel well enough to participate in the day-care program, so keep her home until she starts feeling better.

Type of Illness	Symptoms	How It's Transmitted	Is It Okay to Send Your Child to Day Care?
Pink eye (Conjunctivitis)	Redness, itching, pain, and discharge from the eye	Pink eye is spread from person to person as a result of direct contact with secretions from the eye. Excessive eye rubbing, allergies, viruses, or bacteria can also trigger it.	Pink eye is contagious for the duration of the illness or until 24 hours after antibiotic treatment has been started. (If your child's eye discharge is yellowish and thick, ask your doctor for a prescription.) Don't allow your child to return to day care until she's been taking her antibiotics for at least 24 hours, or she could spread the pink eye to other children.
Strep throat	Sore throat, fever, and swollen glands in the neck; if a skin rash is also present, the illness is known as scarlet fever	Strep throat is a bacterial infection that is transmitted via airborne droplets and/or by touching contaminated objects.	Strep throat is contagious until 24 to 36 hours after the start of antibiotic treatment, so your child won't be able to attend day care during that time. She won't be able to go back to day care until she's feeling well enough to participate in the program.
Tonsillitis	Fever, swollen glands under the jaw, a very sore throat, cold symptoms, and abdominal pain	Tonsillitis can be bacterial or viral in origin.	If your child's doctor prescribes antibiotics, keep your child home from day care for at least 24 hours after the antibiotics have been started. Keep her home a few days longer if she's not feeling well enough to participate in the program.
Whooping cough	Cold-like symptoms that linger; about two weeks into the illness, the cough suddenly worsens; when the child coughs, thick mucus is dislodged, causing the child to gasp — or whoop — as she tries to breathe; she may turn red in the face during the cough and then vomit afterward	Whooping cough is spread through airborne droplets or by touching contaminated objects. Children without symptoms can spread the infection.	Whooping cough is contagious for up to three weeks after the start of the cough or up to five days after antibiotics have been started. Keep your child home until she has received five days of antibiotic treatment, assuming she's feeling well enough to return to day care at that point.

(continued)

Table 12-1 *(continued)*

Type of Illness	Symptoms	How It's Transmitted	Is It Okay to Send Your Child to Day Care?
Fever			
Fever	A fever may indicate the presence of an infection	A fever is not infectious.	If your child's fever is mild, and she's feeling well enough to participate in the program, sending her to day care is okay.
Gastroenteritis			
Gastroenteritis (infection caused by camploybacter, E. coli, shigella, or viral infections)	Poor appetite, vomiting, stomach cramps, bloody or watery diarrhea	Gastroenteritis is spread through contact with the stool of an infected person or by consuming contaminated food, milk, or water. It can also be spread through poor hygiene.	Gastroenteritis is contagious when symptoms are present. Keep your child home until the diarrhea has stopped and all stool tests are negative.
Skin and scalp conditions			
Chickenpox	A rash with small blisters that develops on the scalp and body and then spreads to the face, arms, and legs over a period of three to four days; other symptoms include coughing, fussiness, loss of appetite, and headaches	Chickenpox is caused by a viral infection that is spread from person to person through direct contact with an infected person. The incubation period is two to three weeks.	Chickenpox is contagious from two days before to five days after the rash appears, so keep your child home during this time.
Fifth disease	A rash on the face that is accompanied by a red rash on the trunk and the extremities; child may also have a fever and sore joints	Fifth disease is caused by a viral infection (human parvovirus B19) that is spread via exposure to airborne droplets from the nose and throat of infected persons.	Fifth disease is most contagious during the week before the appearance of the rash. By the time the rash has shown up, your child is unlikely to be contagious. Your child may not feel well enough to go to day care while the illness is at its most severe, but

Type of Illness	Symptoms	How It's Transmitted	Is It Okay to Send Your Child to Day Care?
			after she starts to feel better, she can return to day care.
Head lice (pediculosis)	Itchy scalp, the presence of either live *lice* (wingless insects that crawl into the hair) or *nits* (tiny egg-shaped deposits that are firmly attached to the hair)	Head lice are spread via direct head-to-head contact or by sharing items of clothing such as hats.	Head lice are contagious until the child's head has been treated with an anti-lice shampoo. Keep your child home until you've started the treatment.
Impetigo	A rash featuring oozing, blister-like, honey-colored crusts that may be as small as pimples or as large as coins	Impetigo is contagious until the sores are dry. It can be spread through contact with the sores. The infection can then be spread to other parts of the body by the child's fingers.	A child can return to day care after antibiotic treatment has commenced (oral antibiotics or antibiotic ointment) and the sores have dried out.
Red measles	Initial symptoms include a fever, cough, red eyes, runny nose, red spots in mouth, and swollen neck glands; then a blotchy red rash spreads from face to neck to body over a three-day period	Red measles are spread via direct or airborne contact with saliva, phlegm, or contaminated objects.	Your child is contagious from four days before until four days after the rash appears. She can return to day care any time after the fourth day after the rash appears, provided she feels well enough to participate in the program.
Rubella (German measles)	Mild fever, headache, cough, red eyes, runny nose, swollen glands at the back of the neck, a mottled or raised red rash that spreads from the face to the neck over a 12- to 24-hour period	Rubella is spread through direct contact with phlegm, saliva, or contaminated articles.	Rubella is contagious from seven days before until four days after the rash appears. Your child should stay home from day care for a full seven days after the rash appears and avoid having any contact with any non-immune pregnant women, including substitute child-care providers.

Source: The Mother of All Baby Books *by Ann Douglas (John Wiley & Sons, 2002). See* www.themotherofallbooks.com.

Nothing to sneeze at

According to the National Association for Sick Child Daycare, working mothers miss between 5 and 29 days of work each year because of the need to stay home to tend to sick children — something that represents an annual cost to U.S. employers of between $2 and $12 billion.

If your child is already being cared for at home, you don't have to worry about spreading your child's illness to other children, but you still need to consider your nanny's health and well-being. If your child has an active outbreak of scabies or some other highly unpleasant infectious disease, give the nanny time off with pay until the outbreak is under control.

Caregivers may have extenuating circumstances

Of course, your child isn't the only one who may end up going AWOL from childcare on occasion. Your nanny or family day-care provider may also end up needing to wave the white flag from time to time.

In the following list, I explain a few reasons why you may find yourself scrambling to line up backup childcare in a hurry.

- ✔ **A sick kid:** Your family day-care provider may have to close up shop temporarily if she has a sick kid at home. (Hey, if it can happen to you, it can happen to her!) She's likely to keep the day care open if her child is only mildly ill, but she won't be doing you any favors if she allows your child to come into contact with her sick child. (Of course, nannies can find themselves being hit with the proverbial sick-kid curveball, too. So don't assume that having an in-home child-care provider will necessarily get you off the hook in this particular department.)

- ✔ **Health problems:** Health problems can be a major wild card for anyone, child-care providers included. If your nanny or family day-care provider were to experience a gallbladder attack or an appendicitis attack that required emergency surgery, she would need to take a few weeks off work to recover. She may also need to take some time off work to get over a particularly nasty flu bug. And because many health problems come on quickly and require immediate treatment, you may have to swing into action mode immediately if your nanny announces that she's scheduled for major surgery.

✔ **Maternity leave:** Your family day-care provider may not have been planning to have any more children when you first enrolled your child in her program, but perhaps she changed her mind along the way (or maybe the Stork managed to track her down). Regardless of the circumstances that led to her pregnancy, she's likely going to need to close up shop for at least a few weeks after she has her baby. (She may keep it open if she has a family member who's willing to fill in for her, but that's highly unlikely. And even if she's kind enough to make this offer, you may not necessarily feel comfortable having a stranger parachuted in to care for your child while the family day-care provider is recovering from the birth.)

✔ **Jury duty:** In a perfect world, nannies and family day-care providers would never get summoned for jury duty. But, they do get summoned, and they're legally obligated to serve on the jury if they make the final cut. Although the vast majority of jury trials are short and sweet, some last for months — even years. (Can you imagine what bad luck it would be to have your nanny selected for an O.J. Simpson-type case? The kids would be practically grown before you ever got her back!)

✔ **A family emergency:** Your nanny or family day-care provider gets a telephone call in the middle of the night to say that her mother has just had a serious stroke. She calls you from the airport at dawn to say that she's hopping the next plane out of town and has no idea when she'll be back. The challenge with this particular situation is that you are unlikely to know what you're dealing with for a couple of days, so you'll basically be treading water until you have a few more facts.

✔ **A household emergency:** A flash flood occurs in early summer and your family day-care provider's basement is flooded with sewage. Her insurance company warns her that it would be unhealthy for her family to live in the house until the house has been properly cleaned and sanitized, so they relocate to a hotel. Obviously, keeping her family day-care business up and running from her nearby hotel room simply isn't an option, so she regretfully informs you that she has to close up shop for the next few weeks.

The only way you can protect yourself from having your childcare disappear in a flash along with your child-care provider is to opt for center-based child-care (see Chapter 6). Although I can still think of a few situations that may cause a child-care center to close its doors with little or no notice — a financial crisis that prevents the day care from making its weekly payroll or a health and safety violation that causes the state health department to revoke its license — these situations are far less common. So if reliability is of paramount importance to you, you may want to go the center-based child-care route. (See Chapter 2 for a detailed discussion of the pros and cons of your various child-care options.)

Putting Your Backup Plan in Place

After you become aware of some of the reasons that you're likely to need a child-care backup plan, you need to come up with a couple of backup plans for your family. I know, I know: I've been leading you to believe that you needed to come up with only a single plan. And if you're blessed with exceptional good luck, that may be all you need.

But if you're like most parents, you probably want to come up with an entire laundry list of arrangements that can work under various types of circumstances: For example, "If the nanny calls in sick on a Monday, I can always call Mom. If it's a Tuesday, I can work from home in the morning and then take the kids over to the neighbor's in the afternoon," and so on. Coming up with a single solution that meets your emergency child-care needs around the clock 365 days a year, after all, is pretty difficult.

And consider this: The backup plan that works perfectly as a short-term care solution may not work out quite so well as a long-term care plan. If your short-term care solution involves calling in favors from friends, neighbors, and relatives, you may soon find yourself with no favors left to call in. (And no friends, neighbors, or relatives who are willing to pick up the phone when you call!) So take time to consider your short-term and long-term child-care needs separately in the following sections. They're two entirely different animals.

Short-term care options: Pinch-hitting for a day or two

Most working parents find themselves in need of short-term backup care every now and again, either because their regular child-care provider is unavailable or because their child is too sick to go to day care. Mull over these tips on coming up with a backup care arrangement that works in both situations.

When your child-care provider is unavailable

The telephone rings at a few minutes past 6 a.m. You groan as you stumble out of bed. Your sixth sense tells you it's your nanny calling to say that she can't make it into work this morning. And today's the day of your annual performance review at work — not exactly the best day to miss work dealing with a child-care snafu.

Brainstorming child-care solutions when you haven't even had your morning cup of coffee is pretty difficult, which is why coming up with your child-care backup plan ahead of time is a good idea. Then you simply make a phone call or two and then calmly go on with your day (and maybe even back to bed for 20 more minutes).

Contemplate these ways you may choose to deal with your need for short-term childcare the next time the need arises:

✔ **Take advantage of any flexible working arrangements your employer has to offer.** If your company allows its employees the option of working from home on occasion or working flexible hours, take advantage of one or both of those options. (Obviously, research your options ahead of time as opposed to in the heat of the moment.)

✔ **Find out if your employer has any emergency child-care spaces available.** Some employers reserve a certain number of emergency child-care spaces in an area child-care center and then make these spaces available to employees who need backup care. In many cases, employers provide these spaces at or below cost — sometimes even for free — so find out what is available through your employer or your partner's employer. (See Chapter 4 for more on how your employer can help to ease your child-care woes.)

✔ **See if a family member is willing to occasionally pinch-hit.** Your retired mom and dad may not have any interest in getting into the child-care business on a full-time basis, but they may be happy to help out on days when your regular child-care provider is unavailable or your child is feeling under the weather. Just make sure you have a rough idea of how available they're likely to be before you assume that they're at your beck and call. If they're busy with volunteer work and other community projects four days a week, you only have a 20 percent chance of them actually being available when you hit the panic button.

✔ **Come up with your own emergency child-care roster.** Maintain a list of family day-care providers in your neighborhood who would be willing to take care of your child if they happen to have a vacancy in their day care on a day when you need care. (***Note:*** Because you can't predict ahead of time who will and won't have a vacancy when the moment of truth arrives, err on the side of caution by having too many rather than too few names on your list.)

✔ **Take a half-day of vacation.** If you're having trouble finding someone who's available to pinch-hit for the entire day, arrange for a friend or neighbor (or your partner, if you have one) to stay with your child during those hours of the day when you absolutely have to be at work. Then take a half-day of vacation to cover the rest of the day.

✔ **Hire a temp through a child-care agency.** I put this option at the bottom of the list, both because it tends to be pricey ($15 an hour with a four-hour minimum is fairly typical) and because many parents don't feel comfortable with the idea of asking an agency to send in a complete stranger to provide emergency child-care for the day. However, depending on your work situation and your degree of family support (or lack thereof!), you may have little choice but to make that call. After all, what are you supposed to do if your child comes down with the chickenpox on a morning when you're scheduled to defend a client in court or perform emergency brain surgery? (Talk about the mother of all dilemmas!)

When your child is ill

Of course, sometimes the situation that has you singing the early morning child-care blues is a situation involving your child rather than your child-care provider: Your child wakes up with a fever and a mysterious looking rash, for example.

If you find yourself in this situation, you have four basic child-care options:

- Arranging for someone to come into your home to care for your child until she is well enough to go back to day care (an option I discuss earlier in this chapter)

- Arranging for a family day care to care for your child (only an option if the family day-care provider can keep a sick child away from the other children and still provide appropriate care and supervision to this child — no easy feat!)

- Arranging for care in the child's own child-care center (only an option if the center has the ability to isolate sick children from the other children)

- Arranging for care in a separate child-care center that specializes in caring for children with minor illnesses (a *sick child day-care center*)

Deciding whether sick child day-care centers are an option

If you decide to go the sick child day-care center route, you may be concerned that such a center could be a breeding ground for disease, which isn't actually the case. Such centers adhere to highly rigorous health practices to prevent the spread of illness. They also restrict themselves to caring for mildly ill children (for example, children with head colds, low-grade fevers, ear infections, and other garden-variety illnesses). If a child develops the symptoms of a more serious illness, the program will probably exclude her.

Here's a list of the types of symptoms and illnesses for which a child would be excluded from a typical sick child day-care center:

- Fever and a stiff neck, lethargy, irritability, or persistent crying
- Diarrhea, which is defined as either
  - Passing three or more loose stools in an eight-hour period
  - Passing more stools than normal
  - Passing watery stools that aren't fully formed
- Exhibiting one or more of the following symptoms:
  - Signs of dehydration
  - Blood or mucus in the stool
  - Diarrhea attributable to salmonella, campylobacter, or giardia

✔ Diarrhea attributable to shigella and E. coli, until the diarrhea has cleared up and two stool cultures taken 48 hours apart each test negative for these two bacteria

✔ Vomiting three or more times

✔ Vomiting accompanied by any signs of dehydration

✔ Infectious illnesses such as *pertussis* (whooping cough), measles, mumps, chickenpox, rubella, or diphtheria during the contagious stages (unless the center can isolate the child from children with other illnesses)

✔ Untreated infestations of scabies

✔ Untreated infestations of head lice

✔ Untreated tuberculosis

✔ Untreated rashes

✔ Abdominal pain (either intermittent or persistent)

✔ Difficulty breathing

✔ Extreme lethargy (the child has no interest in playing)

✔ Undiagnosed jaundice

Sizing up a sick child day-care center

If you're considering using the services of a particular sick child day-care center (which, by the way, are still in relatively short supply, even in major cities), look for evidence that the center is meeting American Academy of Pediatrics, American Public Health Association, and U.S. Department of Health and Human Services recommendations concerning best practices for sick child day-care centers.

Ask the center director these key questions when you're shopping for a suitable sick child day-care arrangement.

✔ **Does your program focus exclusively on providing care to sick children?** If not, what provisions are in place to prevent the other children in the center from becoming ill? If the program provides care to both sick and well children, the sick children should have their own separate space within the facility, and they shouldn't come into contact with healthy children.

✔ **What procedures do you use to prevent the spread of disease?** In addition to looking for evidence that the center director has a solid grasp of routine health and safety procedures, you want to look for evidence that the staff understands the need to be extra rigorous in order to prevent a center-wide outbreak of illness from occurring. For example, any furniture, fixtures, equipment, or supplies that have been used by sick children should be thoroughly cleaned and sanitized before being used by other children.

✔ **Is it possible to keep children with gastrointestinal illness or liver infections from mildly sick children being cared for at the center?** Children who show symptoms of gastrointestinal illness or liver infections should be segregated within the sick child day-care center to prevent the spread of these types of illnesses and infections to children with other minor illnesses (head colds). To reduce the risk that these illnesses will spread from one group of children to the next, staff members shouldn't allow supplies, toys, and equipment to move between the two groups unless these objects have been cleaned and sanitized thoroughly in between uses.

✔ **Are children with chickenpox welcome at the center?** If so, what procedures are in place to prevent the chickenpox from spreading to other children in the center? If the sick child day-care center provides care to children with chickenpox, those children should be cared for in a separate room with an external ventilation system.

✔ **What types of information do you collect from parents when a child is placed in the center?** According to the American Academy of Pediatrics, American Public Health Association, and U.S. Department of Health and Human Services, sick child day-care centers should make a point of collecting the following types of information for each child:

- The child's specific diagnosis and details about how that diagnosis was made (for example, was the illness diagnosed by the parents or by a physician?)

- The current status of the illness, including the potential for the spread of disease, details about any modifications that may need to be made to the child's diet or activity level as a result of the illness, and an assessment of how long the illness is likely to continue

- Details about the child's overall health and any medications the child is currently taking (either at home or at day care)

- Details about how the parents may be contacted to discuss the child's progress during the working day and the name, address, and phone number of the child's primary healthcare provider

You don't have to worry that you're going to spend hours and hours filling out paperwork on your child's first day at the center. Most sick child day-care centers ask parents to pre-register, so most of this health information is already on file. You also need to sign release forms authorizing the center to administer any medications that you have supplied and giving them permission to seek emergency medical assistance for your child if she requires such assistance and you're unavailable.

Of course, caring for the child's physical health is only part of the job. The sick child-care center should also have policies in place that are designed to make the child feel as comfortable as possible while he's spending time at the center. The American Academy of Pediatrics, American Public Health

Association, and U.S. Department of Health and Human Services recommend that sick child day-care centers

- Match each child up with a caregiver who knows the child (obviously, this may not be possible if the center specializes in caring for sick children and this is the first time your family has used the center, but it's a possibility if your child is being cared for at her regular child-care center)

- Ensure that low enough caregiver-child ratios are maintained to allow the child-care provider to provide plenty of individual care and emotional support to the sick child (caregiver-child ratios for children under the age of 2 should be no greater than 1:3 and shouldn't exceed 1:4 for children ages 2 through 6)

Bottom line? You know that you've stumbled upon a truly crème de la crème sick child day-care center if the center staff seems to be every bit as concerned about your child's psychological well-being as they are about his physical health.

When the days turn into weeks or (gulp) months: Longer-term care options

Sometimes your need for backup childcare may extend for weeks or months rather than mere days. If you find yourself in this situation, some of the solutions that may have worked well as a short-term stopgap measure may no longer be options. For example, your employer probably won't let you tie up one of the company's emergency child-care spaces indefinitely or your neighbor who agreed to pinch-hit for you for a couple of hours would want to turn this into a multi-week gig. But, of course, you don't know for sure unless you ask. And when you're searching for childcare, you discover quickly that you don't want to leave any stones unturned.

If you're lucky, you'll have time on your side: The child-care provider can give you the heads-up about her upcoming knee surgery a couple of weeks ahead of time so that you don't have to quickly come up with a suitable backup arrangement.

Assuming you have the luxury of time, consider one of the following options:

- **Hiring a child-care provider through a child-care agency.** Even though you can expect to pay about $15 an hour for childcare that you book through an agency, if you're looking for care for only a week or two, you may decide to bite the bullet and find a way to come up with the necessary cash. If, however, you're going to be in the market for a replacement care arrangement for many weeks or months, this particular option could break the bank pretty quickly.

✔ **Seeing if a family member is available to help you out.** Desperate
times call for desperate measures, so don't be shy about asking family
members if they can help. If you can't get any one person to commit to
pinch-hitting for the entire five-week period that your nanny is out of
town helping her ailing mother to get back on her feet after heart
surgery, then you may need to put together a patchwork quilt of care
arrangements. Perhaps your mother-in-law is available for the first two
weeks, your mother for the next week, and your sister-in-law the following week. That only leaves you with one week to cover on your own by
drawing upon family days and/or vacation days. (Hey, it sure beats kiss-
ing your entire year's vacation goodbye in one fell swoop!)

✔ **Tapping into the child-care grapevine.** Maybe a friend or acquain-
tance knows of someone who is available for a short-term child-care
contract — perhaps a college student who is looking for work or a
stay-at-home mother whose children have just started school full-time
and who is looking for a way to ease back into the paid labor market
gradually. What you want to do is let anyone and everyone in your life
know about your impending child-care crunch. You never know where
the child-care lead of your dreams may come from.

Where things get challenging is if you don't know upfront that your need for
backup care is going to be long-term — if, for example, you're operating
under the assumption that your nanny will be back on her feet within a
couple of days after her wisdom teeth extraction, but she has an allergic reaction to one of the painkillers and ends up having to stay in the hospital for a
week or two. In this case, you're likely to fumble around for a while before
you finally settle on a temporary child-care solution that can meet your
needs until your regular child-care provider gets back on her feet.

Chapter 13

Not Workin' 9 to 5: Childcare during Off-Beat Hours

In This Chapter

▶ Locating childcare when you work evenings, weekends, or overnight shifts

▶ Discovering child-care options for home-based workers

▶ Checking into baby-sitting co-ops, morning-out programs, and other part-time solutions

Finding childcare is tough enough when you work standard hours. Your task is immeasurably tougher if your work schedule is anything but 9 a.m. to 5 p.m. In fact, a study conducted by the Minnesota Department of Children, Families, and Learning revealed that a significant number of parents working nonstandard hours don't even feel that they have the luxury of choice: More than one-quarter of the parents interviewed by the study's researchers revealed that they "had to take whatever child-care arrangement they could get" for their kids. So much for *choosing* childcare.

Although the news is certainly bleak on this particular child-care front, in this chapter, I show you how to make the best of a less-than-ideal situation. I alert you to opportunities when you can modify existing child-care arrangements to meet your family's unique child-care needs and draw your attention to lesser-known forms of childcare that can help chase away some of your child-care worries.

Mr. Saturday Night: Finding Childcare When You Work Nonstandard Hours

Given how tough it is to find anything but 9 a.m.-to-5 p.m. childcare, you'd figure that only a handful of parents required care outside of standard working hours — that most people happily show up for their shifts at the Acme Widget Factory first thing in the morning, put in eight hours, and then arrive home by dinner time that same day. Nothing is further from the truth.

Nonstandard hours have become a fact of life for approximately one in three American families. According to a recent article in the *Journal of Marriage and the Family*:

- ✔ In 31.1 percent of families with children under the age of 14, at least one parent works evening, night, or rotating shifts.

- ✔ In 46.8 percent of families with children under the age of 14, at least one parent works weekend shifts.

What makes the situation even more frustrating is that parents are responsible for finding childcare to accommodate these nonstandard schedules rather than employers, despite the fact that employers are the ones who come up with these schedules. (A recent study conducted by the University of Maryland concluded that when workers agree to work nonstandard hours, they typically do so because their employers have required them to do so, not for reasons of personal choice.)

Like many parents, you may find yourself in need of childcare to cover evening, overnight, weekend, or rotating shifts. In the following sections, I talk about what types of childcare are most likely to meet your family's needs in these particular situations.

Resolving your evening child-care crunch

Most child-care centers and family day cares shut their doors around dinnertime, and most nannies are happily heading home around the same time — something that can leave you feeling like your quest for evening childcare is totally hopeless.

Finding evening childcare isn't hopeless, but it's not a cakewalk either. You want to start by finding out what options are available. Find out if any child-care centers specialize in providing evening childcare. Ask your friends and neighbors if they know of a child-care provider who's willing to do after-hours childcare (or if your friends and neighbors are willing to care for your child while you're at work).

After you size up those alternatives and consider the logistics involved in shuttling your child to day care late in the afternoon and then back home at night after she's fallen asleep, you'll probably decide that having someone come to your house to take care of your child would be a whole lot simpler. (See Chapters 9 and 11 for more on this particular option.)

Having a child-care provider come to your house *is* a whole lot simpler, but this option is also a lot more expensive. Unless, of course, you can find a relative who's willing to give you a break on the price. But when relatives give you a break on the price, a hidden cost can be involved. (See Chapter 10 for more on the sometimes-risky business of hiring relatives to provide childcare for you.)

Finding overnight child-care solutions

If you're in the market for overnight childcare, you're likely going to have to make like Blanche DuBois and learn to rely on the kindness of strangers. (Well, friends and relatives, at least.) Odds are you're going to have to call in all your favors — and then some — to find your way around this particular child-care roadblock.

And what a roadblock it is. Overnight childcare is, without a doubt, the toughest type of childcare to find, unless you luck out and find a child-care center or family day care in your neighborhood that provides overnight child-care. Failing that, you probably have to do what the majority of shift-working parents do: Arrange for someone to sleep at your house on the nights when you're doing the graveyard shift or take your child to a friend's, relative's, or neighbor's house to sleep (a far less attractive alternative, but often your only choice).

If you work for a major company that has a large number of employees on shift, you may want to talk to your company's human resources manager about the challenges you're facing finding satisfactory overnight childcare. The HR manager may be able to provide you with leads on childcare in your community. And who knows? If enough employees raise the issue of child-care, maybe the company will do something about the problem — for instance, contract with an area child-care center to provide overnight child-care services to company employees. Sometimes it pays to speak up! (See Chapter 4 for more on getting your employer to help you resolve your child-care challenges.)

Troubleshooting your weekend child-care headaches

Weekend child-care may be a headache to arrange, but at least you have a few more options available than you do with evening or overnight childcare. In addition to turning to friends and relatives or hiring an in-home child-care provider (see Chapters 9, 10, and 11 for more on these options), you may be able to find a teenager or college student looking to do some childcare on the weekends (see Chapter 14). You may even find a family day-care provider whose husband works weekend shifts and who is happy to work weekends, too. (See Chapter 7 for the do's and don'ts of going the family day-care route.)

What you're unlikely to find is a lot of child-care centers opening their doors on the weekends. Like it or not, most child-care centers are designed to meet the needs of parents who work a standard 9 a.m. to 5 p.m., Monday through Friday, schedule.

Till shift work does us part

Child-care headaches aren't the only problems that shift-working parents have to contend with. According to a study reported in the *Journal of Marriage and the Family,* they're also more likely to end up in divorce court. Researchers at the University of Maryland found that the risk of divorce was six times higher in families with young children when one of the parents in the family worked midnight shifts.

Figuring out what to do about childcare when you work rotating shifts

Rotating shifts can be the most frustrating schedules to accommodate when lining up childcare. Unless you have the world's most flexible and accommodating nanny, friend, relative, or family day-care provider at your disposal, you may end up with a patchwork quilt of child-care arrangements: The arrangement that works the week you're on midnight shifts; the arrangement that works the week you're on evening shifts; and the arrangement that works the week you're on day shifts.

Notice I didn't even mention child-care centers here. I didn't mention them because, unless you're lucky enough to find a child-care center willing to follow your shift schedule to the tee (something that's only likely to happen if your employer's operating or funding the child-care center), you're probably going to be out of luck. Finding a space in a child-care center is hard enough when you work only days, evenings, or nights, let alone all three!

Balancing Deadline with Playtime: Deciding on Childcare When You Work from Home

Whether you're running your own business from home or working for an employer who allows you to work from home on a full- or part-time basis (a working arrangement that is referred to as *telecommuting* or *teleworking*), if you have young children, you need to figure out what you're going to do about childcare.

If *timeshifting* is an option (in other words, doing your work at a different time of day), you may be able to get off scot-free in the child-care department. If, for example, you're hired to write a computer software manual, you could potentially do all the writing at night after your kids are in bed or on weekends when your partner or another relative is available to run interference with the kids, so that you can get some writing done.

However, this strategy works only if you're prepared to stick with a part-time work schedule. Unless you're prepared to burn the candle at both ends, you're going to have a hard time squeezing in a full 40-hour workweek on evenings and weekends. (Remember, you still have to do your regular shift as a parent from 9 a.m. to 5 p.m. — or should I say from 5 p.m. to 9 a.m.!)

Most home-based workers who are running anything but very part-time businesses quickly discover that they're in the market for childcare. The question then becomes which type — an in-home child-care arrangement or an out-of-home child-care arrangement?

Knowing when in-home childcare is your best option

In-home childcare can be the ideal solution if you have a baby and a business to run. You may find that hiring a nanny or arranging for a relative to care for your baby in your home works extremely well so that you can pop out of your office periodically to visit with or feed your baby.

Having your baby just a few steps away can work out particularly well if you're intending to breastfeed. Your child-care provider can come get you when your baby needs to be fed and then take over again when your baby is finished nursing. This arrangement may not work out quite so well, however, if having your baby under the same roof as you is highly distracting (for example, you're so busy listening for your baby's cries that you can't focus on your work).

You and your child may outgrow this particular child-care arrangement when your baby morphs into a toddler. (Hey, sounding professional when you're talking to a client on the phone is hard when a toddler's wailing and pounding on your office door with a toy hammer.) Granted, you can find ways to work around this problem — like moving your office to a part of the house that your toddler can't get to very easily — but that's not possible for every family. Ultimately, you have to decide whether the in-home child-care arrangement that worked so well during your child's baby days is still meeting your family's needs.

Understanding when out-of-home childcare is a better alternative

Some home-based workers choose to go with out-of-home child-care arrangements right from the start. They may anticipate that an in-home child-care arrangement is only likely to meet their family's needs for a relatively short period of time and decide upfront that they want to spare themselves (and their child) the upheaval that goes along with changing child-care arrangements. Or they may simply have a strong preference for out-of-home child-care and decide to go this route right from day one.

You're most likely to gravitate toward an out-of-home child-care arrangement if you feel establishing clear boundaries between your family and your business is important. In other words, you want to be 100 percent in business mode during the day and 100 percent in baby mode when you pick up your child from day care at the end of the day.

Parents who opt for in-home childcare inevitably find that the boundaries are a whole lot blurrier: You're in business mode for a couple of hours, and then you make a quick switch into baby mode over your lunch hour before heading back to work for a couple of hours in the afternoon. (Or until your baby's next feeding.)

There's no right or wrong way to handle the work-family boundary issue. Your decision comes down to personal preference: What feels right to you and what works best for your family and your business? You'll find it easier to decide whether in-home or out-of-home childcare works best for you if you give some thought to the all-important question of boundaries — specifically, how comfortable you are allowing your family life to intrude on your working life, and vice versa. Setting boundaries is by far the toughest aspect of being a home-based worker.

The Perils of Part-Time: Lining Up Part-Time Childcare

Part-time childcare can be surprisingly difficult to find. When you start knocking on doors, you quickly discover that a lot of child-care centers and family day-care providers are unwilling to accept part-timers because of the potential for reduced revenue and because the ever-changing parade of children can make for a chaotic child-care environment. And most nannies and other in-home child-care providers are reluctant to settle for part-time employment when they could be collecting a full-time paycheck somewhere else.

Fortunately, the situation isn't entirely hopeless (although you may feel that way at times). You simply need to know where to find part-time childcare in your community. But before you start searching for part-time childcare, you need to be clear about whether you're looking for regular part-time childcare or occasional part-time childcare. They are two different beasts. In the following sections, I discuss where regular part-time childcare and occasional part-time childcare fit into the child-care universe and what your basic options are for lining up each type of care.

Finding regular part-time childcare

Before I start walking you through the menu of regular part-time child-care options, I want to point out that the term *regular part-time childcare* tends to get used in two entirely different ways:

- **To refer to part-time childcare that occurs on the same day or days each week.** For example, you require childcare for your child every Wednesday, Thursday, and Friday because you have a part-time job in an office and you've been hired to work those three days. Obviously, if your boss suddenly changes your days of employment, you face a major child-care crisis: Your child-care provider may not necessarily be available to care for your child on Tuesdays, even though your employer now needs you to work that day.

- **To refer to part-time childcare that's required on a regular basis, but the actual hours and days of care fluctuate from week to week.** For example, you may require one day of childcare this week, but four days next week. This fluctuating pattern is very common if, like me, you're a self-employed freelance writer. Sometimes the editorial assignments come fast and furious, and you'd benefit from round-the-clock childcare if it were available. And then you have times when the phone stops ringing, your bank account balance goes down, and you can afford to pay for only a few hours of childcare at a time — enough hours to allow you to send out some more story pitches and book proposals, thereby generating more work for yourself, and hence, the need for more childcare.

Not surprisingly, lining up regular part-time childcare is a lot easier when your child-care needs fall into the first category: You contract to purchase so many hours of childcare per week, and the days and hours of childcare remain consistent from one week to the next. Finding a child-care provider who's willing to take you on if you're not sure how many hours of childcare your family will require from week to week is a lot tougher. What follows is a bird's-eye view of your basic options in each situation.

When the days and hours of care remain consistent

You'll have the most luck finding childcare that meshes with your family's schedule if you

- ✔ Find a family day-care provider who accepts part-timers and has a space open on the right days of the week

- ✔ Hire an in-home child-care provider to come to your home on the days of the week when your family needs childcare (something that may appeal to a grandparent who isn't up to caring for her grandchildren on a full-time basis but would love to spend a couple of days with them each week)

If you have to look outside the family for a part-time child-care provider, you may have better luck finding a nanny who's willing to work part-time hours if you arrange to share her with another family so that your two families collectively provide her with full-time employment. Or a family that has a full-time nanny in place may agree to have her watch your child at the times when you need care, as long as you share the cost of those hours. See Chapters 9 and 11 for more about the ins and outs of hiring nannies and other in-home child-care providers.

If you're interested in having your child cared for in a child-care center, you may luck out and find one willing to accept part-timers, but, frankly, this arrangement is a bit of a long shot. Many child-care centers are reluctant to accept part-timers unless they're guaranteed to fill the other half of the child-care space that your family's using on a part-time basis. (If your child requires childcare on Wednesdays, Thursdays, and Fridays, for example, that child-care space doesn't generate any revenue for the center on Mondays and Tuesdays, unless a family needs care for its child on those two days of the week.)

You can overcome this financial hurdle by offering to pay for a full-time space, even if your child only uses it on a part-time basis, but that can be a costly proposition. You can also present the child-care center director with a ready-made child-care solution: For example, show up with a friend or neighbor who's looking for Monday and Tuesday childcare so the center director knows she's able to fill the other half of your child's child-care space.

Just don't be surprised if the center director doesn't go for your proposition. She may be justifiably concerned about what may happen down the road if the other family decides that it no longer needs its half of the child-care space. Who would be responsible for finding another family to fill the other half of the child-care space: the center or you? And the director may simply not want to introduce an extra child into the day-care environment. Imagine how crazy it would be if the day-care staff had to deal with a different mix of children every day because all the children in the center attended on a part-time basis. The director simply may not want to start down what she may see as the slippery slope to total day-care chaos! So go in prepared to make the best possible case for yourself, but just be prepared for the possibility that you'll get a thumbs down nonetheless. (Remember, I told you this one was a long shot.)

When the days and hours of care fluctuate

You know that old expression about finding yourself between a rock and a hard place? Well, that's exactly where you're likely to find yourself when you're looking for regular part-time care if your work hours fluctuate from week to week. Your child-care needs aren't consistent enough for the job to be very appealing for a child-care provider to take on your family as a regular client, yet you need care often enough that you can't meet your child-care needs by begging favors from friends and neighbors. A rock and a hard place indeed.

You may as well scratch child-care centers off the list right away. The vast majority of child-care center directors would look at you like you had horns growing from your head if you told them you wanted to arrange childcare for your child but weren't quite sure what hours of care you'd need from one week to the next. And those directors who *would* give you the time of day are likely to be operating the types of programs that child-care experts advise parents to steer away from: center-based care that operates on a drop-in basis. (Because the group of children attending these programs varies from one day to the next, the atmosphere tends to be much more chaotic than in a program where the staff and children are consistent from day to day and week to week.) So child-care centers really aren't a particularly good option in your situation.

Although you're more likely to find a part-time space for your child in a family day care, you can run into the same difficulty in terms of the quality of care. If the family day-care provider accepts a lot of part-timers, your child can find himself interacting with a different mix of children every day — something that he can find quite disruptive, and that is bound to add to the child-care provider's stress level as well.

Your best bet is to have someone come to your home on the days when you need care or to find another family that is willing to share their nanny. Because in-home childcare is the most expensive type of childcare, if you're picking up the tab for the nanny on your own, you either need to have an above-average income or a friend or relative who's willing to help you out by providing in-home childcare at a bargain-basement rate. (Before you assume that having a relative care for your child is the answer to your child-care prayers, you may want to read Chapter 10. Anyone who's been there can tell you that relative care comes with its own unique sets of joys and challenges.)

Lining up occasional part-time childcare

If you're at home full-time with your children, your needs for childcare may be much more sporadic. Perhaps you like to meet your old college roommate for a kid-free lunch every now and again or enjoy the odd night on the town with your partner. Because it'd be overkill to try finding a space for your child in a child-care center or family day care or to hire a nanny to meet these occasional needs, you're looking at an entirely different child-care menu than parents who need childcare on a day-to-day basis.

Teenage or college-age baby sitters

If you're looking for evening or weekend childcare, a teenage or college-age baby sitter may be your best bet — assuming, of course, you can find one.

Teenage baby sitters seem to be in chronically short supply these days, thanks to increased academic pressures and the need to have a full slate of extracurricular activities to round out that college application — to say nothing of the perennial lure of boyfriends and part-time jobs. But if you can find a reliable teen with an abundance of common sense, she may be the perfect solution to your occasional part-time child-care needs. (See Chapter 14 for more on hiring a teenage baby sitter.)

If you're not too keen on the thought of leaving your kids in the care of someone who's only a few years older than they are, you may consider hiring a college student instead. College students who are enrolled in programs like early childhood education are often eager to earn a few extra bucks while acquiring experience working with young children. Contact the campus recruiting office at your local college to find out how to go about advertising an employment opportunity to their students. Or visit one of the online job boards that specialize in matching up parents in certain cities with college students who are willing to provide child-care services.

Baby-sitting co-ops

If you're looking for childcare during the day, you won't have much luck finding a high school or college student who's likely to be available when you need her, so you may want to consider moving to Plan B — a baby-sitting co-op.

A *baby-sitting co-op* (short for cooperative) is a group of parents who agree to trade baby-sitting services on a non-cash basis. A co-op functions like any other type of bartering system, but, in this case, you and the other co-op members are only swapping child-care services.

Baby-sitting co-ops can also meet your needs for evening and weekend care, so if you're not a big fan of teenage and college-age baby sitters, but you don't have the money in your budget to pay what mature baby sitters typically demand, a baby-sitting co-op may be just what you need.

What makes a co-op more effective than the one-on-one baby-sitting trades that you may otherwise arrange with a friend or neighbor is that you have a much larger pool of potential baby sitters to draw upon, thereby dramatically increasing your odds of finding someone who's available when you need a baby sitter.

The advantages of going the baby-sitting co-op route are as follows:

✔ **You don't have to come up with any cash for childcare — something that can make it possible for you to enjoy a night out with your partner that may otherwise be beyond your financial means.** Instead of coming up with the money to pay a baby sitter, you simply agree to return the favor by providing childcare for another family in the co-op at some point in the future.

✔ **The other members of the baby-sitting co-op are experienced moms and dads.** Therefore, you're less likely to obsess about whether they're going to be able to spot the difference between your baby's I'm-tired-and-fussy cry and his I'm-seriously-ill-and-need-to-go-to-the-hospital-right-now cry — a perennial worry if you're leaving your child in the care of a less experienced baby sitter.

✔ **You have the opportunity to get to know other families with young children in your community.** A co-op provides you with a ready network of friends to turn to for support and information when you're going through a particularly challenging stage with one of your kids.

Of course, joining a baby-sitting co-op can have its downsides, too. You want to take these points into consideration before making your final decision about joining.

✔ **You must be willing to provide childcare to other people's children.** This point may seem painfully obvious, but I thought I'd better state it in black and white so that you're perfectly clear about what you're getting yourself into. If you can barely manage to tolerate your friends' children when you get together for visits, you may want to think twice about volunteering to take care of some other family's anything-but-angelic tribe of wild children. And you can't postpone this responsibility, by the way. Most baby-sitting co-op systems only allow you to go into debt to the system by so many hours before you're expected to start doing childcare for other families.

✔ **You can choose your friends, but you can't always choose the members of your baby-sitting co-op, particularly if you join one that's already up and running.** Personality conflicts tend to crop up in most baby-sitting co-ops, as do disputes about who's under-using or over-using the system. If you don't want to risk getting dragged on some cheesy TV talk show for an episode on "Baby-Sitting Co-ops Gone Bad," then you may want to pass on this particular child-care option.

Make sure you find out right from the start whether baby-sitting co-op members provide baby-sitting services in their own homes, whether they go to the children's home to provide care, or whether the two co-op members negotiate where the care takes place. You may not necessarily feel comfortable having your child cared for in someone else's home, and you may not want to invest the time required to check out the co-op member's home before bringing your child there to be baby-sat. (Remember, this type of childcare is often of the one-off variety. You may spend more time checking out the baby-sitting member's home than she actually spends baby-sitting your child!)

But don't neglect this step. If your child is going to be cared for in someone else's home, you owe it to your child to check it out as thoroughly as you would any other family day-care setting. You want to pay particular attention to

- ✔ **Cigarette smoke:** This is a biggie because second-hand smoke has been linked to an alarming number of childhood diseases, including respiratory illnesses and ear infections.

- ✔ **Diaper odors in the home:** This can be a red flag that the baby-sitting co-op member's sanitation standards may not necessarily be up to snuff.

- ✔ **Clutter and obvious safety hazards:** If toys are on the stairs and lawn darts are in the foyer, you can feel pretty confident that this particular baby-sitting co-op member hasn't got a clue about what it takes to keep kids safe.

- ✔ **Dirt and dust:** If you can write your name on the top of the TV set and your child starts sneezing the moment you walk through the front door, chances are the co-op member's housekeeping standards may not be up to your standards.

- ✔ **Pets that aren't suitable for young children:** You want to be wary of more than just pit bulls, by the way: Iguanas and turtles can spread salmonella to young children, so they're also bad news. You can learn all about the pros and cons of various types and breeds of pets by reading the American Veterinary Medical Association's online pet guide *Caring for Animals: Practical Advice and Considerations*. You can find it online at www.avma.org/careforanimals/animatedjourneys/petselection/consider.asp.

Although the baby-sitting co-op member may not necessarily consider herself a family day-care provider, for all intents and purposes, that's exactly what she is. And she should be held up to the same health and safety standards as any other child-care professional providing care in her own home. (And, of course, you owe it to other parents to hold yourself to the same standards when you're caring for their kids in your home.)

You also want to consider the impact the baby-sitting co-op has on your family. Is your spouse going to be keen on having you baby-sitting someone else's kids on a Saturday night while he stays home with your own kids? Will your kids be happy having to free up some elbowroom around the dinner table so some other kid they don't know (and may not like!) can join your family for dinner? And when it's time to turn the tables and have someone care for your kids, are they going to be thrilled about eating dinner at another family's house or having someone else's Dad tuck them into bed? These are the types of issues you need to consider before signing on the baby-sitting co-op dotted line!

If you're not particularly impressed by the baby-sitting co-op that's up and running in your community, an alternative is available: You can always start your own. Here's what you need to get your co-op off to the best possible start:

✔ **Handpick your members.** If you draw your members from your own circle of friends, you're less likely to end up with members whose parenting philosophies or housekeeping standards are totally incompatible with your own. And if you handpick members from the same geographical area, you save yourself countless hours in the SUV!

✔ **Resist the temptation to get too big too fast.** Ideally, you want to attract between 10 and 20 families to your co-op. If you have fewer than 10 families, people have a hard time finding someone who's available to provide childcare at the time when they need it. And if you have more than 20 families, people won't have the opportunity to get to know one another well.

✔ **Give some thought to how your system will work.** Some systems work on a points system, and others involve the physical exchange of coupons or barter dollars. In this day and age of computers, sometimes the easiest thing to do is appoint one member treasurer and have her track all the transactions on her computer. She can then mail or e-mail monthly statements to each co-op member. (Obviously, you want to compensate her for her time by giving her co-op system credits worth so many free hours of childcare per month.)

✔ **Come up with a rate structure that's simple but fair.** Issues you need to iron out include what rate families with more than one child should pay (for example, do they have to pay four times as much for an hour of childcare as a family with one child?) and whether an extra fee applies if meals are provided.

✔ **Consider charging an annual membership fee to provide the co-op with a bit of cash to cover postage expenses and other incidentals.** Something in the range of $20 to $40 per family per year should be more than enough and may even provide you with a small surplus to help underwrite the costs of an annual family picnic.

✔ **Put your co-op's rules in writing so that everyone is clear about the expectations from day one.** Most baby-sitting co-ops require families who leave the co-op to pay back any child-care hours they owe the co-op in cash. (This hourly rate needs to be spelled out from the start so that people know how much they could potentially be responsible for if they don't do an adequate number of child-care hours.)

✔ **Ensure that the baby sitter receives adequate information about the child she is caring for.** Insist that parents provide the co-op member who's caring for their child with a signed medical consent form and an information sheet about their child (a sheet containing emergency contact information for the parents as well as information about the child's health, food likes and dislikes, allergies, and so on).

✔ **Look for other ways of making your co-op pay off.** Find out whether businesses in your community are willing to offer a special discount to your members — perhaps discounts on children's clothing or children's meals. Offering this kind of membership perk helps you attract and retain members to your co-op, so this venture is definitely worth pursuing. You may have a better chance of negotiating these types of discounts if you join forces with other baby-sitting co-ops in your community. After all, there's strength in numbers.

Morning-out programs

Morning-out programs are free or nearly free programs operated by churches, synagogues, recreation facilities, and other community groups to give stay-at-home parents a bit of a break.

Sometimes morning-out programs are referred to as *drop-in programs,* but if you get word of a drop-in program in your community, make sure that the people operating it are talking about the same thing. Sometimes the term drop-in program is used to describe playgroups in which parents stay with their kids. (This kind of program is all well and good, but it's not going to solve your child-care woes if you're looking for someone to take care of your child for a couple of hours while you get a root canal.) And sometimes the term drop-in program is used to describe childcare in a child-care center that is offered to parents on an as-needed basis (and usually for a hefty fee) — something different yet again.

Most morning-out programs take children for only a couple of hours at a time, and you usually have to book a space for your child ahead of time, so make sure you're clear about how the program works. Although morning-out programs work well if you have a child who adjusts well to new situations, it may not be an ideal child-care choice for a child who's slow to warm up to strangers.

If you decide to take advantage of a particular morning-out program, evaluate it ahead of time using the same criteria that you use to evaluate any other center-based child-care arrangement (see Chapter 6). After all, you can't afford to take chances with your child's health and well-being, even if you're leaving her in a particular child-care situation for only a couple of hours.

Friends and relatives

Friends and relatives are another option when you're looking for occasional part-time childcare. Your best friend or your mother may not be available to provide childcare to your children on an ongoing basis, but she may be willing to step in from time to time. Just be aware that all kinds of hidden strings can be attached to using the services of a relative — a topic I discuss at great length in Chapter 10.

Child-care agencies

If all your efforts to find childcare on your own have failed miserably, you may want to consider going the child-care agency route. Most parents consider this option as a last resort because it can be expensive (depending on where you live, you can end up spending as much as $20 per hour to have your child cared for by an on-call nanny supplied by a child-care agency) and because they don't feel comfortable having someone they don't know send a total stranger over to care for their child.

If you do decide to go the child-care agency route, you want to do some digging to make sure that the agency you're dealing with is reputable and experienced and that they carefully screen all of their employees. Otherwise, you'd be just as far ahead flipping open your local phonebook and calling some stranger at random to come over and baby-sit your child. A scary thought, I know.

You also want to find out if you can meet the caregiver ahead of time to see if she's someone both you and your child feel comfortable with. Obviously, this is only possible in situations where you can predict the need for care in advance — like when you're arranging for care while your child recovers from minor surgery, for example. You're unlikely to have the luxury of meeting the child-care provider ahead of time if the first inkling you have that you're in need of her services is on the morning when your child wakes up with the chickenpox!

Although you may be tempted to compromise your standards when you're in the market for occasional childcare because, after all, you're only leaving your child in the care of this particular child-care provider "just this one time," you need to be as vigilant as any other child-care parent. You'd never forgive yourself if something happened to your child because you failed to take the necessary precautions. Your child is counting on you to be vigilant.

Chapter 14

The Baby-Sitters' Club: Finding a Teenage Sitter

Finding a teenage baby sitter has never been easy, but these days it's tougher than ever. Rising academic standards combined with the pressure to participate in the perfect mix of extra-curricular activities so that they'll look sufficiently well-rounded on their college applications means that today's generation of teenagers are busier than ever before — and that's not even factoring in the perennial lure of boyfriends and part-time McJobs. (Things have gotten so bad in my neck of the woods lately that I've been tempted to write to conservation authorities to suggest that they add another item to the endangered species list: the teenage baby sitter!)

In this chapter, I tell you what's involved in finding, interviewing, hiring, and keeping a teenage baby sitter. Assuming, of course, that you choose to go this route. Hiring a teenager isn't necessarily the right child-care choice for every family, as this chapter also explains.

Is a Teenage Baby Sitter the Right Choice for Your Family?

Before you get too far into your search for a teenage baby sitter, you want to make sure that a teenager is what you want. Not every parent feels comfortable leaving her children in the care of a teenager. You're less likely to feel comfortable having your children cared for by a teenager if

✔ Your children are still quite young, and you don't feel comfortable leaving them with someone who may or may not have much hands-on experience with babies and toddlers.

✔ You have a large family — more children than you think a typical teenager is capable of handling alone.

✔ One or more of your children have complex medical needs or behavioral problems that a typical teenager may not know how to deal with.

✔ You simply aren't convinced that the average teenager has the maturity and judgment required to care for other people's children. (Who knows? Perhaps you're having flashbacks to your own teenage years!)

Whether you feel comfortable having your children cared for by a teenager is very much a matter of personal preference. Your best friend may feel comfortable leaving her 6-month old triplets in the care of a 13-year-old, but the family next door may refuse to leave anyone other than an adult relative in charge of its tribe of wild toddlers. What other people's preferences are doesn't matter; you need to know what *you* prefer. And if your mother-in-law starts "tsk, tsking" after you announce your plans to leave your kids with a teenager every Friday night so that you and your partner can indulge in a regular, kid-free meal, ignore her. Clearly, she believes that no one but a graduate of an accredited nanny school should be entrusted with her beloved grandchildren. In this situation, you must find a way to tune out all the conflicting child-care advice that's coming your way and simply go with your gut. With any luck, your gut can offer you plenty of wisdom on the issue of teenage baby sitters.

The Do's and Don'ts of Hiring a Teenage Baby Sitter

You're still with me, so I'm going to make the wild and crazy assumption that you've decided to take the plunge and hire a teenager to baby-sit your kids. Assuming that's the case, be sure to keep these all-important do's and don'ts in mind as you embark on your search for Mary Poppins, Jr.

✔ **Do look for a teenager who has a genuine love of children.** Although all teenagers are motivated to a certain degree by the opportunity to make money, you don't want to hire someone who's hung out her baby-sitting shingle only because she sees an opportunity to make some cold, hard cash. You'll feel a whole lot better about leaving your kids in the care of a neighborhood teen if she happens to mention that she has her heart set on a career in teaching or pediatric medicine.

✔ **Do make common sense one of your key criteria.** Predicting what strange curve balls the baby sitter may have to deal with while holding down the fort is hard, so you want to feel confident that she knows what to do in a variety of circumstances: for example, when she's confronted with a baby with a leaky diaper, a toddler who just ate a crayon, or a preschooler who thinks saying "pee" and "poo" every 30 seconds is hilarious.

✔ **Don't hire the baby sitter across the street for the sake of convenience.** Sure, not having to drive the baby sitter halfway across the planet after you've just enjoyed a romantic night on the town with your sweetie is nice, but you can't hire just anyone simply because she has the right address. (Can you imagine the outcry in your workplace if your boss used a similar hiring criteria? "Yeah, we know she's not particularly qualified, but she lives right across the street.") So check her qualifications before you get too hung up on the whole convenience factor. Leaving your children in the care of an unqualified, albeit nearby, teenage baby sitter simply for the sake of avoiding a late-night trek across town isn't worth it.

✔ **Don't skip the usual reference checks simply because you've known the would-be baby sitter's parents forever.** You're not hiring the parents to baby sit: You're hiring their kid! And you need to be similarly thorough about carrying out reference checks on teenagers who come highly recommended by a trusted friend or someone else whose opinion you value greatly. Glowing personal recommendations may carry a lot of weight, but they don't eliminate the need to check the teenager's references in a standard, business-like manner.

✔ **Don't lose sight of the fact that you're dealing with a teenager.** Even if you're lucky enough to find the most mature, considerate, and reliable 16-year-old on the planet (for example, a girl who turns down a date on New Year's Eve with the guy of her dreams simply because she'd already promised your family that she'd baby sit for you that night!), she's still just 16. So don't plan to leave her alone with your triplet 3-month olds while you're attending an out-of-town wedding. Most 40-year-olds are overwhelmed, exhausted, and more than a little freaked out at the prospect of taking care of three tiny babies, so don't expect an adolescent who may have little experience with babies to magically rise to the occasion.

Landing the Best Baby Sitter

Up until now, I've been talking a lot about the theory of what constitutes the perfect baby sitter. Now it's time to switch into action mode.

Basically, three phases are involved in finding a teenage baby sitter:

- ✔ **The search phase:** When you ask friends and neighbors for referrals

- ✔ **The interview phase:** When you interview the teenager to see whether she has what it takes to be a good baby sitter

- ✔ **The hiring phase:** When you help the teenager settle into the job, and then do what you can to ensure that she sticks around for the long-term

If you're lucky, you whiz through the phases relatively quickly. (For example, a friend lets you know how pleased she is with her new baby sitter and passes along the baby sitter's name. You call the baby sitter and arrange to interview her, and before you know it, you and your partner are enjoying a kid-free dinner in a restaurant that actually features something other than chicken nuggets on the menu!)

If you're not quite so fortunate (for example, your child-care fairy godmother has taken the month off), you can find yourself embroiled in quite a lengthy search before you find a teenager who's suitable and available. (Finding a teenager who is suitable *or* available is pretty easy, but finding someone who's suitable *and* available requires a bit more child-care sleight of hand!)

The search phase: Asking friends and neighbors for referrals

Finding a teenage baby sitter can be a major challenge, depending on where you live. If you're fortunate enough to live in a neighborhood that's positively overflowing with teenagers eager to make a buck, finding a teenager who's looking for work may be relatively easy. But if you live in an area where few teenagers are around, you need to ask friends, neighbors, and anyone you know who works with teenagers for leads on possible baby sitters.

In particular, you may want to ask the following people whether they know any teenagers who are looking for baby-sitting gigs:

- ✔ The instructor of the local baby-sitting or teen first-aid course (check your local phone book or call your local Red Cross for leads)
- ✔ High school teachers
- ✔ The head of the career-counseling department at your local high school
- ✔ Coaches of high-school sports teams
- ✔ Youth-group leaders
- ✔ Members of the clergy

Some parents have resorted to highly creative recruitment methods — like hanging out at the neighborhood swimming pool and approaching suitably wholesome-looking teens. ("Fifteen years ago I was trying to meet guys at the pool," quipped one mother to a reporter from *The Christian Science Monitor.* "Now I'm trying to meet baby sitters.")

If you don't have any luck finding a teenager, you may want to cast your net a little wider and consider recruiting a college student instead. You may have to offer a slightly higher hourly wage, but you're likely to attract a more experienced and mature applicant. If you're interested in hiring a college student, you may want to advertise your job vacancy through the recruitment office of your local community college or through an online recruitment firm that specializes in matching up parents who are looking for baby sitters and college students who are looking for part-time child-care work. See Chapter 13 for more part-time child-care solutions.

The interview phase: Talking to potential baby sitters

After you manage to track down a lead on a teenage baby sitter, seize the moment and schedule an interview as soon as possible. If you allow the baby sitter to languish by the phone too long, odds are some other family will get wind that she's available and snap her up.

When you're setting up a time to do the interview, be sure to pick a time when both you and the kids will be home. After all, one of the most important things you're sizing up during the interview is how well the baby sitter relates to your kids. If the kids hate her from the moment they first lay eyes on her and the feeling appears to be mutual, you want to scratch her off the baby-sitter list right from the get go.

But assuming she manages to make it through the world's toughest pre-screening team (that's your kids, by the way!), you're all set to plunge into the interview. Here are the types of questions you want to ask and the types of answers you should be seeking in response:

- **How old are you?** Although you can land yourself in major hot water if you ask this particular question during a standard employment interview, nothing's stopping you from asking a teenage baby sitter her age. This information is valuable to have because it gives you a rough indication of the baby sitter's maturity level: A typical 17-year-old is generally light years ahead of your average 13-year-old in the maturity department. Of course, as with anything else in life, there are always exceptions. Some kids behave considerably more or less maturely than their age indicates. So be on the lookout for other evidence of the baby sitter's ability to cope with whatever curve balls may come her way during a typical evening of baby-sitting duty. For example, if your 3-year-old suddenly upchucks the entire contents of his spaghetti dinner, would she attempt to comfort him and then put in a call to you — or would she run from the house screaming at the first sign of vomit, convinced she was about to experience a real-life reenactment of one of the scarier scenes from *The Exorcist?*

- **Have you taken a baby-sitting course?** Because teenagers today typically have a lot less hands-on experience in caring for younger siblings than teenagers did a generation ago, baby-sitting courses have emerged as a modern-day substitute for the poor, unfortunate younger sibling who often served as the baby-sitting training ground in days gone by. Most baby-sitting courses feature fairly rigorous curriculums that touch on everything from first aid to child development to pediatric nutrition to CPR, so finding out whether the prospective baby sitter has done her homework by getting the necessary training is definitely worth it.

- **What other baby-sitting experience have you had?** Finding out how much baby-sitting experience the prospective baby sitter has — whether she's an old hand at caring for young children or whether this is the first time she's ever been in charge of anyone other than her own siblings — is important. And while you're inquiring about her past baby-sitting experience, you also want to find out what ages of children she's baby-sat in the past. After all, there's a world of difference between caring for one slightly bookish 8-year-old and a set of highly rambunctious 2-year-old twins!

- **What is the longest time you've ever baby-sat in one stretch?** You need to know whether the baby sitter is likely to wave the white flag after an hour or whether she's likely to have plenty of stamina to get through the entire day. Novice baby sitters are often surprised just how much energy it takes to care for kids — particularly very young children. You want to make sure she's up for the job.

✔ **What would you do if my 3-year-old started crying for me while I was gone?** This question tests the teenager's creative thinking abilities and her knowledge of child development. If she has a bunch of creative — and age-appropriate — ideas about how she would deal with the problem, you've probably lucked out in the baby-sitter department. If, on the other hand, she can't come up with any ideas at all or her ideas demonstrate an extraordinary lack of judgment, you may want to go back to pounding the child-care pavement.

✔ **What is the most difficult situation you've ever encountered while you were baby-sitting, and how did you handle it?** This question is one that everyone dreads during job interviews — but it can be remarkably revealing to potential employers. What you're looking for here is evidence that the baby sitter was able to act maturely and decisively when faced with a particular challenge, and that her response was pretty much what you'd hope for (for example, she neither under- nor over-reacted).

✔ **My 10-year-old insists that he doesn't need a baby sitter anymore. How would you convince him to cooperate if we were to hire you?** You want to see evidence that the teenager understands the sensitivity of this particular situation (it's normal for a 10-year-old to question the need to be baby sat when he sees himself as completely grown up!) and has a concrete game plan in mind — perhaps taking your child to area attractions where he wouldn't otherwise be allowed to go on his own so that he reaps some sort of benefit from being baby sat.

✔ **Do you have a driver's license?** You may not necessarily be keen on allowing a teenage baby sitter to chauffeur your children around town in your car — or, even worse, the rust-bucket that may qualify as her own means of transportation. But when the baby sitter has her own set of wheels, she can get herself to and from your house on the nights when she's baby sitting for your family. Having to pick up the baby sitter when you're trying to get ready for a night on the town and then drive her home after you get home can turn into a major headache — and this task may be a logistical near impossibility if you're a single parent. If you do allow her to drive your kids around town, you definitely want to give her an unofficial driver's test to ensure that her driving skills measure up to your exacting standards. So ask her to take you for a spin around the block to see how well she does at abiding by the rules of the road. You can't afford to take chances where your children's safety is concerned.

✔ **Are you available to baby-sit on weekdays?** Some teenagers are understandably reluctant to baby-sit on weekdays when they're likely to be busy with schoolwork and extracurricular activities. Finding out upfront whether the teenager you're thinking of hiring is only available on Saturday nights or whether you can count on her to stay with your kids in the middle of the week while you attend your Wednesday-evening fitness class is important.

✔ **How late are you available to baby-sit?** If the teenager you're thinking of hiring plays on a sports team that practices at 6 a.m. on a Sunday morning, you may find yourself saddled with an 11 p.m. curfew. If you think that's overly confining (after all, you'd have to commit to taking in the early show rather than the late show at the movies), then you need to find a baby sitter who can stay out a little later.

✔ **Do you know anyone else who may be able to fill in for you on nights when you're busy?** Because teenagers tend to lead very busy lives, asking whether she can provide her own backup — perhaps pass along the name of a sibling or a cousin who also does some baby sitting — is always worth it. Of course, you still need to arrange to interview the backup baby sitter to see whether she makes an acceptable substitute, but this situation is better than going back to the drawing board entirely.

✔ **What do you charge?** Do your homework ahead of time so that you know if the rate the baby sitter quotes you is what you'd expect to pay — or whether she's simply a pig-tailed, underaged extortionist! Assuming you're willing to pay her what she's asking, find out whether she's willing to accept checks or whether she's a cash-only kind of gal.

The hiring phase: Helping the teenage baby sitter learn the ropes

You can get your relationship with the new baby sitter off to the best possible start and increase the likelihood that she'll be willing to baby-sit for your family for the long-term by helping her ease into her new job. Adopting the following four-part strategy will probably work well for your family and the new baby sitter:

✔ Schedule a dry run

✔ Make your baby sitter feel welcome

✔ Go over the ground rules with the baby sitter and the kids

✔ Let your teenage baby sitter know how much you appreciate her

Scheduling a dry run before you exit stage left

One of the best ways to see whether a particular teenager is up to the challenge of baby-sitting for your family is to schedule a dry run on a day when you're going to be at home anyway. You can hire her to entertain your child while you do some chores that are more easily done without a baby or toddler underfoot (think house painting!) or while you enjoy a bit of uninterrupted time to yourself (a very rare commodity for any parent with young children, as you know).

Go this route only if you can take a step back and let the baby sitter do her job. If you're going to second-guess her every decision or bark out orders from the next room at every opportunity, you'll merely drive her crazy and undercut her authority in the eyes of your children. If you know in your heart that you don't have what it takes to let the baby sitter take over while you're at home, arrange for someone else to be on hand for the baby sitter's dry run and meet a friend for coffee. Perhaps your partner or your mother may be a little more inclined to simply let the baby sitter get on with the show!

Making the baby sitter feel welcome the first night

If you did much baby-sitting during your own teenage years, you no doubt have fond memories of those families who went out of their ways to make you feel welcome. Perhaps they made a point of having your favorite flavor of pop on hand, or they simply let you know that you were welcome to listen to their Madonna albums after the kids were in bed. (Grown-ups who actually understood your obsession with the Material Girl? What could be cooler than that?!!)

Well, now you can return the favor by making the next generation of teenage baby sitters feel welcome in your home. You can do something as simple as tipping off the baby sitter to the location of your diet cola stash or letting her know that she's welcome to flip through — even borrow! — back issues from your *Rolling Stone* magazine collection. (Just not any of the issues featuring interviews with Madonna. Some things are sacred, right?)

Setting ground rules for the baby sitter and the kids

Kids are notorious for trying to con the baby sitter the moment their parents pull out of the driveway. So do the baby sitter (and yourself) a favor by briefing her on your family's ground rules before you leave.

At a very minimum, make sure that the baby sitter knows

- ✔ Where you have written down your emergency contact information (on the refrigerator door or beside the phone)

- ✔ Where the telephones are located and (in the case of particularly high-tech telephone models) how they work

- ✔ How to arm and disarm the home security system and what to do if it goes off accidentally (for example, should she call the security firm, the police department, or both?)

- ✔ Where the first-aid kit, fire extinguisher, flashlight, and spare house-keys are kept

- ✔ Where the water shut-off valve and fuse box are located

- ✔ What you want her to do if the smoke detector or the carbon monoxide detector goes off

✔ How to administer any medication that your child may require (for example, injectable ephedrine for an allergic reaction)

✔ What parts of the house are baby-proofed and what parts of the house are entirely off-limits to your kids

✔ Where your child's bedroom is located and what the baby sitter needs to know about her bedtime routine to get her to settle down to sleep (for example, how many stories you typically read to her, what time she gets tucked in, and so on)

✔ Where your baby's diapering supplies are kept, what she should do with wet and soiled diapers, and where she can wash her hands

✔ Where the kitchen is located and which foods she and your children are welcome to eat while you're out

✔ How to feed an infant (for example, propping up a bottle for an infant is unsafe, and babies should never be allowed to take food of any sort to bed)

✔ Why supervising young children while they're eating is important and what to do if a child chokes

✔ Which household appliances she's allowed to use while you're out and how they work

✔ What you want her to do if you're delayed in traffic or unable to make it home on time (you want to make sure that she realizes that she needs to stay with your child until you get home or get in touch with the person who you've indicated can assist her in such an emergency — perhaps your child's grandmother)

✔ A bit about your child's likes and dislikes so that she doesn't inadvertently serve up your 2-year-old's most hated vegetable for dinner

✔ Your family's rules about having friends over when you're out (both your children's friends and the baby sitter's friends)

✔ How you feel about her talking on the phone while you're out (you probably don't have a problem with her making the occasional short phone call, but you don't want her to tie up the phone line the entire time you're gone, nor do you want to encourage her to spend all her time gabbing on the phone and ignoring your children)

✔ Your family's TV rules (what shows your kids are allowed to watch and how much viewing time they're allowed)

✔ Your family's video-game rules (which games are acceptable for which kids and how much time they're allowed to play)

✔ Your family's Internet rules (whether you allow your kids on the Internet and, if so, what types of Web sites they're allowed to visit and what other types of activities they're allowed to engage in online)

Do what some other parents do: Summarize this information in a baby-sitter binder. With this binder, you can record in one central place all the information you need to pass along to the baby sitter every time she comes over. If the baby sitter forgets how to operate your microwave oven when she needs to make lunch for your toddler, she can flip open the baby-sitter binder and follow the simple instructions that you've written out. The alternative — scrawling the important information on a scrap of paper that immediately gets turned into a paper doll by your craft-obsessed 2-year-old — doesn't work nearly as well.

You'll probably find that having two types of pages in your baby-sitter binder works best:

- ✔ Permanent pages that remain in the binder at all times

- ✔ Temporary pages that get replaced with new information every time the baby sitter comes over

As a rule, you want your permanent pages to contain the following types of information:

- ✔ Your street address

- ✔ Basic instructions on how to get to your home (something that's particularly important if you live in a rural area)

- ✔ Your home phone number

- ✔ Your cell phone number

- ✔ Emergency contact information for the ambulance, fire department, police, poison control center, and other emergency services in your area

- ✔ The name and phone number of a neighbor or other trusted adult who the baby sitter can turn to for assistance in the event of an emergency

- ✔ Details about any allergies or medical problems your child is currently experiencing, as well as the specifics about any medications she's currently taking:

    - • The name of the medication

    - • How often the medication is to be administered

    - • How much of the medication is to be administered each time

    - • Information about any possible side effects

- ✔ A consent form signed by the parents authorizing the baby sitter to administer medication to your child

✔ A consent form signed by the parents authorizing the baby sitter to seek emergency assistance on your child's behalf if you are unavailable

✔ The name and phone number of your child's doctor

✔ The full names and birth dates of each of your children and their medical insurance numbers (information the baby sitter's likely to need in the event of a medical emergency)

The temporary pages in your baby-sitter binder should contain the following types of information:

✔ Details about where you're planning to spend the evening and how you can be reached while you're out (for example, the name and phone number of the restaurant you're dining at, the name and phone number of the friends' house you're dropping by afterwards, your cell phone number, and so on)

✔ Details about any medications your child is taking on a short-term basis (for example, if he's currently taking any antibiotics to help clear up a sinus infection)

✔ Details about any visitors, phone calls, or deliveries you're expecting

✔ Details about any special arrangements the baby sitter needs to know about (for example, "Kira has a soccer practice at the park down the street at 7 p.m.")

You can turn your baby-sitter binder into a two-way communication tool by adding some blank pages for your baby sitter to record phone messages and other important bits of information. (The baby sitter can use these pages to leave you a note reminding you of an upcoming exam schedule at school and the fact that she's unavailable to baby sit the weekend before her big math exam.)

Some families also leave a small amount of cash in a plastic pouch in the back of the baby-sitter binder in case the baby sitter needs an emergency cab fare or some other small amount of cash.

Showing your appreciation for your teenage baby sitter

Competition for teenage baby sitters can be fierce — so fierce that you may be reluctant to pass your baby sitter's name on to even your very best friend for fear that your friend may lure your baby sitter away with a juicier hourly wage. (In this case, you won't just be in the market for a new baby sitter, you'll be looking for a new best friend, too!)

Although your odds of holding on to a particular teenage baby sitter indefinitely are pretty much slim to none (as the years go by, she's likely to be lured away by a better-paying part-time job or find that her evenings and weekends get increasingly busy with boyfriends, schoolwork, and other academic and social demands), you'll want to do what you can to keep her working for your family as long as possible. (Not only are teenage baby sitters a major headache to replace, but also if the baby sitter has been baby sitting for your family on a regular basis, odds are your kids have become quite attached to her by now.)

Here are few tips on keeping your teenage baby sitter happy over the long-term:

- **Be prepared to hold up your end of the bargain.** This may seem like a total no-brainer, but sometimes parents fail to honor their commitments to their teenage baby sitters — something that can result in an immediate blacklisting from every teenage baby sitter on the block! If you book a teenage baby sitter for a particular evening, stick to the hours you've contracted her for rather than calling her midway through the evening and telling her that you're going to be late: She may have already made plans to go out with other friends after her baby-sitting shift is finished. And if you book her services but have to cancel at the last minute because one of your kids just came down with the flu, pay the baby sitter anyway: She's just lost out on an evening of baby sitting (and consequently income) through no fault of her own.

- **Don't expect your baby sitter to extend you a line of credit.** Be prepared to pay your baby sitter in cash when services are rendered — at the end of each evening. Paying your baby sitter by check is only acceptable if she's already indicated to you that she's willing to accept that method of payment, otherwise, you may be creating a major inconvenience for a kid whose bank may be halfway across town.

- **Don't cheap out when paying your baby sitter.** Pay your sitter well. Do an informal survey of family members and friends to get the lowdown on what they're paying their own sitters and offer at least the going rate. If your wages are rock-bottom, you risk having your baby sitter lured away by another family who's willing to pay her what she's worth.

- **Offer your baby sitter a raise from time to time.** Your baby sitter is much more valuable to your family now that she's mastered your family's routines and learned how to deal with your child's little idiosyncrasies (for example, his insistence that the person tucking him in kisses his teddy bear goodnight, too). So make sure the wages you're paying her reflect her true value to you. If you haven't given her a salary increase since the day she started working for your family, she's probably overdue for a raise.

- **Be prepared to work around your baby sitter's schedule.** Your teenage baby sitter may have to drop off the face of the earth momentarily during certain times of the year — like when she's in the middle of exams or her basketball team is blazing toward glory in the playoffs. Don't give her the gears if she has to take a couple of weeks off every now and again. Otherwise, she may decide baby sitting for you isn't worth the hassle.

✔ **Keep your baby sitter gainfully employed.** The teenager who makes it possible for you to enjoy that sanity-saving evening out with your partner or your best friend is less likely to succumb to the pressure to take a job at a convenience store if you're giving her a steady stream of hours and income. If, on the other hand, you only call to book her about once a month, she's going to have a much greater incentive to start looking for other ways to start earning some cash. This is definitely one of those "use it or lose it" propositions.

Safety reminders for less experienced sitters

An inexperienced teenage baby sitter may not be aware of all the potential hazards to a child's health that can be found in a home, so do a quick walk-through of your home before the sitter arrives to eliminate as many of the following hazards as possible. (In situations where eliminating the risk is impractical or impossible, make sure that the baby sitter knows of the potential risk and how to minimize it.)

✔ **Unsafe leftovers:** You may realize that the spaghetti sauce in the refrigerator dates back to the time of the dinosaurs, but the baby sitter doesn't know that. So if your 5-year-old asks for spaghetti as a bedtime snack, chances are the baby sitter will let him eat it. To prevent instances such as these, purge your refrigerator of any unsafe leftovers before the baby sitter arrives. Otherwise, you're basically forcing her to play food-poisoning roulette every time she opens the refrigerator door.

✔ **Foods that are unsuitable for kids:** Unless your teenage baby sitter has taken a baby-sitting course that covers the ins and outs of feeding kids, she may not have an adequate understanding of which foods are appropriate for young children. She may eye that package of microwave popcorn in your kitchen cupboard and think it's the perfect snack for your 2-year-old, not realizing that popcorn poses a significant choking risk to children under the age of three. Because you probably don't want to declare your house a popcorn-free zone for the foreseeable future (after all, if you have older kids, popcorn may be a favorite snack food), the best way to handle this situation is to alert the baby sitter to the choking risks posed by the following types of foods: popcorn, raisins, nuts, sunflower seeds, wieners (unless they've been sliced into quarters lengthwise), and hard fruits and vegetables (unless they've been grated or chopped into small pieces).

✔ **Cooking hazards:** Make sure you provide the teenage baby sitter with clear guidelines on cooking when the children are in the kitchen: for example, the importance of using the back burners on the stove and ensuring that pot handles are pointed away from the front of the stove. You may also want to establish clear rules about which types of cooking appliances can be used when you're out of the house: for example, the toaster and the microwave can be used, but the stovetop and the broiler are off-limits.

✔ **Drowning hazards:** Children can drown in even miniscule amounts of water, so puddles, wading pools, and undrained bathtubs pose risks to little ones. Convey the following two all-important messages to your teenage baby sitter: First, she needs to know where your children are at all times, and, in the case of very young children, she needs to provide direct supervision the entire time they are awake; and second, the baby sitter needs to remember to drain the bathtub and the wading pool the moment your child is finished using them.

✔ **Toppling TV sets:** The baby sitter may not be aware that allowing a toddler to climb the family TV set is unsafe. Tragically, toppling TV sets result in a significant number of toddler deaths and injuries each year. And according to the U.S. Consumer Product Safety Commission, the majority of the 2,300 children who end up in hospital emergency rooms each year as a result of injuries sustained from falling TVs are four years of age or younger.

✔ **Stranger danger:** Caution your baby sitter not to answer the door unless you have specifically told her that you're expecting someone to drop by and warn her not to let anyone who calls on the phone know that she's on her own with your kids. Otherwise, she can be putting herself and your children at risk.

If your baby sitter hasn't received any training in first aid, offer to pay for her to take a course. You'll feel a lot better leaving her in charge if you know she's capable of dealing with potential emergencies.

Part V
The Part of Tens

The 5th Wave   By Rich Tennant

"I've been taking Samantha to a child-care center for more than three weeks now. One of these days I hope to get up the nerve to take her out of her car seat and drop her off."

In this part . . .

This part of the book is where I get to play David Letterman and create a few top-ten lists of my own. (Because Dave doesn't spend much time talking about childcare on his late-night TV show, I don't think he'll mind me encroaching on his turf.)

These chapters are packed with useful, nitty-gritty, need-to-know information — in this case, how to ease your child into a new child-care arrangement, how to feel more connected with your child's day-care "family," and how to spot the warning signs that your child-care arrangement's in trouble. I also include a list of ten highly helpful child-care resources and organizations — essential information for any parent trying to navigate the child-care maze.

Chapter 15

Ten Tips on Easing Your Child into a New Child-Care Arrangement

. . . .

In This Chapter

▶ Preparing your child for what to expect

▶ Knowing how to say goodbye quickly and with confidence

. . . .

Your child's first day at a new child-care arrangement doesn't have to be the stuff of which nightmares are made. (Honestly.) In this chapter, I give you some practical things you can do to help make the transition as stress-free as possible for the entire family.

Scheduling a Dress Rehearsal

Arrange for your child to visit the child-care center or family day care before he officially starts so that he can have a chance to meet his child-care provider ahead of time — something that can make that first morning a whole lot less stressful for all concerned.

If you're hiring an in-home child-care provider, you may want to arrange to be at home for her first day on the job so that you can help ease the transition for both her and your child. (Even if they've already met on one or two previous occasions — during the job interview and during a subsequent get-acquainted visit, for example — that first day can still be a bit rough.) If your child takes to the child-care provider immediately, and you start to feel like your presence is no longer required, you can always come up with a list of errands to run that'll get you out of the house for a while.

Giving Your Child Some Day-Care Prep

If your child is old enough to enjoy reading stories and watching children's videos with you, you may want to ask a bookseller, a children's librarian, or your friendly neighborhood video store manager to recommend a few titles that deal with going to day care or having a nanny. After you read the story or watch the video together, you can discuss the specifics of your child's new child-care arrangement.

Just one small caveat if you decide to take this particular bit of advice: Make sure that the book or video you choose describes the type of child-care arrangement that you're going with. If you recruit a nanny to come into your home and then read your child a book about center-based childcare to prepare her for the experience, she's bound to wonder why tons of other kids haven't magically appeared on the scene. After all, isn't that what day care is all about?

Prepping Your Child-Care Provider

You can make your child-care provider's job 100 percent easier if you provide her with the inside scoop on your child's likes and dislikes, his daily routines, and anything else you that think she needs to know in order to provide him with the best possible care (for example, how well he copes with changes to his day-to-day routine, what techniques work best in soothing him, and so on).

If you give her this information ahead of time — ideally in written form, so that she can refer to it later — you save her from having to figure out all this stuff on her own through trial and error.

Enrolling Mr. Bunny in Day Care, Too

Transitional objects — also known as *comfort objects* — can help ease the transition between home and day care. If your child has a much-loved stuffed bunny or other favorite toy animal, she may find it comforting to have this special friend to hug if she's feeling lonely or scared. If your child's not the stuffed animal type, she may prefer to bring a picture of you or something that belongs to you with her. That way, if she starts missing you, she can go look at the picture or hold on to that plastic Starbucks travel mug that she's come to associate with you. (Mom = Starbucks!)

Even very young babies can take comfort from transitional objects. What works well with newborns is a shirt or other object that carries Mom's unique scent. Breathing in that familiar scent can be tremendously calming and reassuring to a newborn who's feeling a little out of his element — literally.

Leaving the Rush Hour Mentality at the Day-Care Door

Rather than trying to rush through the day-care drop-off, which only tends to heighten your child's anxiety on that all-important first day, build a bit of slack into your schedule. Ideally, you want to have the luxury of spending at least 15 minutes helping your child settle into her new day-care arrangement that first morning and every other morning during the days and weeks ahead.

Fifteen minutes seems to work well. Exiting any sooner may leave your child feeling as though the transition was too abrupt, but lingering too long may only serve to heighten her anxiety.

Remembering to Walk the Walk and Talk the Talk

Consider what message your body language and voice tone are sending to your child when you're saying your goodbyes. Your attempts to reassure your child that you're leaving him in good hands will all be in vain if your body language and voice indicate to him that you're feeling ambivalent and anxious yourself. What you want to do instead is give your child the message that you feel thoroughly confident in his new day-care arrangement and that you're looking forward to finding out all about his day when you pick him up after work.

And don't assume that your pre-verbal baby or toddler isn't picking up on these cues: Studies have shown that young children are surprisingly tuned into the emotions of the important people in their lives. So if you're positive and upbeat, your child is likely to pick up on — and possibly even mimic — your mood.

Keeping Your Goodbyes Short and Sweet

If your goodbyes are starting to resemble a scene from one of the sappier daytime soaps, perhaps the time's come to get on with the show (the day-care show, not the soap opera!). Keep a smile on your face, even if your child is crying, and reassure her that you *will* be back again at the end of the day. Of course, you also want to validate your child's feelings by letting her know that you understand that it's tough to say goodbye (you'll miss her, too!), but that you'll be back to pick her up at the end of the day.

Trying the Old Disappearing Act — Not!

Resist the temptation to sneak out the door the second your child looks the other way. Although you may manage to avoid *this* rendition of the "I Want My Mommy Blues," you're likely to end up creating an even bigger problem for yourself. Now that you've exited once, your child may rightly conclude that you're likely to sneak out again. This fear can lead your child to become extremely clingy — and not just at day care, I might add. That one not-so-great escape from the day-care center could cost you your "going-to-the-bath-room-alone" privileges for many months to come!

Here's something else to think about. According to child development experts, those kind of day-care great escapes can damage your child's trust in you — a pretty hefty price to pay for the sake of avoiding a few early-morning tears.

Minimizing the Other Changes in Your Child's Life

Avoid making other changes to your child's routine while he's getting used to a new day-care arrangement. That may simply be too overwhelming for him. (How would you feel if someone asked you to adjust to some massive changes at work at the same time that you were trying to cope with a divorce or a death in the family?) So you may want to hold off on moving him from a bed to a crib or adding a new puppy to the family until your child is a little more settled into his new day-care routine and better able to cope with these added changes.

Having Someone Else Handle the Day-Care Drop-Off

If your child has an extremely difficult time bidding you a fond farewell, you may want to arrange for your partner or trusted friend to handle the day-care drop-off instead. Doing so may help to make the early-morning goodbyes a little less wrenching for her and for you!

Chances are you'll only need to use the services of the day-care surrogate for a short time: Most children tend to settle into a new day-care arrangement relatively quickly. If they don't, it could be because another underlying problem is present — an issue I discuss in Chapter 17.

Chapter 16

Ten Ways to Feel Connected to Your Child's Day-Care "Family"

In This Chapter

▶ Getting the lowdown on what your child experiences at day care

▶ Finding ways to get involved in your child's day-care experience

After your child starts day care, he'll spend his days in the company of other adults and children you likely know little about — something that can leave you feeling like you're living with some pint-sized double agent who's leading a double life! Here are ten things you can do to feel more connected to the other major players in your child's life — your child's day-care "family."

Schedule a Day-Care Reconnaissance Mission

You'll be amazed how much you can discover about your child's day-care experiences simply by observing how she responds to her caregiver and how her caregiver responds to her. So do yourself and your child a favor and schedule a reconnaissance mission — in other words, a visit to her child-care center or family day care. Hey, if you're living with a double agent, engaging in a bit of spy work yourself only makes sense!

Stay in the Loop about Your Child's Day-Care Experiences

You're less likely to feel out of touch with your child's day-care experiences if the child-care provider makes a point of communicating with you on a daily basis — both about cute things he did or said (kids this age are always doing or saying something cute) as well as anything out of the ordinary that may have happened at day care that day.

If, for example, your child happened to come within chomping range of the resident day-care barracuda (some 18-month-old who's determined to latch her teeth onto the nearest chunk of human flesh whenever the opportunity arises), you want to hear about the bite on your child's leg when you pick him up at day care, not discover this bite for yourself a couple of hours later when you're helping him change into his pajamas. Whether this caregiver-parent debriefing takes place verbally at the end of the day or if the child-care provider has another means of communicating this important information to you — perhaps calling you at work shortly after the incident occurred or writing a note in your child's day-care diary or logbook — doesn't matter. What matters is that you feel confident that you're on the receiving end of a steady stream of need-to-know information about your child.

Start a Day-Care Photo Album

Send a disposable camera to day care with your child and ask the child-care provider if she would take a few snapshots of your child whenever she's having a particularly good time. You can use these snapshots to start a day-care photo album at home for your child — an album that your child will enjoy looking at with you and that will encourage her to talk to you about the fun times she has at day care.

Encourage Your Child to Talk about His Day

Give your child a chance to share the highlights of his day-care day — either in the car on the way home or when you sit down at the dinner table. (Of course, this strategy works a lot better if your child is verbal. You'll have a hard time getting much of a dialogue going with a 6-month-old! In this case, you'll have to rely on other people to fill in the blanks about your child's day-care day.)

Scan the Bulletin Board When You Drop Off or Pick Up Your Child

If you make a point of scanning the day-care bulletin board on a daily basis, you get a pretty good idea of what's on the day-care menu — literally and figuratively! You find out what's likely to show up on your child's plate at lunch time and snack time *and* what types of crafts, activities, and field trips are scheduled for that week or month — something that's bound to leave you feeling a lot more in the know.

Read the Day-Care Newsletter

If the child-care center or family day-care provider publishes a monthly newsletter, make a point of reading it from cover to cover. Like the day-care bulletin board, the newsletter can provide you with valuable information about what's going on behind the scenes — information that helps you feel more connected to your child's day-care experience.

Get Involved with Day-Care Activities

If your child's day-care center is planning a trip to a pumpkin patch or an apple orchard, you may want to consider taking some time off work to tag along on the trip (provided, of course, that your work schedule allows you to take the odd bit of time off during the day).

But even if you're unfortunate enough to be an employee of Ebeneezer Scrooge Enterprises (a company that isn't exactly known for being progressive in supporting employees' requests for time off to be with their kids), you can still find other ways of being involved behind the scenes with your child's day care, such as volunteering to bake a batch of dinosaur-shaped cookies when it's dinosaur month at day care.

Know the Names of Your Child's Day-Care Friends

Ask your child to introduce you to some of her friends at day care (or, if your child isn't old enough to manage these social niceties on her own, ask the child-care provider to make the necessary introductions). Being able to greet these other children by name each morning when you drop your child off at day care helps you feel like you're a part of her day-care life.

Invite Some of Your Child's Day-Care Friends to Your House

You have a better opportunity to get to know your child's day-care friends if you invite some of his closest buddies to your house for a play-date or a birthday party. Your child will also get a huge kick out of introducing his day-care friends to his favorite toys, to say nothing of his pet goldfish.

Get to Know the Other Day-Care Parents

To feel more connected to your child's day-care life, make a point of getting to know the other day-care parents. Introduce yourself to some of the other moms and dads when you're doing the daily drop-off and pickup. Offer to serve on the day-care center's parent council. (Not only will you get to know other families with children enrolled at the day-care center, but you'll also get to have your say about important center policies.) And be sure to participate in any open houses or other special events organized by the family day-care provider or day-care center staff because these events can offer an ideal opportunity to get to know the other parents.

If you're really ambitious, you may even consider organizing a potluck dinner for the other day-care families as well as the day-care center staff (or, in the case of a family day-care arrangement, the family day-care provider and her family). You may be amazed how much bonding can take place over a bowl full of mystery casserole!

Chapter 17

Ten Signs That Your Child-Care Arrangement Is in Trouble

In This Chapter

▶ Spotting the warning signs that the quality of care has deteriorated

▶ Being on the lookout for signs of child abuse

Although you may be tempted to bury your head in the sand rather than face the fact that your child's child-care arrangement could have some problems, you owe it to your child to switch into Day-Care Detective mode at the first sign of trouble. This chapter gives you ten important warning signs to look out for when trying to decide whether there's a problem.

The Child-Care Provider No Longer Puts Much Effort into Her Job

If you notice things slipping on the quality front (for example, the home-cooked lunches that the family day-care provider took such pride in preparing for the children in her care have been replaced with servings of canned pasta and her once-spectacular arts and crafts table now consists of little more than a stack of coloring books), you definitely want to take her aside and let her know that you've noticed a decline in the quality of care. Ask her if something is going on in her life that's making it difficult for her to give her full attention to the children in her care. If she's willing to work on the problem, you may be willing to give her another chance; but if she becomes angry or defensive, you probably want to start shopping around for another child-care arrangement.

Your child-care provider may be suffering from burnout, an all-too-common affliction in the child-care profession, unfortunately. Or perhaps her half-hearted efforts on the child-care front are an indication that she's battling depression or struggling with some sort of substance abuse problem.

The Child-Care Provider Doesn't Get Along Well with Your Child

If the child-care provider seems to have unrealistic expectations of your child or you suspect that she just plain doesn't like him (for example, she's consistently impatient with him and her body language indicates she really doesn't want anything to do with him), you may want to talk to her about what you've observed and ask her if she's willing to work on the problem.

If she's not, odds are your child would be a lot happier in another child-care arrangement. (Would *you* want to spend your days in the company of someone who makes it blatantly obvious that she thinks you're a huge pain in the you-know-what?)

The Child-Care Provider Has Difficulty Handling Criticism

If the child-care provider tends to become angry and defensive every time you raise a concern about your child's care — or, even worse, she tries to convince you that your child's to blame for the conflicts between the two of them — then you may want to shop around for someone who can handle constructive criticism in a more professional manner.

The Child-Care Provider Doesn't Follow Through on Your Instructions

If you've made it clear to the child-care provider that you don't want your toddler watching TV while she's at day care, but the TV set always seems to be blaring when you show up unexpectedly during the day, then you may wonder how many of your other instructions are blatantly ignored. You need to feel confident that the child-care provider respects your authority as your child's parent and follows through on any important instructions you give her regarding your child's care.

The Child-Care Provider Doesn't Respect the Privacy of the Children in Her Care

If the child-care provider is in the habit of passing along confidential information about the other children in her care or gossiping about their parents, you may want to think twice about sticking with this particular child-care arrangement. Do you really want this woman airing your dirty laundry the moment you step out the front door?

You and the Child-Care Provider No Longer See Eye to Eye on Child Rearing

Maybe the child-care provider was terrific when your child was a baby, but now that your baby has moved into the toddler stage, you and the child-care provider don't see eye to eye on important issues such as disciplining, toilet-training, and feeding a toddler. Bottom line? If you're worlds apart on everything related to child rearing, you may be better off parting ways.

You're Constantly Worried about Your Child While You're at Work

Parents who choose to ignore mother's intuition (or father's intuition!) do so at their own peril. If you're having a hard time concentrating on your job because you're worried sick about your child, your feeling is generally a pretty clear sign that serious trouble is brewing in Child-Care Paradise.

The Child-Care Provider Won't Let You Drop by the Day Care Unexpectedly

You have the right to check on your child at any point during the day-care day, whether you've given the child-care provider advance notice of your intention to drop by or not.

If the child-care provider refuses to let you see your child, this refusal should serve as a warning that something's seriously wrong, in which case you want to remove your child from such a child-care arrangement *immediately*.

The Child-Care Provider Doesn't Answer the Phone When You Call

Having the phone ring and ring when you expect the child-care provider to pick up the call can be very worrying. If it happens once or twice, you'll probably assume the child-care provider was simply momentarily too busy to get to the phone. But if it happens over the course of an entire day, you're likely to become quite frantic, wondering if something terrible has happened to your child.

If it turns out that the child-care provider turned off the ringer on the phone during naptime and then forgot to turn it back on, you'll want to make it perfectly clear to her that you expect her to be reachable by phone throughout the day-care day, naptime included. If she doesn't take your concerns seriously or, worse, she makes you feel like you're an overly hysterical parent, you'll clearly want to rethink your choice of child-care provider.

You're Concerned That the Child-Care Provider Could Be Abusing Your Child

If you notice a sudden change in your child's behavior that can't be explained by other circumstances in his life (for example, the arrival of a new brother or sister or a move to a new house), you should at least consider the possibility that your child could be being physically or sexually abused at day care. There is generally cause for concern if your child

✔ Exhibits marked behavior changes (cries more or less than usual, suddenly seems indifferent to you, or is uncharacteristically agitated and jumpy)

✔ Is suddenly reluctant to go to day care or to be with his child-care provider

✔ Is unusually fearful of adults and/or closed spaces

✔ Doesn't want anyone to touch him

✔ Is unwilling to allow anyone to dress him or change his diaper

✔ Has developed nervous mannerisms or seems more dependent than usual on comfort objects (for example, a stuffed animal or favorite blanket)

✔ Is extremely aggressive when he's playing with other children

✔ Engages in sexual acting out such as inappropriate sexual behavior or excessive masturbation

✔ Is experiencing sleep problems such as insomnia, nightmares, or a refusal to sleep alone, or insists on having the light left on at night

✔ Starts wetting the bed again at night or starts having accidents during the day after being fully potty trained

✔ Has trouble walking, sitting, going to the bathroom, or swallowing

✔ Shows symptoms of pain, itching, bleeding, and bruises in the genital or anal area or in the throat

✔ Seems to be experiencing a large number of injuries when he's at day care and/or comes home with lacerations, burns, unusual bruises, bite marks, fractures in unusual places, welts, skin discoloration, and/or torn clothing

✔ Gives inconsistent explanations about any injuries that he's received or talks about being abused by his child-care provider

If you suspect abuse, pull your child from the child-care arrangement immediately. Contact the police and your local child-protection authorities, and ensure that your child is examined by a medical doctor. Find out what types of counseling services are available to your child. Your child is likely to need some extra support to cope with this traumatic experience.

Chapter 18

Ten Child-Care Resources and Organizations

In This Chapter

▶ Finding out about the major child-care organizations

▶ Locating Web sites that can assist you in your child-care search

*1*f you like to research things in a bit more depth than your average guy or gal on the street, you're in for a treat. This chapter contains ten child-care resources and organizations you definitely want to know about. (I've listed the organizations in alphabetical order rather than ranking them in order of usefulness. So don't mistakenly assume that I'm not a big fan of ZERO TO THREE just because it shows up last on the list — one of the perils, I suppose, of having an organization name that starts with the letter "Z"!)

And while you're merrily surfing from one child-care Web site to the next, don't forget to make a quick pit-stop at my own child-care Web site: www. childcare-guide.com. You'll find a few extra goodies I wasn't able to shoehorn into this book — your reward for dropping by!

Child Care Aware

Child Care Aware; phone 800-424-2246; www.childcareaware.org.

Child Care Aware is a project of the National Association of Child Care Resource and Referral Agencies. The Child Care Aware Web site (which is easily the most user-friendly child-care Web site for parents you'll find anywhere) features tip sheets on choosing childcare, a newsletter called the *Daily Planet,* and a database that allows you to search for child-care resource and referral agencies in your area. (You can also find out the location of your nearest child-care resource and referral agency by calling Child Care Aware.)

Child Care Bureau

U.S. Department of Health and Human Services, Administration of Children, Youth and Families, Child Care Bureau, Switzer Building, Room 2046, 330 C St., SW, Washington, DC 20447; phone 202-690-6782; www.acf. dhhs.gov/programs/ccb.

A program of the U.S. Department of Health and Human Services, Administration of Children, Youth and Families, the Child Care Bureau is an excellent place to turn to if you're looking for information about child-care tax credits and child-care financial assistance. The Child Care Bureau is federally mandated to enhance "the quality, affordability, and availability of child-care for all families" and is responsible for administering federal funds to states, territories, and tribes to assist low-income families in accessing quality childcare when the parents work or participate in education or training. The Child Care Aware Web site also features information on conducting a thorough child-care search, as well as links to other useful Web sites.

Ecumenical Child Care Network

Ecumenical Child Care Network, 8765 West Higgins Rd., Suite 405, Chicago, IL 60631; phone 773-693-4040; www.eccn.org.

As the name implies, the Ecumenical Child Care Network (ECCN) is a network of Christian child-care programs operated by churches and other religious organizations. The ECCN offers a self-study program for churches that allows them to improve the quality of their child-care and early childhood education programs.

National Association for the Education of Young Children

National Association for the Education of Young Children, 1509 16th St. NW, Washington, DC 20036-1426; phone 800-424-2460 or 202-232-8777; www.naeyc.org.

The National Association for the Education of Young Children (NAEYC) is a highly influential association of early childhood educators and others involved in the care and education of young children. The NAEYC administers a highly respected child-care accreditation program for child-care centers and family day cares. (You can get a good idea of what constitutes quality in an out-of-home child-care program by checking out the accreditation criteria on the NAEYC Web site.)

National Association for Family Child Care

National Association for Family Child Care, 5202 Pinemont Dr., Salt Lake City, UT 84123; phone 800-359-3817 or 801-269-9338; www.nafcc.org.

The National Association for Family Child Care is a national organization that represents family and group home (residential care) child-care providers. The association administers a child-care accreditation program for family day cares that promotes excellence in family day care (also known as "family childcare").

National Child Care Association

National Child Care Association, 1016 Rosser St., Conyers (Atlanta), GA 30012; phone 800-543-7161; www.nccanet.org.

The National Child Care Association is a professional trade association that focuses exclusively on licensed, private child-care and education programs. The association offers a child-care accreditation program for child-care providers and early childhood educators. The site includes a search tool that allows you to locate an NCCA child-care program in your area as well as an extensive list of childcare-related links.

National Child Care Information Center

National Child Care Information Center, 243 Church St. NW, 2nd Floor, Vienna, VA 22180; phone 800-616-2242; TTY: 800-516-2242; nccic.org.

The National Child Care Information Center (NCCIC) — a project of the Child Care Bureau — serves as a clearinghouse for information about childcare. The NCCIC Web site features numerous articles and links of interest to parents. The site is definitely worth checking out.

National Institute on Out-Of-School Time

National Institute on Out-of-School Time, 106 Central St., Wellesley, MA 02481; phone 781-283-2547; www.niost.org.

The National Institute on Out-of-School Time is the only child-care organization in the country that focuses exclusively on so-called "out-of-school time" (the childcare that school-aged children require during the hours when they're not in school). The Institute's Web site is an excellent source of information on the unique child-care needs of school-aged children. You'll find links, articles, and research reports galore.

National Resource Center for Health and Safety in Child Care

UCHSC at Fitzsimons, National Resource Center for Health and Safety in Child Care, Campus Mail Stop F541, P.O. Box 6508, Aurora, CO 80045-0508; phone 800-598-KIDS; nrc.uchsc.edu.

The National Resources Center for Health and Safety in Child Care is an excellent source of information on child-care health and safety information. You can download a copy of *Caring for Our Children: National Health and Safety Performance Standards for Out-of-Home Childcare Programs* (a mammoth document that spells out the best health and safety practices for child-care centers and family day cares) and access detailed information about child-care legislation in each state by visiting the center's Web site.

ZERO TO THREE

ZERO TO THREE: National Center for Infants, Toddlers, and Families, 2000 M St. NW, Suite 200, Washington, DC 20036; phone 202-638-1144 (administration) or 800-899-4301 (bookstore); www.zerotothree.org.

ZERO TO THREE'S mission is "to promote the healthy development of our nation's infants and toddlers by supporting and strengthening families, communities, and those who work on their behalf." ZERO TO THREE's Web site includes articles and lists of frequently asked questions about childcare.

Index

• D •

FOR DUMMIES®

The easy way to get more done and have more fun

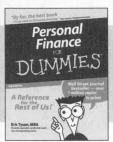

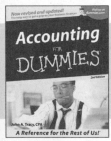

FOR DUMMIES®

A world of resources to help you grow

HOME, GARDEN & HOBBIES

0-7645-5295-3

0-7645-5130-2

0-7645-5106-X

Also available:

Auto Repair For Dummies
(0-7645-5089-6)

Chess For Dummies
(0-7645-5003-9)

Home Maintenance For
Dummies
(0-7645-5215-5)

Organizing For Dummies
(0-7645-5300-3)

Piano For Dummies
(0-7645-5105-1)

Poker For Dummies
(0-7645-5232-5)

Quilting For Dummies
(0-7645-5118-3)

Rock Guitar For Dummies
(0-7645-5356-9)

Roses For Dummies
(0-7645-5202-3)

Sewing For Dummies
(0-7645-5137-X)

FOOD & WINE

0-7645-5250-3

0-7645-5390-9

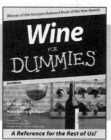

0-7645-5114-0

Also available:

Bartending For Dummies
(0-7645-5051-9)

Chinese Cooking For
Dummies
(0-7645-5247-3)

Christmas Cooking For
Dummies
(0-7645-5407-7)

Diabetes Cookbook For
Dummies
(0-7645-5230-9)

Grilling For Dummies
(0-7645-5076-4)

Low-Fat Cooking For
Dummies
(0-7645-5035-7)

Slow Cookers For Dummies
(0-7645-5240-6)

TRAVEL

0-7645-5453-0

0-7645-5438-7

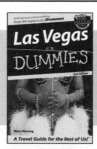

0-7645-5448-4

Also available:

America's National Parks For
Dummies
(0-7645-6204-5)

Caribbean For Dummies
(0-7645-5445-X)

Cruise Vacations For
Dummies 2003
(0-7645-5459-X)

Europe For Dummies
(0-7645-5456-5)

Ireland For Dummies
(0-7645-6199-5)

France For Dummies
(0-7645-6292-4)

London For Dummies
(0-7645-5416-6)

Mexico's Beach Resorts For
Dummies
(0-7645-6262-2)

Paris For Dummies
(0-7645-5494-8)

RV Vacations For Dummies
(0-7645-5443-3)

Walt Disney World & Orlando
For Dummies
(0-7645-5444-1)

Available wherever books are sold. Go to www.dummies.com or call 1-877-762-2974 to order direct.

FOR DUMMIES®

Plain-English solutions for everyday challenges

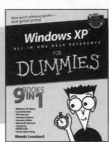
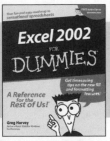

FOR DUMMIES®

Helping you expand your horizons and realize your potential

INTERNET

The Internet FOR DUMMIES
0-7645-0894-6

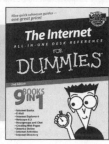

The Internet ALL-IN-ONE DESK REFERENCE FOR DUMMIES
0-7645-1659-0

eBay FOR DUMMIES
0-7645-1642-6

Also available:

America Online 7.0 For Dummies
(0-7645-1624-8)

Genealogy Online For Dummies
(0-7645-0807-5)

The Internet All-in-One Desk Reference For Dummies
(0-7645-1659-0)

Internet Explorer 6 For Dummies
(0-7645-1344-3)

The Internet For Dummies Quick Reference
(0-7645-1645-0)

Internet Privacy For Dummie
(0-7645-0846-6)

Researching Online For Dummies
(0-7645-0546-7)

Starting an Online Business For Dummies
(0-7645-1655-8)

DIGITAL MEDIA

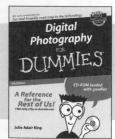

Digital Photography FOR DUMMIES
0-7645-1664-7

Photoshop Elements 2 FOR DUMMIES
0-7645-1675-2

Digital Video FOR DUMMIES
0-7645-0806-7

Also available:

CD and DVD Recording For Dummies
(0-7645-1627-2)

Digital Photography All-in-One Desk Reference For Dummies
(0-7645-1800-3)

Digital Photography For Dummies Quick Reference
(0-7645-0750-8)

Home Recording for Musicians For Dummies
(0-7645-1634-5)

MP3 For Dummies
(0-7645-0858-X)

Paint Shop Pro "X" For Dummies
(0-7645-2440-2)

Photo Retouching & Restoration For Dummies
(0-7645-1662-0)

Scanners For Dummies
(0-7645-0783-4)

GRAPHICS

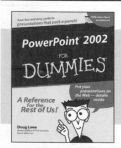

PowerPoint 2002 FOR DUMMIES
0-7645-0817-2

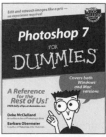

Photoshop 7 FOR DUMMIES
0-7645-1651-5

Macromedia Flash MX FOR DUMMIES
0-7645-0895-4

Also available:

Adobe Acrobat 5 PDF For Dummies
(0-7645-1652-3)

Fireworks 4 For Dummies
(0-7645-0804-0)

Illustrator 10 For Dummies
(0-7645-3636-2)

QuarkXPress 5 For Dummies
(0-7645-0643-9)

Visio 2000 For Dummies
(0-7645-0635-8)

FOR DUMMIES®

The advice and explanations you need to succeed

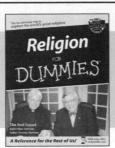